Dinah Zike's

Foldables® and VKVs®

for
Phonics, Spelling
and Vocabulary

Dinah-Might Adventures, LP
P.O. Box 690328
San Antonio, Texas, 78269
Phone (210) 698-0123
Fax (210) 698-0095
ORDERS ONLY: 1-800-99-DINAH
Visit our website www.dinah.com

Copyright © 2007 Dinah Zike
1st Edition 2007, 2nd Edition 2009, 3rd Edition 2010
Published by Dinah-Might Adventures, LP, San Antonio, Texas
www.dinah.com 1-800-99DINAH

ISBN-13:978-1-882796-26-7
ISBN-10:1-882796-26-8

Editors
Jill Houghton, Judi Youngers, Rhonda Meyer, Ignacio Salas-Humara, Jan Manzanero
Book Design and Layout
Ignacio Salas-Humara
Photography
Ignacio Salas-Humara
All photos copyright © 2007 Dinah-Might Adventures, LP

Samantha

Dedication
With Love to
our precious
Samantha,
from her
Aunt Dinah.

Aunt Dinah

Thank You!
Thank you to the many teachers, students, and parents who contributed Foldables® to this book.
A special thank you to Julie and her children and the Dinah Zike Academy after-school group.

The words and pictures used in these lessons as *real world print* (RWP) came from numerous newspapers, magazines, flyers, and advertisements from across the U.S. -- all valuable teaching tools. The vast
majority of the words and phrases used on the Foldables® and VKVs™ were found in the following
publications, or supplements to these publications:
USA Today, San Antonio Express-News, Austin American-Statesman.

Dinah Zike's

Foldables® and VKVs®

for

Phonics, Spelling and Vocabulary

A Photographic Reference Guide for Kinesthetic Learning

PreK - 3rd Grade

All contents copyright © 2007, Dinah Zike
Dinah-Might Adventures, L.P.
San Antonio, Texas

Table of Contents

Table of Contents

Dear Friends and Educators,

I am frequently asked, "When did you invent *Foldables*?" and "How did you become the 'hamburger' and 'hotdog' lady?" It is a story that I enjoy sharing with teachers and students, and I'd like to share it with you as I think it will provide a historic reference for the 3-D instructional strategies presented in this book.

I first started designing and using paper-based manipulatives when I was in sixth grade. Originally, I used them as study aids to help organize my own notes in junior high and later in high school and college. I discovered they also worked as study aids for students I tutored. Throughout HS, I tutored students who needed just a little extra help. Later, to make money for college, I worked with students with severe learning disabilities. I continued to design paper-based study aids, or manipulatives, and invented names for the folds I was using to make the manipulatives -- hamburger, hotdog, taco, burrito, and shutterfold were some of my first terms because they were easy for my "students" to remember. I adopted, or borrowed, the terms *mountain* and *valley* from origami books and programs.

Sometimes I got ideas for new manipulatives from greeting card folds or folded advertisements, but most of the time, I would just take paper and fold it to illustrate something I personally needed to remember or something I needed to teach others. This was the beginning of *Foldables*, even though they were not called that at the time, and when I tell you I started Junior High School in 1966 and graduated from high school in 1970, you will be able to do the math -- I've been designing, using, and teaching others to use my three-dimensional graphic organizers for 40 years.

After graduating from college I became a teacher. I taught school during the week and presented workshops and continuing education sessions for schools and conferences on the weekends. With the help of excited, creative teachers who attended my presentations, my three-dimensional graphic organizers began to spread across the US, and I remember how thrilling it was to receive my first letters from teachers who were using my manipulatives in other countries.

In the 1970's and early 1980's, my folds and manipulatives were met with resounding approval in my teacher workshops, but when I presented my ideas for 3-D manipulatives to major publishing companies, I was met with rejection. I was told that the strategies were too time consuming, they were too dependent upon student production and writing, they were too artsy-craftsy for upper level students, and innumerable other negative critiques. For several years I sent out query letters trying to find a publisher to print books that contained instructions on how to make and use my three-dimensional graphic organizers. You have to remember, this was over thirty years ago, and the world of education was paper based, but the paper was used to produce "ditto sheets" or duplicated worksheets, not 3-D study aids. To put this time in perspective, know that it was before most of the brain research was published, before cooperative learning was an accepted practice, and years before two-dimensional graphic organizers began to appear in nearly every educational publication -- supplemental and required -- as duplicable sheets. And, the duplicated worksheets we used at this time were made on a crank machine that used a powerful fluid to copy information imbedded on purple masters.

Totally frustrated, and with a file drawer full of rejections, I withdrew all the money I had accrued in my teacher retirement fund, and with a loan from my community bank in Anderson, Texas, I began my own publishing company in my garage in 1984. My first publications were not based upon my folds, even though I was still inventing new folds and using both the old and new manipulatives in my classroom, in my graduate work, and in my staff development training sessions. My company had to make money to succeed, so I began by publishing the thematic units I used in my classroom and taught in my staff development sessions. I also published social studies materials I had developed to teach the history of my state of Texas. I knew these were teaching aids that were needed and easily understood, and they would generate the revenue I needed to publish my book of 3-D manipulatives. (Looking back on this, I think I lacked the self-confidence needed to put what little money I had into a book based solely on my folds because my folding activities had received so many rejections from so many very successful companies!)

In 1986, after two years of garage publishing, I wrote my first book consisting entirely of my folds and 3-D graphic organizers. It was entitled *Dinah Zike's Big Book of Books and Activities*, and like my other self-published books, it consisted of photocopied pages bound using notebook rings or brads. I often gave away parts of it as a handout at my workshops. In 1991, my company published the official copyrighted, bound version of this award-winning book and included black line illustrations to accompany the fold instructions, along with black-and-white photographs. It was one of the first, if not the first, supplemental educational book to use more photographs than black-line art.

Over the years I continued to design, publish, and teach others using my three-dimensional graphic organizers, and they continued to gain in popularity because teachers who used them successfully shared them with others. My folds were spreading across the country, and it was rewarding to see my ideas and hear my terms used by students, teachers, and professors. While presenting the Mary C. McCurdy lecture at the National Science Teacher's Conference in 2000, Glencoe McGraw-Hill approached me to include my 3-D graphic organizers in their textbooks. Michael Oster, my dear friend with McGraw-Hill, coined the term *Foldables*, and today my *Foldables* are an exclusive feature of McGraw-Hill School Solutions. They appear as a study aid in nearly every K-12 McGraw-Hill textbook and many McGraw-Hill ancillaries.

Two-dimensional graphic organizers have been in use for decades, and I am certainly not the first person to fold paper to teach a skill or concept, but I started and popularized the practice of using innumerable three-dimensional graphic organizers as teaching aids and developing them into a supplemental program based upon proven, research-based skills and strategies. When I take Venn diagrams, concept maps, KWL lists, comparing and contrasting activities, and other research based graphic organizers and make them as *Foldables*, they have tabs or layers so main ideas can be written and viewed clearly on the top plane and supporting facts, definitions, and notes can be recorded on underlying planes -- or under the tabs. (See Appendix Two, Research Citations, pages 286-288.)

You will see my *Foldables* used in other people's presentations and publications, but as the originator of *Foldables* and VKVs (visual kinesthetic vocabulary manipulatives introduced in this book), I present this photographic reference guide to you as a compilation of forty years of my experience inventing 3-D graphic organizers. Many of you know and use my many content specific *Foldable* publications; however, this is my first book published specifically for phonics, vocabulary, and spelling, and in it you will find hundreds of ideas on ways you can use *Foldables* and VKVs (Visual Kinesthetic Vocabluary Flashcards) with PreK-3 students to create a print-rich environment.

Have fun and be creative as you use and adapt the *Foldables* and VKVs in this book!

Before

During

After
With Husband Ignacio Salas-Humara

Please support breast cancer research and awareness programs.
Tell those you love to get mammograms.

P.S. This book presents my VKVs (Visual Kinesthetic Vocabulary) for the first time in print! I have used them in workshops for many years, and we teach them at the Dinah Zike Academy, but this is my first publication demonstrating my VKVs for phonics, vocabulary, and spelling. What are VKVs?

In my years of teaching, I have made hundreds, probably thousands, of flashcards -- sight word cards, phonics cards, parts of speech cards, content vocabulary cards. I tried different organizational methods to help me retrieve the appropriate cards when needed, but I was still dealing with hundreds of cards.

I loved making and using sets of stapled word family cards because one "card" made numerous words, and they were kinesthetic. Who knows when these stapled card sets were first used in classrooms? I don't remember using them myself as a student in the 50's, but I did use them as a teacher in the 70's. These cards inspired me to invent other kinesthetic methods for manipulating and forming words. (See page 230.)

Twenty years ago, I began designing VKVs with three goals in mind:

1. I wanted <u>two-dimensional</u> <u>words</u> to become <u>three-dimensional</u>, allowing one or more parts of the word -- initial or final consonant, medial vowel/vowels, root word, blend, prefix, suffix -- to be manipulated and changed to form numerous words.

The flashcards focused student attention on the part of the word being manipulated as well as the stationary part of the word. I hoped that by placing visual and kinesthetic "importance" on a moveable portion of a word, and by having students experience the word base several times while manipulating the VKV, they would transfer to similar words encountered in print what they learned during the experience.

Onset and Rime Analysis

2. I wanted to find a way to decrease the number of word cards I had to organize and store, and yet maintain or increase the number of words presented for student interaction and immersion; therefore, I tried to design flashcards where each card presented two or more words. I was on a mission to invent folds that would kinesthetically present as many words as possible based on a commonality. When I designed one VKV flashcard that presented 12 words, I was ecstatic and students loved it! (See page 159.)

VKV® Three-Word Example: Sound Sequence Analysis and Verb Conjugation:

3. I designed the flashcards using only one sheet of paper, or one strip of paper, that was neither glued nor stapled. You will see a few exceptions to this rule where I use glue (I made the rule, so I can break it!), but the majority of my VKVs are neither glued nor stapled.

The VKV forming the words spring, sprang, and sprung is typical -- one sheet of paper used to form three words without using glue or staples. The VKV below uses one sheet of paper to form five words, but it is an exception in that it works better if the sections are glued together.

VKV® Five-Word Example: Onset and Rime Analysis

Double VKV® Flashcard Example: Contractions

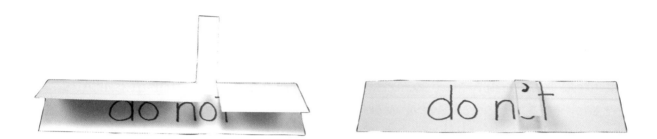

This personal challenge resulted in the VKVs you will find in this book and other books in this series. The more experienced I became as a teacher in the early 80's, the more I realized the need for 3-D graphic organizers to enhance the teaching of phonics, spelling, vocabulary, and grammar in all grade levels. Older students responded positively to the kinesthetic aspect of the VKVs in much the same manner as elementary students. I used these folds when I taught first graders to read, tutored middle school and high school students with learning disabilities, helped ESL and ELL students learn English, and experimented with strategies to prepare students for testing -- GED, SAT, ACT.

Today you will find my *Foldables* and VKVs used to teach a wide range of skills from pre-Kindergarten picture words to college preparatory vocabulary. This book focuses on Pre-K through 3rd grades. The second book in this series is for 4th-12th grades and features vocabulary and spelling activities as well as word lists, test prep, academic vocabulary, and ESL strategies.

Please take the time to read the rest of the introduction for ideas on how to make, store, organize, and use Foldables and VKVs. Have fun and be creative,

DZ

Join Dinah's free **e-group** at www.dinah.com for e-mail updates on the following new publications, seminars in your area, and information on sessions at the Dinah Zike Academy: *Foldables,* Notebook Foldables, and VKVs for Spelling & Vocabulary: *Test-Prep, Academic Vocabulary, and ESL Strategies* *Intermediate to Advanced, 4th - 12th grades*

A Summary of VKVs®

VKVs kinesthetically focus on words, their structure, use,
and meaning. VKVs are referred to as *action flashcards*.

1. VKVs make two-dimensional words three-dimensional, allowing one or
   more parts of the word to be manipulated and changed to form
   numerous words with a common part.

2. VKVs present two, three, four, six, or more words on each flashcard.

3. VKVs are usually made using one sheet or strip of paper that is neither
   glued nor stapled, but shaped in a manner that allows
   strategically designed tabs to be folded or unfolded to form words.

Single VKV® Flashcard Example: Phonogram Syllables

 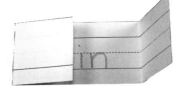 

Double VKV® Flashcard Example: Adding Prefixes and Suffixes to a Base Word

 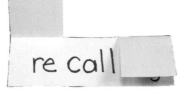 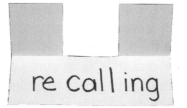

Triple VKV® Flashcard Example: Closed Compound Words

Selecting Paper for Foldables® and VKVs®:
Foldables can be made out of many different kinds of paper depending on the size and shape of the Foldable or VKV and depending on how it is to be used. For Pre-K - 2nd classrooms, I've designed VKVs to be made out of 8½" x 11" paper the majority of the time. This results in continuity of size and facilitates storage of these flashcard-manipulatives. Needless to say, this doesn't mean that VKVs can't be made on a larger or smaller scale when needed. (When working with Pre-K and K students I often use 11" x 17" index weight paper, and when working with high school students, VKVs are made using quarter sheets of notebook paper. I use the following paper:

- 8½" x 11" or 11" x 17" photocopy paper, 20 pound weight; white, pastels, or bright colors
- notebook, or binder paper, primary lined paper, grid paper
- index weight paper (80 pound weight) or cover stock paper (100 pound weight)
- art paper or construction paper (Not my favorite because it tears along creases.)
- poster board or railroad board
- scrapbooking paper, usually square, 12" x 12"
- chart paper, both lined and grid patterns
- butcher paper and/or bulletin board paper on rolls

Selecting Paper for Teacher-Made Manipulatives: When small manipulatives are made by the instructor as examples for student use, I recommend using a sturdy paper such as index weight or cover stock paper. Large manipulatives are made using poster board, chart paper, or bulletin board paper.

Selecting Paper for Student-Made Manipulatives: Young students have difficulty folding thick paper, thus my rule..."*the younger the child, the thinner the paper.*" This means that most Kindergarten students can fold thin photocopy paper more easily than construction paper or art paper.

White or Colored Paper?
The majority of Foldables, and nearly all VKVs, are made using plain white paper due to cost, availability, and readability. It is much easier to read a word written on a white flashcard than to read a word on a colored card. Colors also become clues, and I might not want students to become dependent on that. I frequently use colored paper to make Foldables or VKVs to collect words cut from *real world print (RWP),* or commercial print. I feel more comfortable using the more expensive colored paper if it is to be used by a large group of students or an entire class.

Collect Paper Scraps:
Make and allow students access to a paper scraps box so they can use the scraps to cut letters or pictures to be placed on the front tabs or the inside tabs of Foldables and VKVs. Scraps can also be used as background frames for titles or important words. Note the "*Scrap Paper Box*" and the "*Scratch Paper*" box in the first-grade publishing center on the opposite page. The poster board display featured on page 14 illustrates how a computer-generated title, "Silent Letters," can be framed with scrap paper.

Supplies to use with Foldables® and VKVs®

Construction Supplies:
-sharp scissors to be used by teacher
-Dinah Zike's Dual-Cut Scissors for
  cutting along fold lines
-liquid, water-based glue
-stapler and staples
-large paper clips
-water-based markers (for use
  on light-weight paper)
-permanent markers (for use by teacher
  on poster board and heavy paper)
-crayons and/or colored pencils
-pastels and/or paints for giant
  Foldable bulletin boards
-clothespins for securing glued edges

Decorative Supplies:
-stamps
-stencils
-stickers
-borders
-templates
-special design scissors
-scrapbooking materials
-glitter pens
-decorative hole punches, and more.

Publishing Center Paper:
-quarter and half sheets of photocopy paper
-quarter and half sheets of primary-lined paper and/or
        notebook paper
-quarter and half sheets of large grid paper, continent maps,
        picture frames, clocks, blank time lines, other
        publishing aids.
-8½" x 11" photocopy (20#) and index weight (80#) paper
-11" x 17" photocopy (20#) and index weight (80#) paper

See Dinah Zike's book, **Classroom Organization: It Can Be Done**, for storage and organization ideas for supplies, stations, publishing centers, portfolios, bulletin boards, and more.

How to Make Foldables®:
Instructions for making my most commonly used Foldables can be found at the back of this book, on pages 289 to 309. When Foldables are featured in this book in photographs, instructional strategies, bulletin boards, teacher- or student-made activities, and class or group projects, the instruction page for the Foldable will be noted.

What Size Do I Make Foldables®?
The following is my general rule for determining paper sizes when making Foldables:

If every student in the class is making a Foldable,
use 8½" x 11" photocopy paper, notebook paper, or primary lined paper.

If the Foldable is to be made by the teacher and used by all students to collect words and/or pictures, use 12" x 18" heavy construction paper or 11" x 17" copy paper. This paper works well with short-term use (from a few days to a few weeks) of the manipulative. For long-term use or for more permanent manipulatives, use the more expensive, but infinitely sturdier, 11" x 17" index weight (80#) or cover-stock paper (100#), found in office supply stores.

If the Foldable is for class use, and if large pictures, or lots of quarter-sheet sized student writing cards will be glued onto the front tabs or under the tabs, use poster board, chart paper, or sections of butcher paper.

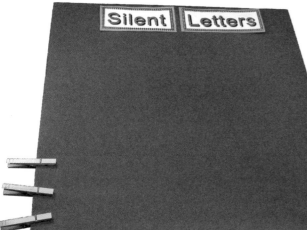

Time-Saving Hint (left): Use clothespins to hold together paper and/or poster board edges while waiting for the glue to dry.

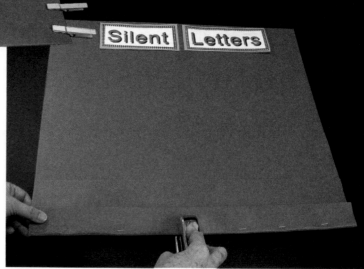

Pocket Chart with Word Strip:
Use poster board to make this wall pocket chart. VKVs and Foldables are stored in the large pocket and displayed in the bottom strip formed by folding and stapling a 1" tab. See the finished pocket chart on page 31.

How to Make VKVs®:
Instructions for making VKVs can be found throughout this book. Photographs illustrate how to fold them, and photographs of finished VKVs are also featured throughout.

What Size Do I Make VKVs®?
Most of my VKVs are based upon a single sheet of paper folded into thirds along the short, or horizontal axis. For PreK, K, 1st, 2nd, and 3rd grade students, I usually use 8½" x 11" regular photocopy paper. For more permanent study aids, I use 8½" x 11" index weight or cover stock paper (80# to 110#). I refer to the basic shapes of VKV flashcards as either single, double, or triple.

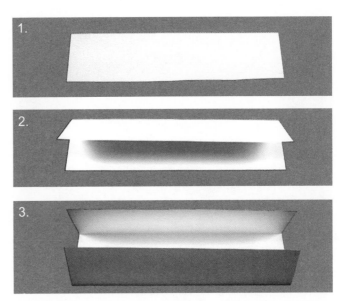

1. **Single flashcard**: A sheet of 8½" x 11" paper cut into thirds along the horizontal axis, or sentence strips cut in half.

2. **Double flashcard**: A sheet of 8½" x 11" paper folded into thirds along the horizontal axis, and cut to form a single strip and a double strip.

3. **Triple flashcard**: A sheet of 8½" x 11" paper folded along the horizontal axis into thirds. All three sections are used.

All the Same Size: Even though VKVs have many different shapes and tab configurations, when folded they are all the same height if they were made from the same size paper. As illustrated below, a single sheet of 8½" x 11" heavyweight paper (80# to 110#) can be cut to form the following:
     a) three single flashcards
     b) one double and one single flashcard
     c) one triple flashcard

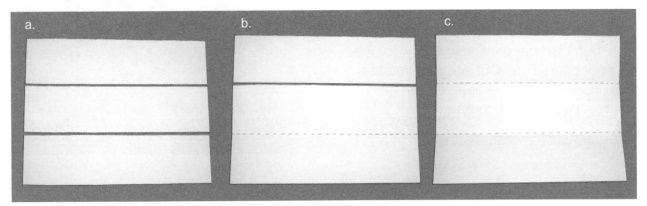

VKV® Flashcard Box: Throughout this book I will recommend that you make different VKV flashcards during the school year and store them in your VKV Flashcard Box. Once again, if all your VKVs are made using 8½" x 11" paper, you can use a box lid from a case of copy paper to collect and organize your flashcards. Dividers can be made by cutting poster board into 4" x 10½" sections and labeling them along one edge. VKV flashcards can also be stored in cereal boxes (see page 32) or in labeled plastic bags.

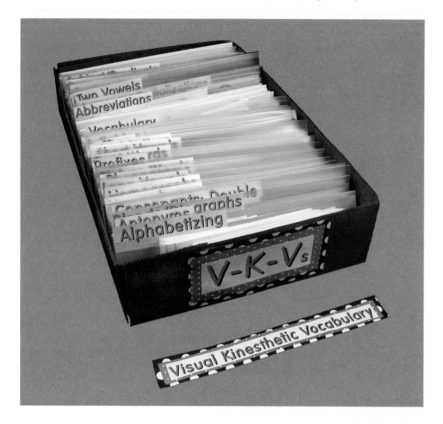

Dual-Cut Scissors (right): Young children with small fingers and poor fine-motor skills can lift tabs easier if there is space between them. I was creating this space by making two cuts -- one on each side of a fold line -- every time I made a VKV or a Foldable. This technique works fine, but it is time consuming. My company now offers Dual-Cut scissors that cut two lines at the same time to form this space. (www.dinah.com)

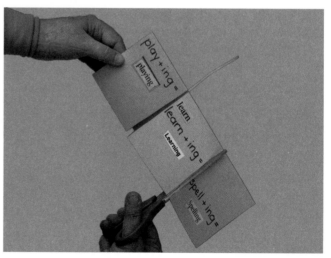

Shrink the VKVs® (below): Even though I have stressed using 8½" x 11" heavy paper (80# or 110#) to make classroom VKVs, VKVs for individual students can be made using any size paper. For example, in the photographs below, compare the VKV (below left) made using a quarter sheet (4½" x 5½") of paper with a classroom-sized VKV made using 8½" x 11" paper (below right).

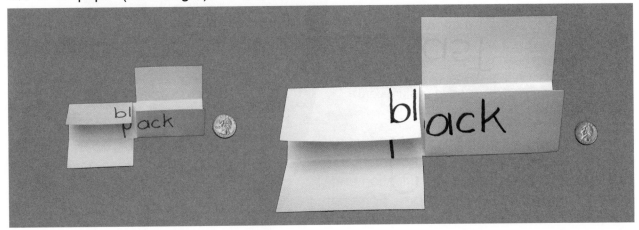

If you want every student in your classroom to have their own VKV to reinforce a new skill or to review a previously learned skill, I recommend using quarter sheets (or half sheets) of paper. This smaller size has advantages -- less paper used, students like things that are miniature, students enjoy using a smaller version of the large classroom flashcard, and this small size will fit in a sandwich bag that provides an inexpensive method of storage.

Supersize the VKVs® (right):
If you have a large group of students and feel you need to make your classroom VKVs as large as possible for easier reading, consider making them out of 11" x 17" heavy-weight paper (80# to 110#) and storing them in a box lid from a case of copy paper.

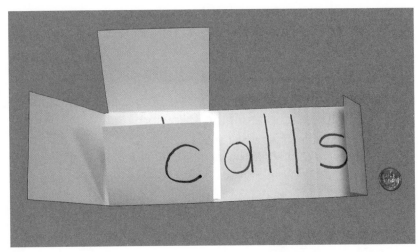

Foldables® Used for Sorting:
Many of the Foldables featured in this book can be used for sorting physical objects, word cards, VKVs, and more. The following Foldables are my favorites for sorting activities:

- -four-door display (right)
- -pyramid diorama
- -display boxes
- -sentence strip holders
- -pocket charts made using poster board
- -top pockets

Collecting and Storing Physical Objects:
Make a list of physical objects that might **safely** be used for skills-based identification and sorting purposes in the classroom. For example, ask parents to help you collect nonperishable, physical objects or small pictures of objects whose names begin with each letter of the alphabet. You might choose to glue pictures to quarter sheets or half sheets of paper.

Collecting Manufactured Letters for Sorting Activities:
Collect and use manufactured sets of letters for the Foldable sorting activities featured in this book. Try to find sets with both upper- and lower-case letters.

- -wooden or rubber blocks (photo bottom right)
- -sets of plastic magnetic letters
- -wooden letters, sold at craft stores. (bottom middle)
- -fabric letters (bottom left)
- -letters and puzzle pictures
- -foam letters, shapes, numbers

Make Letter Cards for Sorting:
Make and use sets of letters for the Foldable sorting activities featured in this book. See pages 128 for examples of the following.

- -letter cards made using stickers
- -letter cards made using stamps or stencils
- -letter cards using letters cut from *word print*

Making Foldables® and VKVs® Tactile:

Tactile Letters and Words:
Place several drops of food coloring into small bottles of white liquid glue to make inexpensive colored glue. Use the colored glue to write letters, sight words, vocabulary terms, and/or spelling words on flashcards or Foldables.

Use either solid lines of glue or dots of glue to form letters or words. Allow the glue to dry for 24 hours before permitting students to use the tactile cards. If the glue is too watery, use cream of tartar as a thickening agent. See page 129.

Magic Letters and Words:
Use white glue to write letters or words on white flashcards. Allow the glue to dry for 24 hours before permitting students to use the tactile cards. Place sheets of scratch paper over the glue words and rub a crayon over the paper until the word appears. See page 215.

Cornmeal Letters and Words:
Dye and use colored corn meal or grits to make tactile letters, or place colored cornmeal or grits in a tub and allow students to write letters or words in the tub of "sand." See page 129.

Sandpaper Letters and Words:
Cut sets of letters out of fine-grained sandpaper to make tactile letter cards. See page 129.

Physical Objects on Tabs (below): In order to make the reading or teaching of concepts more kinesthetic, glue or tape physical objects to the front tabs or under the tabs of Foldables. Note the straw and sticks glued to the front of the *The Three Little Pigs* Foldable as well as the ribbon and other objects used to illustrate colors.

Extension: See page 36 for information on using 2" clear tape to attach science specimens to Foldable Projects. Three-tab instructions can be found on page 293.

Use a Computer and Printer to Generate Copy for Foldables® and VKVs®

Portable Notebook: I use a small, lightweight notebook so I can easily carry it around the class. I use it with large or small groups of students inside or outside the classroom. I am the only person who uses the notebook. Students use classroom desktop computers when available and/or computers in the school computer lab.

Easily Read Fonts: At the Dinah Zike Academy, we often use a font with circle and stick letters when printing labels and titles to be identified and read by beginning readers. The following fonts have circle and stick letters for "a," "b," "d," "p" and "q."

Avant Garde: a, b, c, d, e, f, g, h, i, j,k, l, m, n, o, p, q, r, s, t, u, v, w, x, y, z
A, B, C, D, E, F, G, H, I, J, K, L, M, N, O, P, Q, R, S, T, U, V, W, X, Y, Z

**Aharoni: a, b, c, d, e, f, g, h, i, j, k, l, m, n, o, p, q, r, s, t, u, v, w, x, y, z
A, B, C, D, E, F, G, H, I, J, K, L, M, N, O, P, Q, R, S, T, U, V, W, X, Y, Z**

Vogue: a, b, c, d, e, f, g, h, i, j, k, l, m, n, o, p, q, r, s, t, u, v, w, x, y, z
A, B, C, D, E, F, G, H, I, J, K, L, M, N, O, P, Q, R, S, T, U, V, W, X, Y, Z

Comic Sans: a, b, c, d, e, f, g, h, i, j, k, l, m, n, o, p, q, r, s, t, u, v, w, x, y, z
A, B, C, D, E, F, G, H, I, J, K, L, M, N, O, P, Q, R, S, T, U, V, W, X, Y, Z

Other Easy-to-Read Fonts: Notice the differences in the lower-case letters with and without a tail, and the formation of the capital letter "I" in the following fonts:

Verdana: Aa, Bb, Cc, Dd, Ee, Ff, Gg, Hh, Ii, Jj, Kk, Ll, Mm, Nn, Oo, Pp, Qq, Rr, Ss, Tt, Uu, Vv, Ww, Xx, Yy, Zz

Eurostile: A a, B b, C c, D d, E e, F f, G g, H h, I i, J j, K k, L l, M m, N n, O o, P p, Q q, R r, S s, T t, U u, V v, W w, X x, Y y, Z z

David: A a, B b, C c, D d, E e, F f, G g, H h, I i, J j, K k, L l, M m, N n, O o, P p, Q q, R r, S s, T t, U u, V v, W w, X x, Y y, Z z

Mariam: A a, B b, C c, D d, E e, F f, G g, H h, I i, J j, K k, L l, M m, N n, O o, P p, Q q, R r, S s, T t, U u, V v, W w, X x, Y y, Z z

Tahoma: A a, B b, C c, D d, E e, F f, G g, H h, I i, J j, K k, L l, M m, N n, O o, P p, Q q, R r, S s, T t, U u, V v, W w, X x, Y y, Z z

Outlines and Shadows (below): When printing labels use the font style options of "outline," "bold," and/or "shadow" to make the font easily read and to provide boundaries for coloring.

a.

b.

c.

Make Interesting and Memorable Labels (right): Use a water-based marker to make a border on labels by tracing around the edges of labels (a), or drawing a colorful pattern of dashes, dots, plus signs, Xs, crosses (b).

Use scraps of colored paper or scrapbook paper to frame a title by cutting the paper larger than the label (c) or allowing pieces of paper to stick out from under the labe (d).

d.

Use scissors that cut a design to trim the edges of a label (e).

e.

Use dots discarded from a hole punch to trim the edges of a label (f).

f.

Use shavings of paper discarded after cutting a sheet of paper in half by "shaving off the fold" (g).

Student-created methods are encouraged.

g.

Student-Dictated, Student-Written, and Teacher-Written Print:
A student or students can dictate to the teacher, an adult helper, or to another student who enjoys writing and writes well.

Dictation can be recorded by hand or typed on a computer and printed for multipurpose use. I use my small notebook computer the majority of the time, and you will see print generated from this computer used frequently in the photos in this book. You might chose to code the dictation or copy used with Foldables and VKVs. For example:

    D = student dictated,
    C = copied from student or class writing,
    T = teacher written,
    L = quote from literature (place in quotation marks and give credit to source).

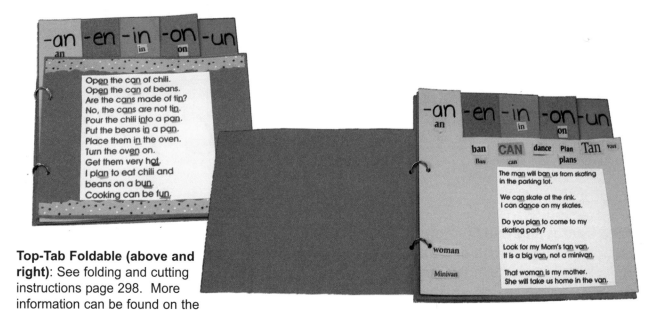

Top-Tab Foldable (above and right): See folding and cutting instructions page 298. More information can be found on the use of this Foldable on page 160.

Teacher-Written Print:
When generating teacher print, remember my **saying** -- "Students like things that are larger than normal and smaller than usual." This applies to books, worksheets, Foldables, and words!

    - Write mini-books using the smallest font possible, and use a magnifying glass to read the copy. See page 252.
    - Use the computer to generate words using the largest font possible, and use a photocopier to enlarge the word even more.

The Importance of Using Print from the Child's World:

The use of print from magazines, newspapers, cereal boxes, advertisements, menus, and other materials is called many things -- *life print*, *commercial print*, and *environmental print*, to name a few. I started calling it *Real World Print*, or *RWP* when I taught first grade in 1985, and have continued to do so through the years.

Real World Print (RWP) and/or Pictures:

Collect print and pictures from many sources to get examples needed when making Foldables and VKVs. For example:

-newspapers use common sight words in titles and in advertisements.

-nature magazines can provide pictures and words for common
   and unusual animals to illustrate the letters in a picture dictionary.

-car magazines provide pictures of wheels which can be used with the *wh-* digraph
   or to illustrate -*ee*- words.

-food and cooking magazines feature pictures of vegetables and fruits.
   They also contain pictures for words that begin and end with blends
and digraphs: *ch*eese, *ch*erry, *ch*icken, *gr*ape, *gr*een onions, *bl*ack beans,
   *bl*ueberries, fi*sh*. (Note the open and closed compound words, too.)

-supermarket flyers describing weekly specials provide pictures of general foods
   and household items.

-agriculture magazines provide pictures of *windmills*, *livestock*, *horses*, and *crops*,
   as well as pictures of *ewes* for homophones and *lambs* for silent letters.

-catalogs are wonderful resources because the pictures featured in them are usually
   small and will fit under the tabs of Foldables and VKV flashcards.
   Catalogs contain pictures of key vocabulary words and nouns -- *shoe*, *shirt*,
   pants, *hat*, *coat*, *dishes*, *toys*.

-sports magazines are filled with action words and other general words such as
   bike, *biking*; *run*, *running*; *swim*, *swimming*; others.

-gardening magazines provide *oi*- words (s*oi*l) and pictures of plants.

-travel brochures are filled with proper and common nouns, compound words, and
   words with prefixes and suffixes. Ask parents who travel for business to
   collect magazines, brochures, and newspapers to provide students with
   various cultural, geographical, historical, and literary experiences.

Photographs of Signs or Labels: Take photographs of print found on signs and labels that are an everyday part of the student's world. Signs can be found in front of schools, businesses, churches, grocery stores, hospitals, fire stations, and other community service locations. Signs are used to label streets and buildings. Take photographs of these frequently observed signs or objects to illustrate skills being studied. For example, when learning short /u/ words, take a photograph of a "Bus Stop" sign and use it on a short /u/ Foldable or VKV.

Photographs of Students in Action:
Take photographs of students to physically illustrate vocabulary terms or words that help teach a skill or concept. For example, when teaching "-ing words" take photos of students jumping, running, singing, clapping, smiling, fussing, hopping, sitting, standing, bending, writing, and reading.

Photographs of Familiar Objects and People:
Integrate photographs of familiar objects and people into picture-word and initial-reading activities.

Take and use photographs of familiar things or actions that define words. For example, take a photograph of one student running and label the photograph, "He/She can run." or "He/She runs." Take a photograph of two students running a race, and label the photograph, "They ran a race."

Free Photos:
Search the internet for copyright-free photographs you can download and use in your classroom.

A Photograph, Magazine Pictures, RWP, and Student Writing (above and right): Ask students to read five *pr* words and five *tr* words to their reading partner and/or use them to write sentences. See page 291.

Film vs. Digital (above): When I first began collecting photographs for what I called "sign language" we used a 35mm camera and had the film developed. With today's digital cameras, it is easy to take photographs and use them immediately. Look for words that teach or reinforce skills on local signs, billboards, highway signs, street signs, and signs found in businesses: exit signs, restroom signs, open or closed signs, and more.

Collecting RWP for Foldables® and VKVs®:
Instead of having stacks of newspapers and magazines that are written for adult readers in an elementary classroom, I do what I call a "Paper Cut."

Cut (or have parent helpers cut out) all age-level-appropriate titles and copy from newspapers and magazines. This allows the censoring of terms that are inappropriate for young readers, and it prevents uncomfortable questions and situations while providing lots of wonderful print. Teachers should review all print before student use.

Old trays purchased at garage sales are perfect for storing, sorting, and carrying the print to work areas. Trays can often be stacked for storage. You will see some of the print in the tray above used in Foldables and VKVs pictured in this book.

Find, Glue, Write, Read, Re-Read (left): Students find the names of animals in RWP, cut them out, and glue them under the appropriate tabs. Students can also dictate the names of animals for the teacher to write. Most Foldables include a combination of RWP, computer-generated copy, and hand-written copy. Students are encouraged to read and re-read the copy under the tabs as it will change over time. See page 293.

RWP and Foldables®:
The colored pencils on the poster to the right were made using 8½" x 11" paper folded into long shutterfolds. The patterns to make the pencil erasers and pencil points can be downloaded at www.dinah.com. Students collect color words and color words used in common phrases, such as "red hot" or "once in a blue moon," and glue them inside the appropriate shutterfold. See page 292.

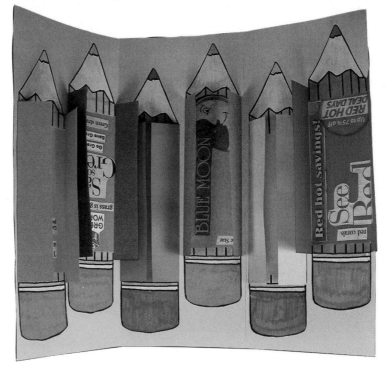

Why Do You Use So Many Examples of the Same Word?: I'm asked this question frequently. I've found that young students, as well as ELL/ESL students, become very dependent upon one type of font for word identification. When they see a new word learned in one font written in a different font from the one on which they learned it, they can stumble or fail to identify the word. My RWP flashcards and Foldables are filled with the same word in many different fonts, sizes, colors, and letter combinations: capitals and lower case, all capitals, all lower case, and with or without affixes. Students become word detectives as they analyze the structure of the words they find.

 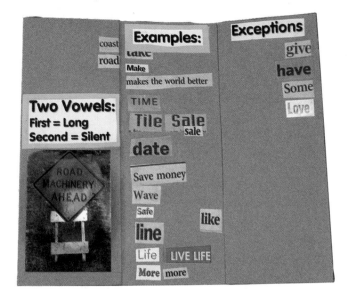

Matchbooks on a Ring (left) and Shutterfold Vowel Collection (right): The CVCe tab of the shutterfold is open to show RWP examples. Note two versions of the each of the words *life*, *more*, and *sale*.

What RWP Words Are Used? During my many years of teaching, I've collected, cut, glued and used with students tens of thousands of words cut from papers, magazines, advertisements, cereal boxes, food labels, and more. You will see several thousand of these words used with and featured on Foldables and VKVs pictured in this book. Over these many years of use, I've developed guidelines for which words I think should be used, viewed, and read by students. These simple guidelines prevent students from placing twenty of the exact same word printed in the same font, size, color, etc. from being placed on learning aids with limited space.

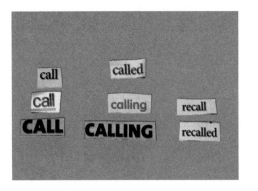

Guidelines
Find and place a featured word ...
... written in all lower case letters.
... written in all lower case letters, but in a different font.
... written with an initial capital letter and lower case letters.
... written with an initial capital letter and lower case letters, but in a different font.
... written in all capital letters.
... written in all capital letters of a different font.
... written in a different or unusual color.
... written with a prefix and/or suffix.
... written as a possessive.

Make an Original and Photocopy for Individual Use (right): Use one sheet of 8½" x 11" paper to make a Foldable or VKV to be used by the class and then photocopy it for individual student use. Photocopy one side (usually the side with the most print) and have students fold, cut, and label their individual Foldable to make it unique. Students continue to add RWP words, write their own words, sentences, definitions, and add more to these study aids. See page 308.

Too Easy, Too Hard, Just Right: You can take advantage of the fact that students find words of varying levels of difficulty, cut, and glue them to a Foldable. The varied word levels allow one to individualize student work. On a photocopied Foldable, have students use a highlighter or crayon to mark words they need to study for spelling tests, or words they need to be prepared to use in oral vocabulary drills or reading activities, or words they are to use in a written assignment. Different colors can be used for different assignments.

One Becomes Many: Photocopy one side of a class- or group-made Foldable, and have students finish the Foldable to make their own personal study guide.

Multi-Tab Example (right): In this example, the outside word list (words on the front of the tabs) were photocopied. Students folded the 11" x 17" photocopied sheet in half like a hotdog with the words to the outside. Students cut between the photocopied words (being careful not to cut through the back of the folded sheet) to form a twelve-tab Foldable. Students continued to collect names of the months and abbreviations for the months on the front tabs, and write about things that happen in each month under the tabs. Information on holidays, birthdays, special family events, and school functions might be included.

Fast Files (left): These notebook paper pockets were used at the Dinah Zike Academy to sort and store small pictures collected from magazines and art copied from the graphics CD (See page 316.)   Academy Director Dr. Judi Youngers made these pockets to keep pictures easily accessible during demonstrations, discussions, and lessons.

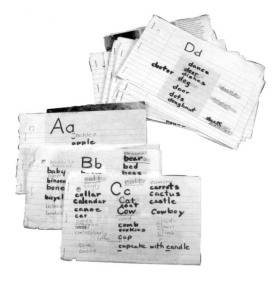

Picture and Word Files (above): Manila file folders can be used to sort and store RWP, photographs, and pictures from magazines.

Envelope RWP Files (above): Any size envelope can be used as a file. Seal the envelope and cut off one of the long edges to form a pocket.

Picture Pocket Book (above): Make thirteen pocket books using 11" x 17" paper, glue them together, and use them to collect pictures. See instructions on page 291, and useful information on page 149.

Glue Sponge (below): Cut a damp sponge that has a heavy mesh scrubbing side, and place it inside a sealable plastic container. With the sponge side down, saturate the mesh with glue, and allow it to soak into the sponge below. Continue until the sponge is completely soaked with glue. Place RWP on the mesh, word-side up, press lightly, and glue RWP onto paper. Rewet with glue and drops of water as necessary.

Smashed Glue Stick: Remove the glue from a glue stick, and "smash" it into the bottom of a sealable, small plastic container. In the example below, we used a colored glue stick that dries clear. Use a drop of water as needed to remoisten the glue glob.

Two-Sided Tape: For easy mounting use small pieces of two-sided (double-stick) tape placed on poster boards, charts, or the front of Foldables. Over time, students place words on the tape. Often the RWP is larger than the piece of tape, so the teacher, an adult helper, or student helpers can glue the extended edges of the RWP as needed. Completed Foldables can be laminated to prevent any exposed tape from adhering to other teaching aids when stored.

Fantastic Foldable® Organizers:
Pocket Foldables, pocket charts, pocket charts with sentence strips, top-pocket Foldables, sentence-strip holders, four-door displays, and display boxes can be used to organize and store RWP flashcards and VKVs. You will see these used on these two pages and throughout this book.

RWP Carrying Case (right and above):
Make eight Foldable display boxes. Glue them together to make two rows of four boxes. Use clothespins to hold them in place while glue dries. Place a two-foot length of ribbon between the two rows of boxes, and then glue the rows together to form a rectangle of eight boxes with a ribbon handle. Use clothespins to hold the rows and ribbon in place. Use the box carrying case to sort words by skills. See page 304.

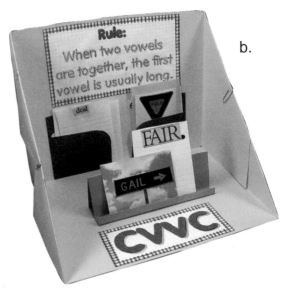

Four-Door Display (below): Made using a
sheet of poster board, this display can be used (a.) without and (b.) with a sentence strip holder. Quarter-sheet word cards illustrating CVVC words with a long vowel sound and word cards with exceptions to the rule were collected and stored in pockets glued to the back of the display. See page 303.

a.

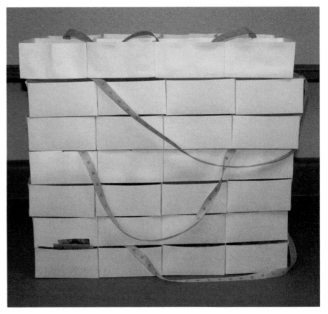

b.

Sentence Strip Holder Bulletin Board Displaying Matchbook Sight Word Cards (above): These sentence strip displays were made using 8½" x 11" paper. Each sentence strip was cut in half to form two small sections and then glued onto a sheet of black foam board. See page 306.

Matchbook Flashcards (right): Fifty sheets of 8½" x 11" paper were made into matchbooks and cut in half to form 100 study cards. Then, 100 high-frequency words were written on the cards. Students found examples of the words in RWP and glued them to the front of the cards. Sentences featuring the words have been written under the tabs by the teacher, students, and parent helpers. See page 292.

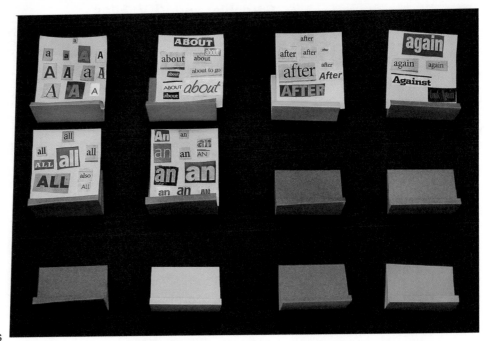

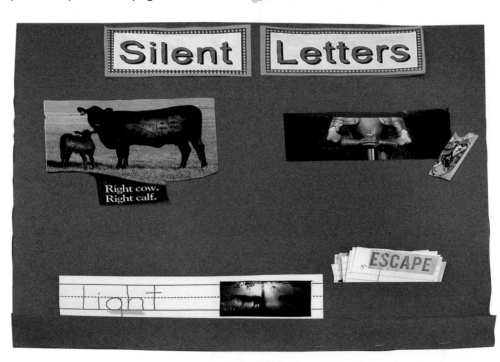

Pocket Chart with Word Strip (above): Use poster board to make large storage pockets. The deep pocket (flashcards are seen protruding from the pocket above) is used for storing VKVs and Foldables, and the stapled strip along the bottom provides a space to display flashcards, picture words, and/or sentence strips.

Foldable® and VKV® Files (left): Cereal boxes can be used to collect and store student- and teacher-made examples of Foldables and VKVs. These box files are perfect for keeping examples of previously made activities at one's fingertips for review and continued immersion throughout the school year. Students can "check out" a box, and take it to their desk for a special study time, and/or these boxes can be placed in learning stations.

This cereal box library was made for the Dinah Zike Academy using sponge brushes to paint cereal boxes with water-based enamel paint. Labels were made using a font style with outlines and shadows, and the labels were colored and glued onto colored paper before gluing them onto the ends of the boxes. These boxes were made to last for many years so we put time and effort into their construction. You can greatly reduce production time by covering the boxes with wrapping paper or contact paper and writing on the box ends with permanent marker.

Powder and Paint: Painted boxes tend to stick together. To prevent this, dust the sides of the boxes with baby powder or talc after the paint has dried thoroughly. This usually helps prevent sticking.

Side By Side: Make Foldables "grow" by gluing them side by side to form multi-page booklets. Most Foldables can be glued together, though two-pocket, two-tab, four-tab, and four-door Foldables are the easiest to use. With a spine or a cover these side by side Fldables become a meaningful collection of student work and progress. Students are proud of these special individual or class books. They "read" them frequently and use them as study guides and reference books. Side by side projects are more interesting than flat poster board projects. During a school year, teacher-made, student-made (and possibly parent-made) side-by-side Foldable booklets can become part of the class-room library.

Examples of these Foldable side-by-side projects can be seen throughout this book. Four examples are pictured below.

Thirteen Two-Pocket Foldables® (above) glued side by side make this 26-page alphabet book.

Four Two-Pocket Foldables® (above) glued side by side make this eight-page blends pocket book.

Six Four-Tab Foldables® (above) glued side by side make this twelve-page heteronym book.

Eight Two-Tab Foldables® (right) glued side by side make this sixteen-page homophone book.

Design Projects to Grow: Continue to immerse students in previously learned skills and previously written print by "growing" Foldables. The "old" skills on the first Foldables glued into a project become easy to students with continued use and exposure. When skills begin to seem easy, students feel smart. Students take an amazing amount of pride in personal and class projects that grow into scrapbooks of their learning and progress. These collections are great study aids.

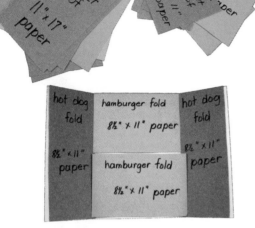

Poster Board Shutterfold Projects (below):

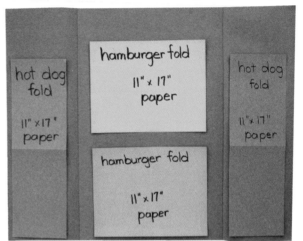

Hotdog Puzzle Pieces (above): Hot-dog shaped Foldables or two quarter-sheet Foldables made using 8½" x 11" paper will fit on the sides of an 11" x 17" shutterfold. Students can plan their projects as if the Foldables are puzzle pieces.

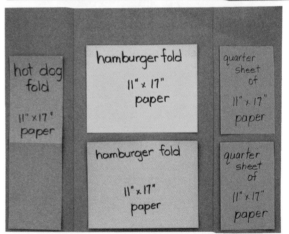

Hamburger and Quarter-Sheet Puzzle Pieces (above): Foldable hamburger folds made using 8½" x 11" paper fit on the inside sections of an 11" x 17" shutterfold. Two quarter-sheet Foldables (below) also fit in the hamburger-sized space.

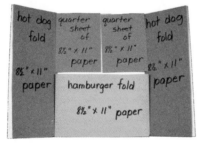

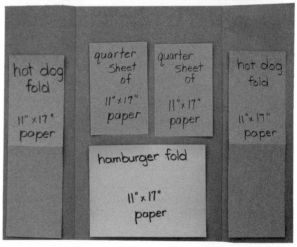

Small Foldables® Within Poster Board Foldables® (below left): The black, poster board accordion below, is being used to collect words that are spelled *ea*, but have three different sounds -- long *e*, long *a*, and short *e*. Notice that three 11" x 17" multi-tab, hot-dog shaped Foldables were glued onto three of the four sections of this large accordion. Look at the puzzle pieces pictured on the previous page, and you will see that two quarter-sheet sized Foldables could have been glued on an accordion section, too. See page 300.

Foldables® in Large Foldable® Projects: Place Foldables made using 8½" x 11" paper or 11" x 17" paper inside the Social Studies poster board, bound-book dictionary (above right). See page 290.

Parent- and Teacher-Made Two-Column Chart (left), Journal Songbook (center), and Four-Door Foldables® (right): Use 11" x 17" paper to make any of the three Foldable projects pictured above. Quarter sheets, half sheets, pop-up activities, folded papers, bound journals, multi-tabbed books, and other Foldables made using 8½" x 11" paper can be made and glued inside these projects.
Two-Column Chart, page 308; Journal Songbook, page 290; Four-Door Foldable, page 299.

Content Project Foldables®: Small Foldables can be glued into larger Foldables to make skills-based projects. Some Foldable projects might grow over a week, a six-week period, or the entire school year. Other Project Foldables might be used to collect unit or skills-based work and information. Skills-based Project Foldables are perfect for content subjects. The examples on this page show how poster board can be used to make large science Foldables that become the "home" for smaller Foldables and quarter sheets or half sheets of paper.

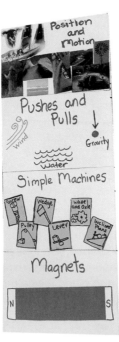

Layered Foldable® Class Project (above): Half sheets of photocopy paper were used for diagrams of monocots and dicots, and circles cut from half sheets of paper were used as a background for displaying physical examples of monocot and dicot seeds.

Laminated with 2" Clear Tape: Use 2" clear tape to laminate physical objects -- seeds, soil, leaves, flowers, roots, feathers, small stones -- to projects.

Three- and Four-Tab Poster Board Foldable® Projects (left): Glue notes, diagrams, vocabulary terms, and Foldables made using 8½" X 11" paper or quarter sheets of paper under the tabs of these large projects.

Introduction Foldables® Within Foldables® and Side By Side

Really Big "Big Books": On the next six pages you will see examples of five two-tab Foldables made with sheets of poster board. These giant Foldables contain smaller Foldables -- pockets, tabbed activities, display cases, dioramas, pocket charts, top-tabs, and more. When the class is finished with all five of the giant Foldables, they will be glued side by side to make a huge vowel *Big Book*.

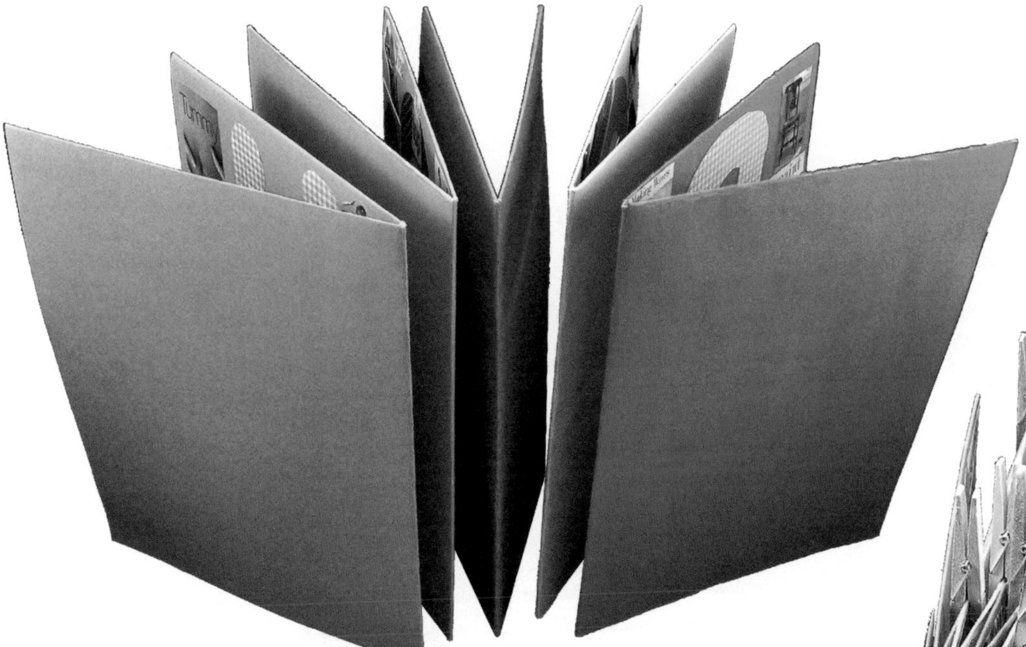

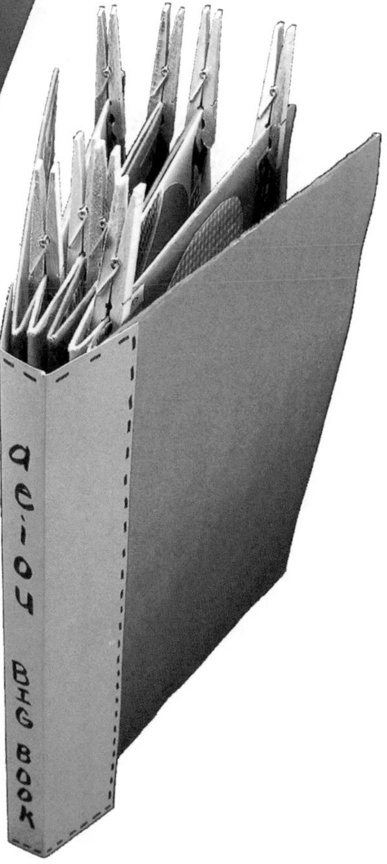

Giant Vowel Big Book (above and right): Two-tab Foldables made using poster board can be glued side by side to form one giant book. Use a strip of poster board to make a book spine. Label the spine and glue it to cover the ends of the Foldables. See inside these vowel books on the following six pages. Instructions for the spine fold and photographs are on page 62.

Make Your Own Big Books: Be creative as you remember that small Foldables can be glued into larger ones. Students love to find the following Foldables glued into Big Books:

- pop-ups
- picture frames
- accordions
- bound journals
- Foldable tables
- layered activities
- tabbed Foldables
- any dimensional Foldables such as pyramid dioramas, four-door dioramas, and display cubes.

Foldables can take days and weeks to complete. Small Foldables can be glued into larger Foldables to make skills-based projects. Some Foldable projects might grow over the entire school year, becoming a collection of student/class work as well as a symbol of progress and achievements.

Giant Two-Tab: This giant two-tab Foldable was made using one sheet of poster board folded into a hamburger and cut to form two tabs. Collect examples of short vowel words and pictures on the left side and long vowel words and pictures on the right.

Always Searching: Pictures might be glued on the front tabs before words are found in RWP. For example, the picture of a chair does not have a word with it yet. Word searches are a constant process, and students become very aware of print.

A Very Special Word: The compound word *pancakes* has a short a in the first word *pan* and a long a in the second word *cakes,* so it was cut and glued to fit in both categories.

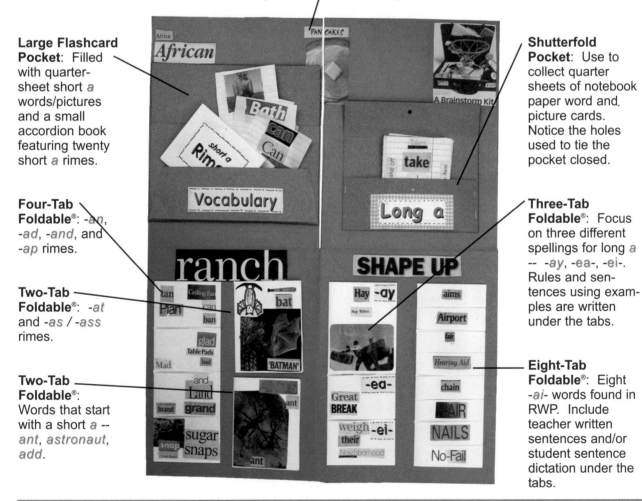

Large Flashcard Pocket: Filled with quarter-sheet short *a* words/pictures and a small accordion book featuring twenty short *a* rimes.

Four-Tab Foldable®: -*an*, -*ad*, -*and*, and -*ap* rimes.

Two-Tab Foldable®: -*at* and -*as* / -*ass* rimes.

Two-Tab Foldable®: Words that start with a short *a* -- *ant*, *astronaut*, *add*.

Shutterfold Pocket: Use to collect quarter sheets of notebook paper word and picture cards. Notice the holes used to tie the pocket closed.

Three-Tab Foldable®: Focus on three different spellings for long *a* -- -*ay*, -*ea*-, -*ei*-. Rules and sentences using examples are written under the tabs.

Eight-Tab Foldable®: Eight -*ai*- words found in RWP. Include teacher written sentences and/or student sentence dictation under the tabs.

Foldables can take days and weeks to complete. Small Foldables can be glued into larger Foldables to make skills-based projects. Some Foldable projects might grow over the entire school year, becoming a collection of student/class work as well as a symbol of progress and achievements.

Giant Two-Tab:
This giant two-tab Foldable was make using one sheet of poster board folded into a hamburger and cut to form two-tabs. Collect examples of short vowel words and pictures on the left side and long vowel words and pictures on the right.

Selecting Words:
Notice the homographs for the word *ear*. Pictures include a human ear and an ear of corn. The homophone for *see* is *sea* and the words and pictures for these words are placed close to each other on the front tab.

Content Vocabulary: Include examples of words students will encounter in other subjects. The word *West* has been used inside the short *e* tab and the word *East* can be used to illustrate long *e*. Point out that these are opposites.

Five-Tab Foldable®:
Words from RWP that begin with a short e were collected and glued to the front tabs. Some of the words selected were easy while others were challenging. Students like the "hard" words.

Two-Tab Foldable®: The short e word *Next* was used as the title of this Foldable featuring -*et* and -*ell* rimes on inside tabs.

Vocabulary Pockets: The two inside pockets are labeled *Know* and *Need to Know*. Quarter-sheet flashcards are placed in the pockets.

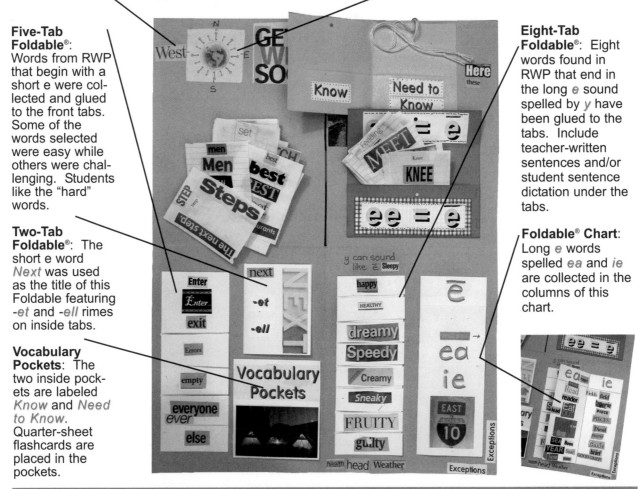

Eight-Tab Foldable®: Eight words found in RWP that end in the long *e* sound spelled by *y* have been glued to the tabs. Include teacher-written sentences and/or student sentence dictation under the tabs.

Foldable® Chart: Long *e* words spelled *ea* and *ie* are collected in the columns of this chart.

Foldables can take days and weeks to complete. Small Foldables can be glued into larger Foldables to make skills-based projects. Some Foldable projects might grow over the entire school year, becoming a collection of student/class work as well as a symbol of progress and achievements.

Giant Two-Tab:
This giant two-tab Foldable was made using one sheet of poster board folded into a hamburger and cut to form two tabs. Collect examples of short vowel words and pictures on the left side and long vowel words and pictures on the right.

Vocabulary Extension:
Include plural forms of singular nouns -- *line*, *lines*; compound words formed with a featured word or sound -- *fire*, *firefighter*; and phrases from RWP -- *For The First Time*.

Very Special Words: The compound word *inside* has a short *i* in the first word *in* and a long *i* in the second word *side*, so it was cut and glued to fit in both categories. The short *i* word *QUICK* was used as a title for the rime section.

Rimes Chart:
Common short *i* rimes are computer generated, printed, colored, and glued under the large tab. Students collect example words from RWP.

Pyramid Foldable®: Even three-dimensional Foldables can be placed within larger Foldable projects because they are designed to fold flat when stored.

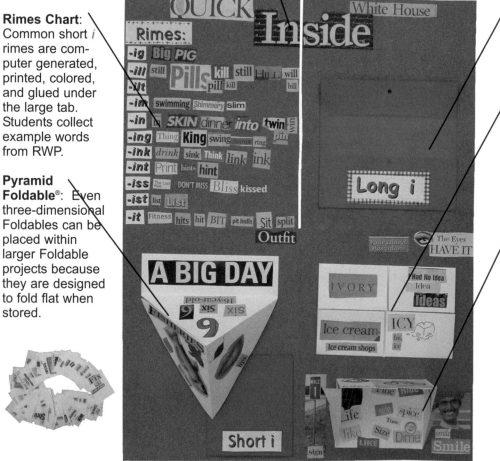

Shutterfold Pocket:
Use to collect quarter sheets of notebook paper word and picture cards.

Small Four-Door:
Four words that begin with the letter *i* and have the long *i* sound have been placed on the front tabs -- *ivory*, *idea*, *ice cream*, *ice/icy*.

Four-Door Display:
This three-dimensional Foldable display can also be placed within larger Foldable projects because it folds flat when stored. This example features CVCe words. Note the word *mile* to the left of the display and the word *smile* to the right -- same rime different onsets.

Introduction Phonics and Vocabulary Big Book -- o

Foldables can take days and weeks to complete. Small Foldables can be glued into larger Foldables to make skills-based projects. Some Foldable projects might grow over the entire school year, becoming a collection of student/class work as well as a symbol of progress and achievements.

Giant Two-Tab: This giant two-tab Foldable was made using one sheet of poster board folded into a hamburger and cut to form two tabs. Collect examples of short vowel words and pictures on the left side and long vowel words and pictures on the right.

Vocabulary Extension: Include plural forms of singular nouns -- *rose, roses*; open compound words formed with a featured word -- *ice cream cone*; and phrases from RWP -- *a dog's life*. Discuss plural and possessive: *dogs and dog's*.

Very Special Words: The compound word *offshore* has a short o in the first word, and a long o (that is r-controlled) in the second word. The word was cut and glued to show its two parts and to illustrate the two vowel sounds.

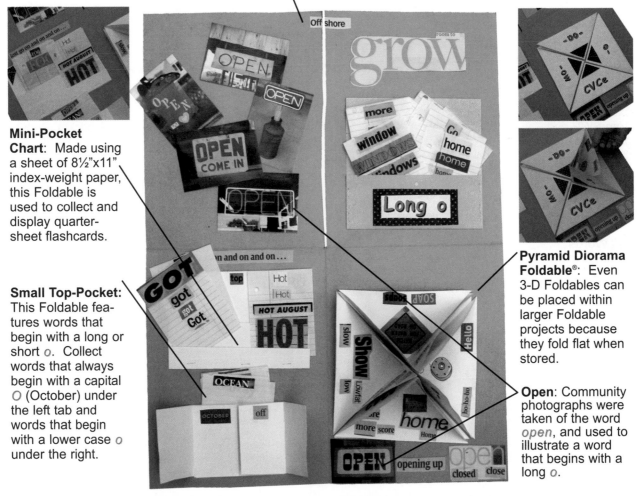

Mini-Pocket Chart: Made using a sheet of 8½"x11" index-weight paper, this Foldable is used to collect and display quarter-sheet flashcards.

Small Top-Pocket: This Foldable features words that begin with a long or short o. Collect words that always begin with a capital O (October) under the left tab and words that begin with a lower case o under the right.

Pyramid Diorama Foldable®: Even 3-D Foldables can be placed within larger Foldable projects because they fold flat when stored.

Open: Community photographs were taken of the word *open*, and used to illustrate a word that begins with a long o.

Foldables can take days and weeks to complete. Small Foldables can be glued into larger Foldables to make skills-based projects. Some Foldable projects might grow over the entire school year, becoming a collection of student/class work as well as a symbol of progress and achievements.

Giant Two-Tab: This giant two-tab Foldable was made using one sheet of poster board folded into a hamburger and cut to form two tabs. Collect examples of short vowel words and pictures on the left side and long vowel words and pictures on the right.

Long *u* RWP: Students will not find many long *u* CVCe words, nor words that begin or end with a long *u*. However, they will find lots of words that have the long *u* sound spelled with these letter combinations: *-ue*, *-oe*, *-oo*, *-ew*, *-ou*, *-ui*.

Very Special Words: The word *unsure* has a short *u* in the prefix *un-* and a long *u* (that is r-controlled) in the base word *sure*, so it was cut and glued across the cut. The short *u* rime *-ut* was used with a giant calendar picture of nuts, and students collected other words with the same rime.

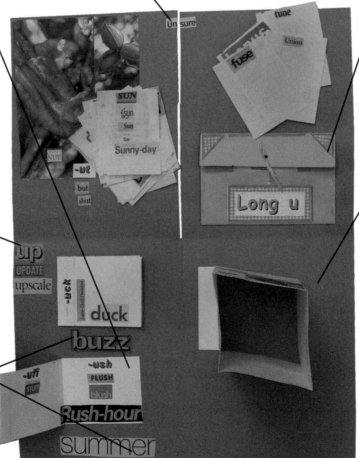

Rime Accordion Booklet: This small accordion booklet features ten short *u* rimes. Students collect example words from RWP and glue them onto the appropriate pages of the book. See the next page for a close-up photograph.

Big Words: Students learn to identify "small" words within "big" words. Notice how the class is collecting words that begin with *up-*.

Large Font: Two short *u* words were found in RWP and glued onto the project -- *summer*, *buzz*.

Shutterfold Pocket: Fill pockets with quarter-sheet flashcards of long *u* words/pictures. Use clear 2" clear tape to reinforce the edges of the pocket. Punch holes and tie the sections together to keep flashcards in place.

Long *u* Cube Project: This small cube project features six long *u* letter combinations. Students collect example words from RWP and glue them onto the appropriate sections of the cube. See the next page for close-up photographs of the cube open and closed.

Shutterfold Pocket Close-Up (right): Make a shutterfold using a heavy paper -- index weight or cover stock. Glue the sides of one half of the shutterfold to form a pocket. You can make one of the sides larger than the other to make a deeper pocket, as shown. Punch holes and tie the pocket sections together to store flashcards.

Standing Cube with a Tab for Gluing (above): Fold and assemble the Cube as described on page 296, but cut off 1" from the bottom of three of the sides. Leave a 1" section on one side, fold it to form a tab, and glue the tab down as illustrated. This will allow the cube to fold flat when the project is closed or to stand when the project is open.

Small Accordion Foldable® Glued into a Project (above): The above accordion was made by folding two sheets of 8½" x 11" paper into hot-dog folds and cutting them in half. This resulted in four (4¼" x 5½") pieces of paper. These four long pieces were folded to form an eight-section accordion. (You can also start an accordian fold using hamburger folds. See instructions page 300.) This accordion was used to collect RWP examples of short *u* rimes.

Rubric Assessment for Foldables® and VKV® Flashcards

How Do I Grade This? I am frequently asked how Foldables are graded. Keep in mind that Foldables and VKVs can be used successfully as instructional strategies for skill introduction, demonstration, practice, drill, reinforcement, and review without grades being taken. However, the majority of teachers using Foldables and VKVs will also use them as a grading tool. Using Foldables and VKVs does not suggest or require a particular assessment strategy. Foldables can be assessed in many ways, including teacher observation with anecdotal notes, student observations and comments on personal strengths and weaknesses, point assignment for a given number of correct responses, and simple to complex rubrics.

Foldable® Assessment and a Simple Skills Rubric: The internet is filled with samples of rubrics that can be adapted and used with Foldables. Most school districts have established their own rubrics. In this book and in my workshops, I only mention a few ways in which rubrics might be used hoping to give you ideas on how to write your own and/or adapt those used by your district.

A very simple, straightforward rubric might include the following: 1. the skill/skills upon which an activity is based; 2. the student action required for the activity; 3. the level/levels of action to be assessed within the activity; and 4. the outcome of the student's actions and performance.

For example, on a Foldable activity over a period of four days, a student might be asked to find ten words in RWP (real world print) that end in the consonant blend -*sh*, read the ten words, and use them orally in simple sentences. If students find and read ten words, they receive an A+, or an S+ for Satisfactory. If students find and read seven words, they might receive a B or an S, and if they find and read five words they might receive a C or an S-. However, students who find only two or three words and have difficulty reading them and/or using them in sentences, would receive a D or a U for Unsatisfactory.

This rubric provides a curve that differs from the more traditional grading method where ten items would be worth ten points each. With this more traditional method, a student would make a C- (70) if they missed three, instead of a B (85) as outlined above. Why give a curve? When using Foldables, the level of student responsibility for and involvement in their own learning process is high compared to the low level of student responsibility and involvement when completing fill-in-the-blank worksheets and workbook pages. For example, students might complete a worksheet that directs them to find -*sh* words and mark them or match them to a picture. This example requires a very low level of performance (recognition) as the -*sh* words and pictures were provided on the worksheet, and there is little space for student production. Worksheets can be completed in minutes and students have very little time to feel "ownership" of their work. Foldables are completed over hours or days, and students are very involved with their production and completion.

Rubric Assessment for Foldables® and VKV® Flashcards

Dinah's Graduated Skills Rubric: I have designed and used simple Rubrics for Foldables that reflect the level of instruction as well as the level of student performance, and I found them to be less threatening for young children (and parents). For example, the rubric pictured to the right is used to assess student understanding of CVCe words.

When the concept is first introduced, I do not grade as strictly as I would once time has been given for mastery. A student who misses two of ten CVCe words during the introduction level of the rubric would receive a 90. Once mastery is expected, the same student who missed two would receive an 80. This rubric gives students a given amount of time to learn, practice, and apply skills. Students are told (or they help determine) when grading will move to the next level -- *I* = *introduction*, *P* = *practice*, *M* = *mastery*.

Student: Lesson: Skill: Date:		Introduction I 5pts. each	Practice P 7 pts. each	Mastery M 10 pts. each
Number Required:	10	100	100	100
Number Correct:	9	95	93	90
Number Correct:	8	90	86	80
Number Correct:	7	85	79	70
Number Correct:	6	80	72	60
Number Correct:	5	75	65	50
Number Correct:	4	70	58	40
Number Correct:	3	65	51	30
Number Correct:	2	60	44	20
Number Correct:	1	55	37	10
Observations and Comments:				

c 2007, Dinah Zike Academy, www.dinah.com

Student: Lesson: Skill: Date:		Introduction I 10 pts. each	Practice P 15 pts. each	Mastery M 20 pts. each
Number Required:	5	100	100	100
Number Correct:	4	90	85	80
Number Correct:	3	80	70	70
Number Correct:	2	70	55	60
Number Correct:	1	60	40	50
Observations and Comments:				

c 2007, Dinah Zike Academy, www.dinah.com

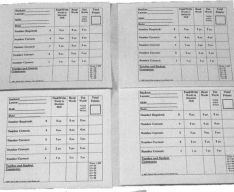

Staple to Student Work: Reduce rubrics so four will fit on one sheet of photocopy paper. Make multiple small rubrics. Staple scored rubrics to Foldables so students and parents can see and discuss the evaluation of student performance.

Example of a Student- and Teacher-Made Rubric: Allow students to help design rubrics to assess their work. For example, students might be asked to make a two-tab Foldable that has the labels *Silent Consonants* on one tab and *Silent Vowels* on the other. In this example (and frequently when using Foldables) the **skill** is stated by the teacher and determined by student needs and district curriculum requirements.

Ask students what they should be required to do (student action) on this Foldable. How they respond to this question will depend on what you have been modeling as the teacher. If you have asked them to find a given number of examples, list them on the front tabs beneath the tab titles, and use a given number of the words in sentences under the tabs, it is likely that students will say something close to what you have asked them to do in the past. Remember to vary what you ask students to do.

Student: Lesson: Skill: Date:	Numbers Assigned Numbers Achieved	Points Asssigned Points Earned	Grade
Assigned Silent Consonants:	4 (5 pts. each)	20	
Number Found:			
Assigned Silent Vowels:	6 (5 pts. each)	30	
Number Found:			
Oral Sentences Using Each of the Ten Words:	10 (2 pts. each)	20	
Number Spoken:			
Paragraphs Under Tabs:	2 (5 pts. each)	10	
Number Written:			
Internal Punctuation:		10	
External Punctuation:		10	
Capitalization:		10	
Teacher and Student Comments:			Final Grade

c 2007, Dinah Zike Academy, www.dinah.com

Next, get students to help you determine the levels of action to be assessed within the activity. Students might think it is harder to find silent consonants than silent vowels, so they feel they should find four silent consonants and six silent vowels. Students decide that they will each have a partner and read their words to their partner. The partner will mark a check on the Foldable in front of words read correctly and a minus in front of words read incorrectly. Students think they should be asked to use each word in an oral sentence after reading it, and that the partners should put a check or minus after the word to indicate if this is done correctly. Students suggest they write a simple paragraph under each tab using three of the words listed on the front. Ten points are given just for writing the two paragraphs regardless of structure and content. Since the class has been working on capitalization and internal and external punctuation, students determine that these will be evaluated as part of their paragraph writing grade and be awarded 30 points.

Example of a Student- and Teacher-Made Rubric (continued):
Once students have helped set the levels of action, they help assign value to the work. In this example, students determined that the entire project was worth 100 points:

20 points	- 5 points for each of the four silent consonant words found, recorded, read
30 points	- 5 points for each of the six silent vowel words found, recorded, read
10 points	- 1 point for each word read correctly
10 points	- 5 points for each paragraph written using three words with silent letters.
10 points	- proper internal punctuation
10 points	- proper external punctuation
10 points	- proper capitalization

_____

100 points Total points on a two-tab Foldable.

One Foldable® Can Provide Multiple Grades: Since students are doing lots of production when using a Foldable, Foldables take much longer to complete than a worksheet. The above example will take several days to complete. The teacher might suggest to students that three separate grades be taken on this exercise. The first grade might be given for the finding and listing of four silent consonants words and six silent vowel words -- 50 points would equal 100%. The second grade could be taken on the reading of the ten words and

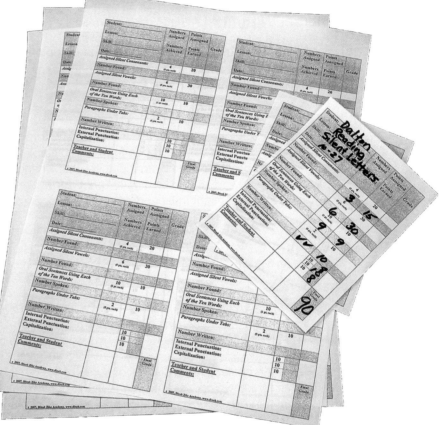

the use of each in an oral sentence -- 10 points for each word (5 for reading and 5 for use in oral sentences) with 100 points available. The final grade could be taken on the writing of the simple paragraphs using six of the words under the tabs -- 50 points would equal 100%. In this example the teacher and students have determined that the entire Foldable is worth 200 points. Three grades, one each for reading, writing, and vocabulary, were collected from this activity.

Note From Dinah: This is not intended to be a scope and sequence for this grade level, nor a list of "must teach" skills or required experiences. State and district guidelines will dictate curriculum planning.

Auditory and Oral Vocabulary:

Students tap out how many words are heard in a simple sentence. Use one-syllable words to form first sentences. Count words as teacher writes simple sentences.

I go. = 2 taps; I can run. = 3 taps; The dog is big. = 4 taps.

Students hear over fifty books or book equivalents of differing genres and by numerous authors.

Students begin to identify genres they enjoy, and they identify favorite authors and illustrators.

Students increase their auditory and oral vocabulary through exposure to reading aloud, audio-taped books, guided reading, shared reading, and independent reading.

Students begin to associate sounds within words with letters and letter combinations.

Students Interact With Print: Students are exposed to print in different fonts, sizes, colors, textures.

Personal Names: Students identify their first name or the first letter of their name.

Students try to write their first name and the names of friends and family.

Some students will be ready for the introduction of their last name.

Writing: Students use drawings to communicate.

Students stay on a topic when communicating through art and "writing."

Students "write" in their own free form (for example "scribble" writing), and some will incorporate words into their personal writing.

Students show an understanding of "print" as written "talk."

Some students might independently begin to show spaces between their scribbles so their written talk corresponds to words.

Letters of the alphabet: Students begin naming and identifying common letters of the alphabet.

(Frequency order of consonant graphemes: r, t, n, s, l, c, d, p, m, b, f, v, g, h, k, w, x, z, j, qu, y.)

Consonants:

Students dentify the most common consonants within CVC words or sight words.

Students find a featured consonant in real world print.

Students find and sort two- or three-letter words with featured consonants and highlight the consonants within the words.

Students learn the names and/or sounds of some of the most common consonants.

Students listen for known consonant sounds at the beginning of common words.

Students listen for known consonant sounds at the end of common words.

Vowels:

Students are introduced to these letters as vowels with special sounds -- a, e, i, o, u.

Students begin identifying short vowel sounds at the beginning of simple words -- at, it, egg.

Students begin identifying short vowels in the middle of simple CVC words -- cat, dog, can.

High Frequency Words:

Students are introduced to and begin to read and write high frequency words:

a, am, and, at, can, come, go, here, I,
in, is, it, like, look, me, my, on, said,
see, the, this, to, up, we, you.

Note From Dinah: This is not intended to be a scope and sequence for this grade level, nor a list of "must teach" skills or required experiences. State and district guidelines will dictate curriculum planning.

Auditory and Oral Vocabulary:

Students hear over sixty books or book equivalents of differing genres and by numerous authors.

Students begin to read books of the genres they enjoy, and they look for books by their favorite authors and illustrators.

Students increase their auditory and oral vocabulary through exposure to reading aloud, audio-taped books, guided reading, shared reading, and independent reading.

Students associate sounds within words with letters and letter combinations.

Students Interact With Print: Students are exposed to various forms of print (magazine, newspaper, advertisements, photographs of signs) that use different fonts, sizes, textures, and colors.

Consonants: b, c, d, f, g, h, j, k, l, m, n, p, q, r, s, t, v, w, x, y, z
Frequency order of consonant graphemes:

r, t, n, s, l, c, d, p, m, b, f, v, g, h, k, w, th, sh-, -ng, ch-, x, z, j, qu-, wh, y

Vowels: Students are exposed to short vowel sounds for -- a, e, i, o, u
Words: Students recognize how many words are in a sentence.
Students vocalize simple sentences using new and review words.

High Frequency Words: a, am, and, at, can, come, go, good, here, I, in, is, it, like, look, me, my, not, on, said, see, the, this, to, up, we, want, went, you.

Phonological Awareness: Letter/Word Knowledge and Letter/Sound Relationships
Sounds:

Students say the order in which two letter-sounds are heard.

Students say the order in which three letter-sounds are heard.

Students recognize the same initial consonant sound in words --
m, s, t, p,n, hard c, f, h, d, r, k, j, qu, y, z.

Students recognize the same final consonant sound in words --
m, s, t, p, n, hard c, f, d, r, -ck, z.

Students recognize the same initial short vowel sound -- a, i, o, e, u.

Students recognize the same medial short vowel sound -- a, i, o, e, u.

Phoneme Blending:

Students form a recognizable word after listening to a short series of separately spoken sounds -- /b/-/a/-/t/=/bat/.

Students use rimes and onsets to form words:

-at, -am, -an, -ap, -ad, -at,

-et, -ed, -en

-it, -ip, -id

-ot, -ox

-up, -ut, -un

Phoneme Addition and Deletion:

Students make a new word by deleting a phoneme from an existing word -- jam, am.

Students make a new word by adding a phoneme to an existing word -- it, bit.

Phoneme Substitution: Students replace the first sound (onset) in a word -- bat, cat, fat, hat, pat, rat, sat, vat.
Syllables: Students blend to form two-syllable words.
Synonyms and Antonyms: Students listen for and use common synonyms and antonyms.

Note From Dinah: This is not intended to be a scope and sequence for this grade level, nor a list of "must teach" skills or required experiences. State and district guidelines will dictate curriculum planning.

Auditory and Oral Vocabulary:

Students hear over fifty books of differing genres and by numerous authors.

Students identify genres they enjoy, and they identify favorite authors/illustrators.

Students increase their auditory and oral vocabulary through exposure to reading aloud, audio-taped books, and guided, shared, and independent reading.

Students read twenty to forty grade-level-appropriate books and discuss them.

Phonological Awareness:

Students show understanding of letter/sound and letter/word relationships.

Vowels: short vowel sounds: a, e, i, o,u
long vowel sounds: a, e, i, o, u
long a sounds: -ay, ai-, -ai
long e sounds: e, -ee-, -ea-, -y
long o sounds: o, -oa-, -ow
long i sounds: -ind, -y, -igh

Vowel Diphthongs: -ou-, -ow, -ow-

Variant Vowel: -oo- (long and short)

r Consonant Blends: cr-, gr-, tr-

l Consonant Blends: bl-, cl-, fl-, sl-

s Consonant Blends: sl-, sn-, sp-

Final Blends: -nd -st, -nt, -nk

Double Final Consonants: -ll, -ff, -ss

Consonant Digraphs: sh-, th-, ch-, -tch, wh-

Consonant Clusters: scr-, spr-, str-

Structural Analysis

Students identify onsets and rimes and use them to read, spell, and write terms.

Students read words with the following patterns: CVC, CVVC, CVCe, CCVC, CVVC.

Students identify r controlled vowels in vocabulary and spelling words: ar, or, er, ir, ur

Affixes:Students identify base words and add affixes.

Common Prefixes including: re-, un-, dis-
Common Suffixes including: -ful, -less
Inflectional Endings:
-s (plurals)
-ed, -ing, -er, -est with no change to base word (comparatives and superlatives)
-ed and -ing dropping the final e
-es for nouns and verbs with no change to base word
-es for nouns and verbs changing final -y of base word to i
-ed and -ing doubling the final consonant of the base word
-er and -est dropping the final e of base word
-s add s to verbs

Suffix: possessives with 's

Common Contractions:
Students read and/or write simple contractions:
I'm; it's, she's, he's; can't, won't, shouldn't, couldn't
I've, you've, we've, they've; I'll, we'll, you'll, they'll

Syllables: Students are introduced to one- and two-syllable words.

Compound Words: Students are introduced to closed compound words -- birdhouse, rainbow.
Students are introduced to common open compound words -- ice cream.

Synonyms and Antonyms: Students listen for and use common synonyms and antonyms.
Homophones and Homographs: Students identify and use homophones and homographs.

Note From Dinah: This is not intended to be a scope and sequence for this grade level, nor a list of "must teach" skills or required experiences. State and district guidelines will dictate curriculum planning.

Auditory and Oral Vocabulary:

Students hear twenty books of differing genres and by numerous authors.

Students identify genres they enjoy, and they have favorite authors and illustrators.

Students increase their auditory, oral, and reading vocabulary through reading aloud, audio-taped books, guided-, shared-, group-, and independent reading.

Students read twenty to forty grade level appropriate books and discuss them.

Phonological Awareness:

Students show understanding of letter/sound and letter/word relationships.

Vowels: short vowel sounds: *a, e, i, o,u*

long vowel sounds: *a, e, i, o, u*

long a sounds: *ay, -ai, -ai-*

long e sounds: *e, -ee-, -ea-, -ey, -y*

long i sounds: *i, -y, -igh, -ie-*

long o sounds: *o, -oa-, -ow, -oe-*

r Controlled: -ar, -air, -are; -er, -eer, -ere, -ear; -ir, -ire; -or, -ore, -oar; -ur, -ure

Vowel Diphthongs: ou-, -ow, -oi-, -oy

Variant Vowels: oo (long and short), -ui-, -ew, -au-, -aw

Consonant Blends: initial, medial, and final

Hard and Soft Consonants: c can also sound like /s/, g can also sound like /j/

Consonant Blends: initial, medial, and final -- two and three letters

Consonant Digraphs: initial, medial, and final -- sh-, th-, ch-, -tch, wh-

Word Endings: -dge, -ge, -ige, -nge, and -rge

Structural Analysis

Students gain mastery of onsets and rimes and use them to read, spell, and write terms.

Students identify base words and add affixes:

Prefixes: re-, un-, dis-, (See "Twenty Most Common Prefixes", pages 154-155.)

Suffixes: -ful, -less, -er, -est (See "Twenty Most Common Suffixes", pages 184-185.)

Suffixes: Inflectional Endings

-s and -es to form plurals

-s and -es w/o changing the base word

-es changing the final y of the base word to i (nouns and verbs)

-ed and -ing without changing base word

-er and -est to form comparatives and superlatives by dropping final e of base

-double the final consonant before adding inflectional endings

-drop the final e of a base word before adding inflectional endings

-change consonant -y to -i before adding endings

-add -s to verbs

Suffixes: possessives with 's

Contractions: Students read and/or write simple contractions:

is: she's, he's

are: we're, they're, you're

not: can't, won't, shouldn't, couldn't

have: I've, you've, they've

Compound Words: Students use common closed, open, and hyphenated compound words.

Syllabication: Students are introduced to the rules and patterns of syllabication -- one-, two-, and three-syllable words.

Synonyms and Antonyms: Students identify and use synonyms and antonyms.

Homophones and Homographs: Students identify and use homophones and homographs.

Note From Dinah: This is not intended to be a scope and sequence for this grade level, nor a list of "must-teach" skills or required experiences. State and district guidelines will dictate curriculum planning.

Auditory and Oral Vocabulary:

Students know the meanings of words encountered frequently in grade-level reading and oral language contexts.

Students expand their vocabularies and learn the rhythm of language by listening to good literature.

Word Recognition - Vocabulary:

Students quickly recognize frequently encountered words in print, whether found in connected text or in isolation (e.g., the meshed list of 300+ Fry and Dolch basic sight words; see page 217). The number of words students can read fluently will increase throughout the school year.

Students use structural, syntactic, and semantic cues—including letter sounds, rimes, base words, and affixes—to read and understand frequently encountered words; decode unknown words or word parts; and determine meanings, including multiple-meaning words.

Students determine the meanings of words and phrases in context, including synonyms, homonyms, multiple-meaning words, content vocabulary, and literary terms. Strategies and resources include context clues, concept mapping, and environmental sources.

Students self-monitor and construct definitions by predicting and self-correcting, and by applying knowledge of language, sound/symbol/structural relationships, and context.

With strong reading-writing connections developed by the time they are in third grade, students find wide exposure to literature—both fiction and non-fiction—to be a rich source of new oral and written vocabulary.

Students learn to recognize signal words in various kinds of texts, including words that cue chronological order, cause and effect, and similarities and differences.

Spelling

Students correctly spell frequently encountered words: multi-syllabic, r-controlled, most consonant blends, contractions, compounds, and common homophones.

For less frequently encountered words, students use structural cues (letter-sound associations, rimes, morphemic cues, syllabication) and environmental sources (word walls, word lists, dictionaries, spell checkers).

Reading-Writing

As they become more discerning readers and writers, students read and write for their own purposes, often becoming experts on topics that interest them.
- Students explore a topic, then state in their own words what they learned.

- Students read thoughtfully, comprehending shades of meaning and interpreting the significance of stories as appropriate for their maturity level.

- Students make comparisons between authors, books, and characters.

- Students question authors' purposes and perspectives and begin to identify the styles and distinguishing characteristics of certain authors.

- Students' writing exhibits personal style and voice in both narrative form (varied word choice and sentence structure, character description) and informational form (examples, transitions, grammar and usage).

- By using mentor texts, students begin to manipulate language, make conscious word choices, and use language descriptively and figuratively at a beginning level to paint a picture or set a mood.

- Through nonfiction studies, students learn to articulate and categorize thier observations and sharpen their skills at interpreting, analyzing, and synthesizing what they read.

- Students develop their writing skills by writing "a little, a lot": fiction and non-fiction, responses to literature, short reports, directions, and procedures.

- Students no longer rely on drawings as key elements to convey meaning, but rather use them for illustrative purposes.

- Students create and understand simple charts or diagrams that communicate information in nonfiction text.

Grammar, Usage, Revision, and Mechanics

Student writing shows:
- subjects and verbs in agreement
- correct verb tenses
- nouns and possessives used and spelled correctly
- correct use of commas in a series
- use of quotation marks and capitalization in dialogue

Students write daily and revise selected first drafts, both individually and with feedback from classmates.

Layered Book Foldable® (above)
instructions on page 295.

Side by Side Pocket Foldable® (below)
instructions on page 291.

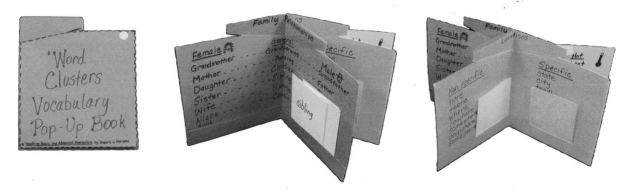

The term *affixes* refers to a letter, or clusters of letters, that add meaning to a base word. Affixes are added before or after a base word. Affixes are often added syllables; however, the single letter *s* is also considered an affix. Letters and letter clusters added to the beginning of words are called *prefixes*. Letters and letter clusters added to the end of words are called *suffixes*. Affixes can change words in several ways, including the following:

-from singular to plural
-from present tense to past or future tense
-from a noun to a verb
-from an adjective to an adverb
See pages150-155 on prefixes and pages 178-189 on suffixes.

Content Application: Make VKVs for words with affixes and/or combining forms encountered in math, science, social studies, and health.

Examples: *tri*angle, *tri*cycle, *Tri*ceratops   *mid*night, *mid*way, *mid*summer
*tele*phone, *tele*scope, *tele*vision   *uni*verse, *uni*form, *uni*corn

VKV® Flashcard: Add an Affix
1. Close a double flashcard, then fold it in half.
2. Cut along the fold line of the top tab to form two tabs.
3. Write the prefix of a selected word under the first tab, and the root word under the second tab. Write the prefix with its last letter next to the center fold line, and write the root word with its first letter next to the fold.
4. Open and close the tabs to view the prefix and the root word separately, or open both tabs at the same time, joining the prefix and root word to form the vocabulary word.
5. On the back of the VKV, write sentences using the base word with and without affixes.

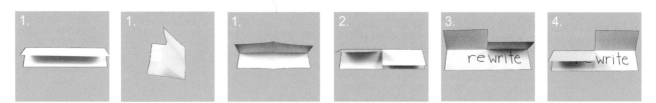

Alternate VKV®: Do the same for a vocabulary word with a suffix. See example below.

Procedure: With the right tab closed, raise the left tab to view the stem word. Read the stem word. Close the left tab. Raise the right tab and read the suffix. Close both tabs. Raise the left tab, read the stem word, and immediately raise the right tab and read the word formed -- *talk, talked*.

VKV Flashcard: Accordion Affixes

1. Fold a half sheet of copy paper into an eight-section accordion book. See photographs (a-e) below.
2. Cut a 3" strip off the right side of the top seven sections leaving the bottom eighth section whole (f).
3. Glue the accordion sections together using clothespins to hold them in place until the glue dries (g).
4. Write a suffix on the extended tab so that the first letter is next to the accordion fold (h).
5. Select and write five words on the accordion strips aligning the last letter of each word next to the edge of each accordion section as illustrated in the photographs.
6. Fold and flip the accordion section to add the suffix to each of the words listed.

Ten-Word VKV®:

7. Fold the affix tab to the back and read the words without an affix. Fold the affix tab so that it shows, and read the words with the affix.

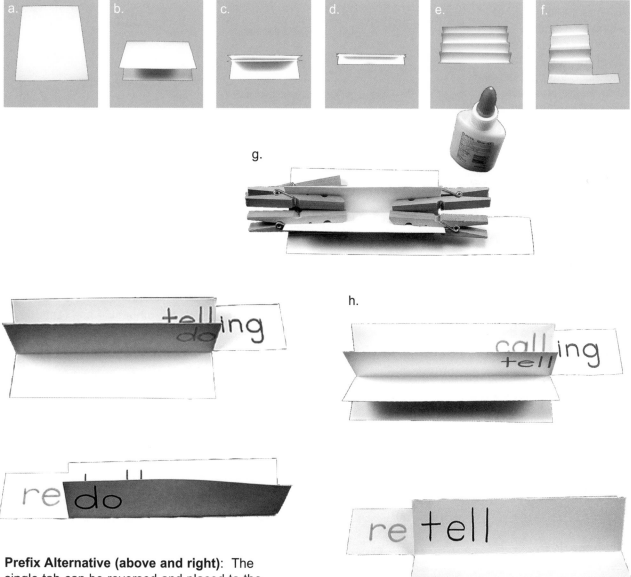

Prefix Alternative (above and right): The single tab can be reversed and placed to the left to create prefix accordion VKVs.

VKV® Flashcard: One Affix Fold-Over

1. On the right edge of a single flashcard, write a word that has a prefix.
   Alternative: Glue a word collected from RWP to the right edge of a single flashcard.
2. Fold the left edge over to cover the prefix.
3. Open and close the left tab and analyze the stem/root word with and without the prefix.

Suffix Alternative (not pictured):
Write a word or glue a word collected from RWP to the left edge of a single flashcard. Fold the right edge over to cover the suffix. Open and close the right tab to analyze the word with and without the suffix.

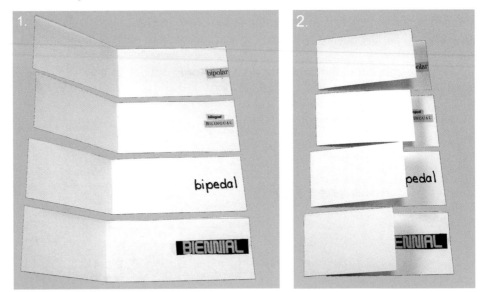

VKV® Flashcards: Affix VKV® Ring

1. Fold a single flashcard in half.
2. Write a word on the left side so that the last letter is next to the fold, and write an affix such as "s" on the right side of the fold. Alternative: Glue a word cut from RWP across the fold so the suffix is to the right of the fold or a prefix is to the left.
3. Place a picture of each word on the back sides, or write sentences using the words.
4. Punch a hole through the folded flashcard along the short edge. Store the VKV cards on a large ring.
5. Look at one side of the word cards on the ring and read the word. Look at the other side and read the word again adding the affix.
6. Reverse all VKV flashcards so the pictures or sentences are showing. Repeat step 5.

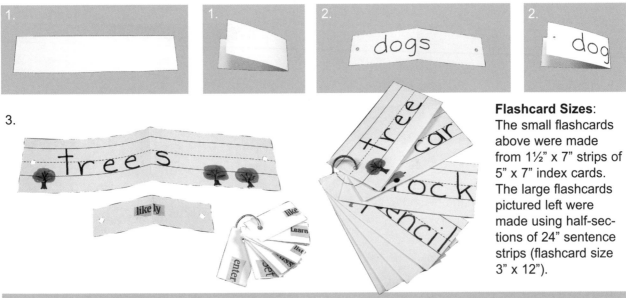

Flashcard Sizes:
The small flashcards above were made from 1½" x 7" strips of 5" x 7" index cards. The large flashcards pictured left were made using half-sections of 24" sentence strips (flashcard size 3" x 12").

VKV® Flashcards: Two Affix Fold-Over

1. Write a word with a prefix and a suffix in the center of a single flashcard.
    Alternative: Glue a word collected from RWP that has a prefix and suffix.
2. Roll the right edge over to cover everything except the prefix. Fold.
3. Open to expose the entire word. Roll the left tab over to cover everything except the suffix. Fold.
4. Alternate opening and closing the left and right tabs to read the word with and without the prefix and with and without the suffix. Read the stem/root word without an affix.

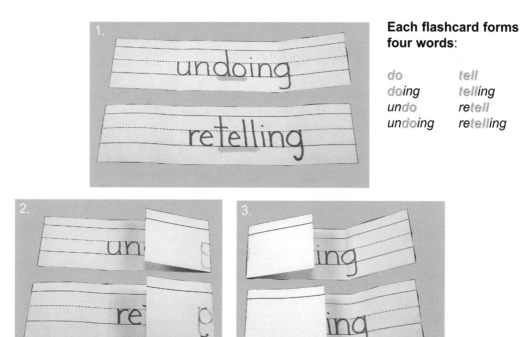

Each flashcard forms four words:

do	tell
doing	telling
undo	retell
undoing	retelling

Two-Column Pocket Chart Foldable® (below): Use a sheet of 11" x 17" paper or poster board to make a two-column Pocket Chart Foldable, and use it to collect examples of words with prefixes and suffixes. Students write examples of words or collect examples from RWP and place them on quarter sheets or single flashcards. Encourage students to use the collected words to write sentences on the backs of the cards. Store the flashcards in the pockets.

VKVs® Glued To Chart: VKV flashcards can be glued onto charts or bulletin boards as seen in the example above. Note that other VKV cards are stored in the pockets of the affix chart pictured. See page 309.

Alphabetizing

Phone books, seating charts, indexes, dictionaries, glossaries, and the sections of this book are alphabetized. Students need to learn how to use alphabetized information and how to alphabetize information for others to use. See other alphabetizing ideas on pages 118-119, Dictionary Skills.

Content Application: Have students use Foldables or VKVs to alphabetize two, three, or four of their spelling words. Selected math, science, or social studies vocabulary words, interesting words from a library book, and items on the lunch menu are also good resources for finding words to alphabetize.

Alphabetizing Strips (right): Sequentially type or write letters of the alphabet using a large font on a long strip of paper or several sections of paper. If sections are used, tape or glue them together to form a long alphabetizing strip as illustrated in the photograph. On small strips of paper, write words to be alphabetized by either sequential first-letters or sequential second-letters. To alphabetize the words, lay them on the alphabet strip. The words in the photograph were alphabetized by second letters.

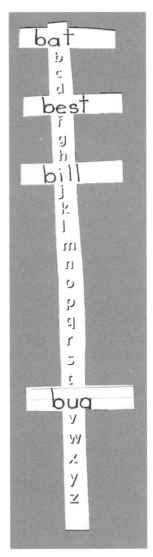

Alphabet Pocket Books (below):

Make thirteen two-pocket books. Glue them together to form a 26-pocket book, and sequentially label each pocket with a letter of the alphabet. Students will become familiar with alphabetic sequencing as they use the pockets to collect examples of vocabulary words and/or pictures that have been written or glued onto quarter sheets or single flashcards.

Beginning Activity: Have students randomly select one word from each of two, three, or four pockets and alphabetize the words by initial letters.

Advanced Activity: Have students alphabetize the flashcards collected in one pocket by second, third, or fourth letters. See page 291 for Pocket Foldable instructions.

Extension: Giant Bound Book Dictionary

Use the words and/or picture cards collected in the pockets to make a giant classroom dictionary. See photograph on page 118.

Pocket Foldables® (below):

Use a two-pocket Foldable to collect words that start with letters found in the first half and second half of the alphabet. Make word cards using student-written words, teacher-written words, or words cut from RWP (Real World Print), and sort them into the appropriate pockets.

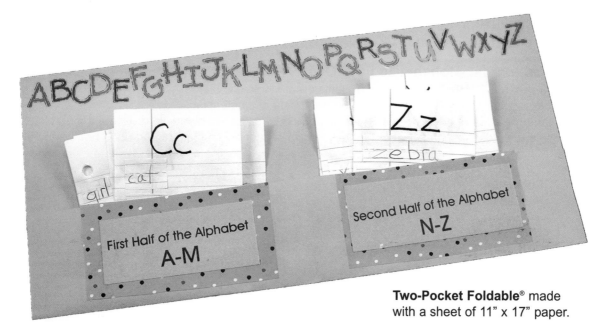

Two-Pocket Foldable® made with a sheet of 11" x 17" paper.

Foldable® Book Jackets (right):

Make book jackets to collect examples of letters and/or words beginning with each letter of the alphabet. Letters or words can be student-written, teacher-written, and/or words cut from RWP. Store these "books" in a bookshelf made out of recycled boxes (see illustration), and arrange them in alphabetical order. See page 307 for Foldable book jacket instructions.

As shown in the examples, stickers or inked stamps can also be used to label the spines of the book jackets.

Make several alphabetizing VKV flashcards. With practice using the VKV flashcards, most students will be able to transfer what they learn about alphabetizing to other situations in which they have to alphabetize words or use something arranged in alphabetical order. It is not necessary to make flashcards each time you wish to alphabetize words; however, continue to make a few alphabetizing VKV flashcards and add them to the *Alphabetizing* section of your VKV Flashcard Box, page 16, throughout the school year.

VKV® Flashcards: Alphabetize Fold-Over VKV®

1. Write words to be alphabetized to the far left side of single flashcards.
   Alternative: Glue RWP words to the far left side of single flashcards.
2. Fold the right edge of each flashcard around and cover all letters of the word except the first letter.
3. Arrange the words in alphabetical order based upon sequential first letters and upon non-sequential first letters.

Sequential
First Letters

  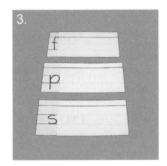

Non-sequential
First Letters

 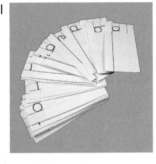

Alphabet Accordion Pocket Chart (left): This giant Foldable pocket chart was made using 7 sheets of poster board folded into fourths and taped together. Four-inch pockets can be folded along the bottom of the poster board and used to sort and alphabetize word cards. The alphabetized words in the pockets to the left are: desk, goat, house, jump, and pencil. See page 131.

Sight Word Alternative: This giant pocket chart can hold VKV flashcards that begin with the initial vowels or consonants that form our alphabet. Use as a sight word dictionary.

VKV® Flashcards: First Letter Alphabetizing VKV®

1. Begin with sheets of 11" x 17" cover stock or index weight paper. Laminated 12" x 18" art paper may also be used.
2. Make a fold 1/3 of the paper's width along the short edge.
3. Fold the paper in half and then fold in half again to form four sections with pockets. (See below.)
4. Staple or glue the pockets closed along the outer edges only.
5. Refold along the central fold lines to make an accordion as illustrated.
   Optional: Label the pockets 1st, 2nd, 3rd, 4th, or leave the pockets unlabeled.
6. Students select two to four word cards. Each word should begin with a different letter.
7. Students determine which of the selected words come 1st, 2nd, etc. when alphabetized.
8. Students place the words in the pockets so that only the first letter shows. Students check their alphabetizing skills by viewing the order of the first letters.

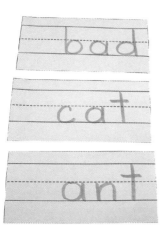

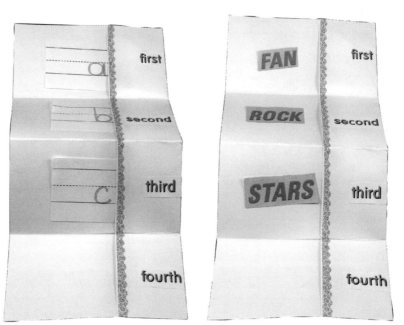

Sequential first letters.   Non-sequential first letters.

Above: Use single flashcards (left) or words cut from RWP, (upper right) and the accordion pocket described above to display sequential and nonsequential first-letter alphabetizing.

Alphabet Alternative (left): Fold five sheets of index weight 11" x 17" paper into sixths. Sequentially label the pockets with the letters of the alphabet and use them as directed above. Place two-inch, single flashcards, or words cut from RWP in the accordion pockets to alphabetize sequential first-letter words.

Begin using the alphabet sections individually and then tape them together to form a long alphabet chart that can stretch down a hall or sidewalk. Use this mobile alphabet chart to take alphabetizing and word studies out of the classroom.

This is a vertical version of the horizontal alphabet pocket chart pictured at the bottom of the opposite page, and it too can be used for word sorts -- initial consonants, final consonants, blends, digraphs, and vowels.

⬭VKV® Flashcards: Fold-Back Alphabetizing

1. Fold single flashcards into sixths or eighths, depending on the length of the words to be alphabetized.
2. Write words to be alphabetized on the strips. Beginning at the far left edge of a folded single flashcard, write the first letter of a word and continue to write the word so that only one letter appears in each folded section of the card. There may be remaining blank sections after the word.
3. Make cards for words that begin with sequential letters. For example, the cards might be for the following words: *rhino, snake, turkey*.
4. Fold the cards so that only the first letters show.
5. Arrange the first letters in alphabetical order.
6. Open the cards to view the words in alphabetical order.

Sequential First Letter Alphabetizing:

Alphabetizing flashcards should be made using sequential initial letters. For example, use words beginning with a, b, and c or words beginning with r, s, and t.

Examples:	VKV Flashcards:	Alphabetized:
	turkey	*rhino*
	rhino	*snake*
	snake	*turkey*

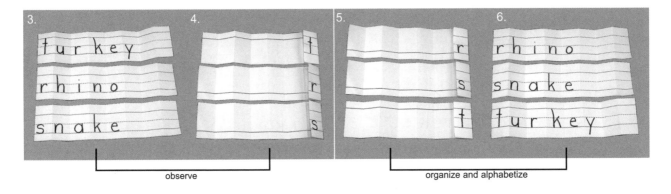

observe   organize and alphabetize

Non-Sequential First Letter Alphabetizing:

As students master sequential alphabetizing using VKV folded flashcards, make the same flashcards for words that have random, non-sequential initial letters. Begin with two and three words, and gradually add words. Continue until students can alphabetize several words.

Examples:	VKV Flashcards:	Alphabetized:
	jam	*bat*
	bat	*jam*
	wind	*wind*

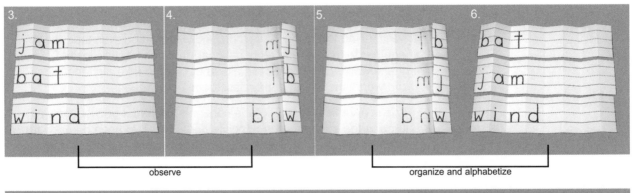

observe   organize and alphabetize

Begin teaching alphabetizing skills by using the first letter of words. With mastery of this skill, progress to alphabetizing by the second letter.

VKV® Flashcards: Second Letter Alphabetizing

Students who feel comfortable alphabetizing sequential and nonsequential first-letter words are ready to learn how to alphabetize to the second letter. Begin with only two words and gradually add more.

1. Fold single flashcards into sixths or eighths, depending on the length of the words to be alphabetized.
2. Write words to be alphabetized on the strips. Beginning at the far left edge of a folded single flashcard, write the first letter of a word, and continue to write the word so that only one letter appears in each folded section of the card. There may be remaining blank sections after the word.
3. Make cards for words that begin with the same letter. For example, the cards might be for the following words: *come, cup, candy*.
4. Since all the words in this exercise begin with the same letter, fold back the common initial letter, making the second letter appear first.
5. Arrange the second letters in alphabetical order.
6. Open the first letter, and view the words arranged alphabetically.

Examples:	VKV Flashcards	Alphabetized
	come	*candy*
	cup	*come*
	candy	*cup*

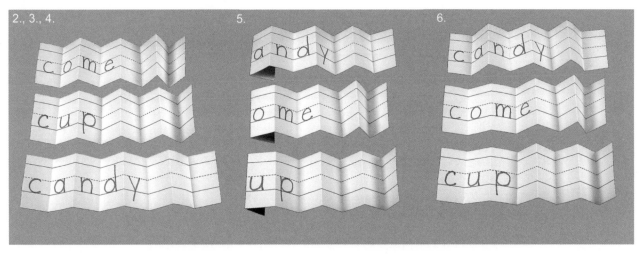

Examples:	VKV Flashcards	Alphabetized
	big	*bat*
	bat	*bet*
	bet	*bit*

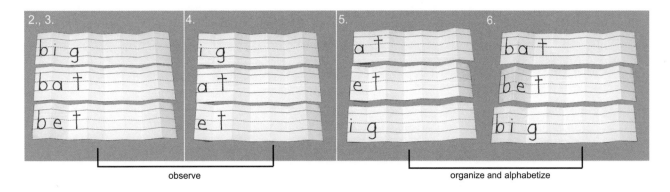

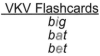

observe   organize and alphabetize

⟨VKV⟩ Flashcards: Analogy Fold-Over VKV®

1. Begin with a long sentence strip.
2. Fold the strip in half leaving the left side 1" longer than the right side.
3. Open and fold the long side (left) around, aligning the edge 1" from the end of the short side (right). Crease the paper. This will form a central "spine" in the strip.
4. Fold each of the sides, left and right, into thirds as demonstrated in the photograph.
5. Open to find six large sections and one small center section.

(Continued on next page.)

1.

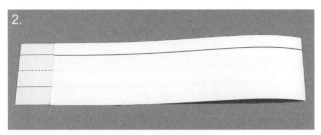

2.

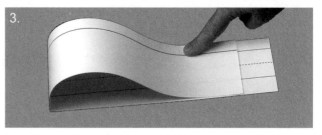

3.

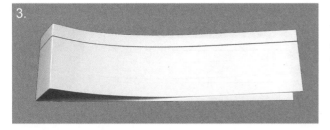

3.

Making a Book Spine: As pictured to the left, the folding procedure illustrated in steps 1-3 makes a spine. Use larger sheets of paper to make spines for book jackets (see page 307) or book covers (see page 68).

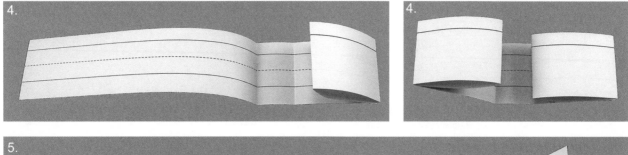

4.

4.

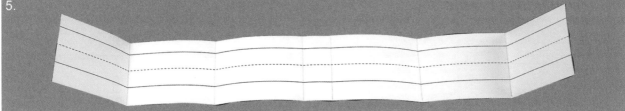

5.

Analogies

Analogies compare two ideas or events that are similar, or have something in common. Read *bird:air::fish:water* as, *Bird is to air as fish is to water.*

Content Application: Help students write analogies for science, math, and social studies concepts. A few examples of content analogies are included in the list below.

car:drive::plane:fly
dog:bark::cat:meow
ear:hear::nose:smell
girl:woman::boy:man
hot:cold::warm:cool
cold:winter::hot:summer
toe:foot::finger:hand
up:down::high:low
wet:rain forest::dry:desert
fall:winter::spring:summer
sunrise:morning::sunset:night

beginning:end::start:finish
sun:day::moon:night
tiger:cat::wolf:dog
ham:pig::beef:cow
wings:butterfly::fins:fish
tiger:India::lion:Africa
empty:full::less:more
morning:breakfast::noon:lunch
zoo:animals::garden:plants
freezing:ice::boiling:steam
two:four::three:six

6. Write an analogy on the card as illustrated. Write the *as* symbol in the center section. Write words in the open folded sections, and the *is to* symbols on the fold lines between the words.

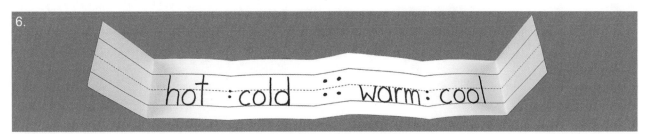

7. Fold and unfold the tabs to the left and right to read the analogy. Leave words covered and see if students can determine what word or words might be used to complete the analogy. Students might come up with alternative analogies. Write student variations as analogies on the back of the flashcard.

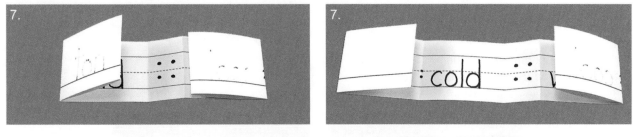

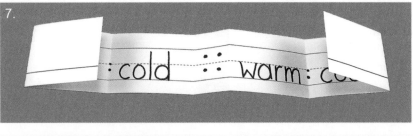

Make several antonym VKV flashcards. With practice using the VKV flashcards most students will be able to transfer what they learn about antonyms to other situations in which they find antonyms in use. It is not necessary to make flashcards every time you discover an antonym; however, continue to make a few antonym flashcards and add them to the *Antonyms* section of your VKV Flashcard Box, page 16, throughout the school year.

Content Application: Have students find antonyms for some of their spelling words, terms encountered in literature, or math, science, and social studies vocabulary terms.

(VKV®) Flashcards: Antonym Flip-Flop VKVs·

1. Fold a single flashcard strip into thirds.
2. On the top and bottom sections inside the open strip, draw or use pictures of antonyms as seen in the example. Write a sentence using the antonyms in the middle section of the strip.
3. Raise the bottom tab and write the word illustrated on the top section with the *fat rat* picture -- write the word *fat*.
4. Fold the top and bottom tabs down and write the word that is illustrated on the lower tab with the *thin rat* picture -- write the word *thin*.
5. Open and close the tabs to view antonyms, words, and matching pictures.

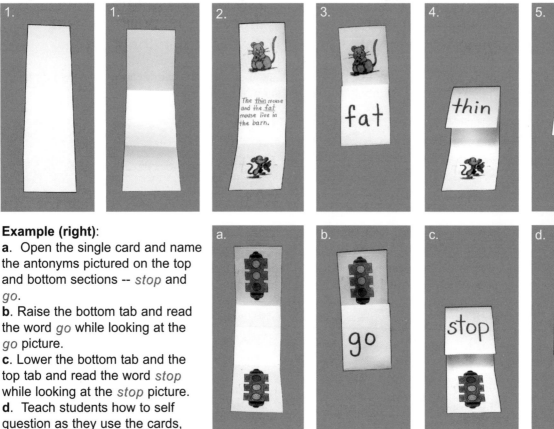

Example (right):

a. Open the single card and name the antonyms pictured on the top and bottom sections -- *stop* and *go*.

b. Raise the bottom tab and read the word *go* while looking at the *go* picture.

c. Lower the bottom tab and the top tab and read the word *stop* while looking at the *stop* picture.

d. Teach students how to self question as they use the cards, and demonstrate how students can manipulate the VKV to answer their own questions. When they see *go* they should ask themselves, "What is the opposite of *go*?" When they see *stop* they mentally ask, "What is the antonym for *stop*?

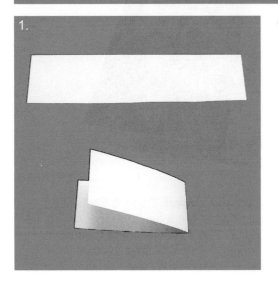

VKV® Flashcards: Antonym Fold-Over VKVs®

1. Fold a single flashcard in half.
2. Write a word on one side of the fold line, and its antonym on the other. Example: *night* and *day*
3. Turn the card over so the words are facing down. Place a picture of each word on this side, or write a sentence using each word. For example, draw a picture of *night* on the back of the word *night* and a picture of *day* on the back of the word *day*.
4. Punch a hole ½ inch in from the short edge of the folded card and store the VKV cards on a large ring.
5. Have students look at one side of the word cards on the ring, and try to determine the antonym of each word. Students turn the card to check their answer.
6. Reverse all VKV flashcards so that the pictures or sentences are showing. Repeat step 5.

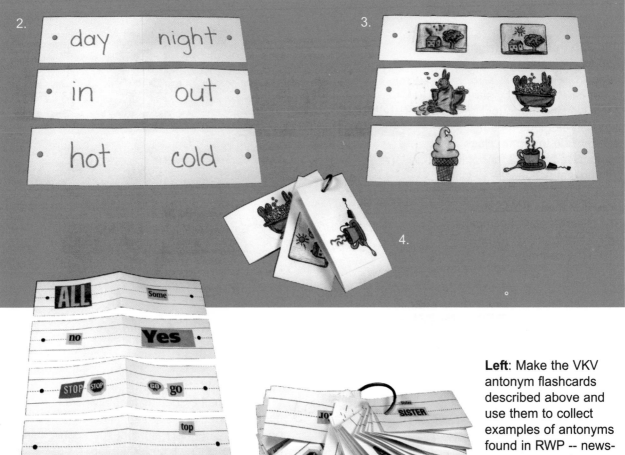

Left: Make the VKV antonym flashcards described above and use them to collect examples of antonyms found in RWP -- newspapers, magazines, advertisements, catalogs, and other print sources.

Two-Tab Foldables® (left and above): Two-tab Foldables, made using poster board folded like a hamburger, provide room for all students in the class to contribute to the Foldable by writing or gluing examples of words under the tabs. The teacher or designated students may write student-dictated information under the tabs, and/or students and the teacher collect and glue examples of words found in RWP.

Two-Tab Foldables® (right): Two-tab Foldables made using 11" x 17" or 12" x 18" paper can be used by students working in groups, or they can be glued together side by side to form a class book. See page 68 for book binding instructions.

Note that these Foldables use photographs of common antonyms found on signs within the community.

Two-Tab Foldables® (left): Use 8½" x 11" paper to make small Foldables for individual student use . As with all Foldables, students can write on quarter sheets or strips of lined paper and glue these sections under the tabs. Copy can also be generated on a computer, printed, and glued onto the Foldable as illustrated in these photographs.

Two-Tab Matching Foldable®:

1. Fold a sheet of 11" x 17" or 12" x 18" paper so that one third is left uncovered.

2. Fold the paper in half along the long axis to form two long columns. Cut along the fold line of the inside small section to form two tabs. Make a fold about ½" above the bottom fold.

3. Label the tabs.

4. Place an equal number of quarter sheets of paper to the inside on both sides of the fold.

5. Staple along the ½" fold line to hold the papers in place.

6. Write or glue a word on a quarter sheet of paper under the left tab of the Foldable, and write or glue it's antonym on a random sheet under the right half.

7. When complete, students select a word card from the left section and search to find its antonym on the right.

8. Students can write sentences on the quarter sheets, or glue computer-generated copy onto them. Encourage students to find examples of the featured antonyms used in RWP, and to also glue these examples into the Foldable.

Words Under Tabs (above, left side):
big
thick
near
good
on

Words Under Tabs (above, right side):
bad
thin
off
little
far

1.

2.

3.

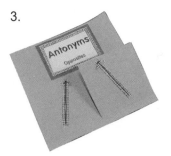

4.

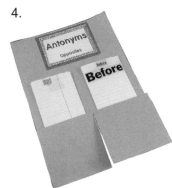

5.

6., 7.

See another example page 106

Four-tab Foldables can be folded in half and glued together (side by side) to form a larger multipage book. See pages 120, 124, 125 for other examples.

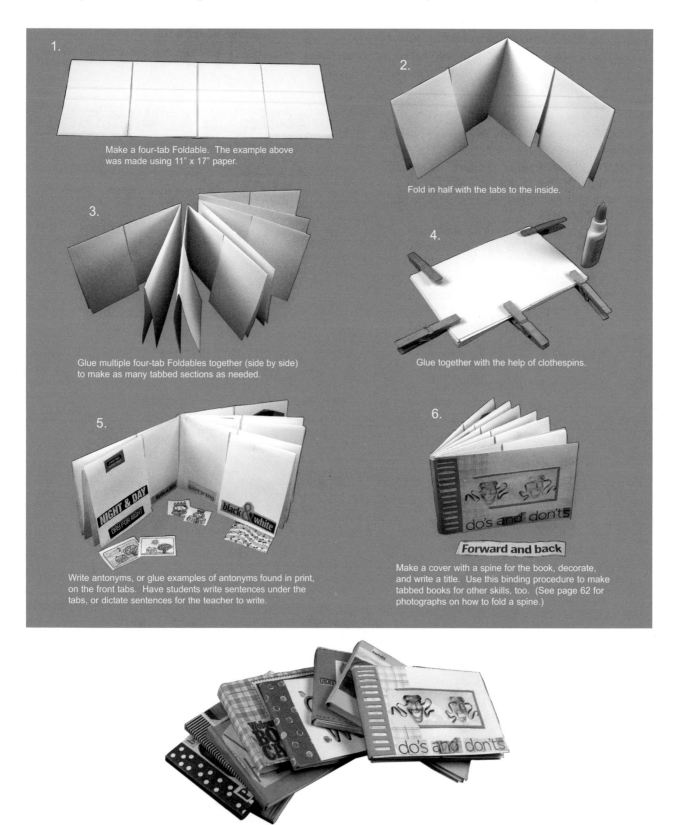

1.

Make a four-tab Foldable. The example above was made using 11" x 17" paper.

2.

Fold in half with the tabs to the inside.

3.

Glue multiple four-tab Foldables together (side by side) to make as many tabbed sections as needed.

4.

Glue together with the help of clothespins.

5.

NIGHT & DAY
DAY FOR NIGHT
queen or king
black & white

Write antonyms, or glue examples of antonyms found in print, on the front tabs. Have students write sentences under the tabs, or dictate sentences for the teacher to write.

6.

do's and don'ts
Forward and back

Make a cover with a spine for the book, decorate, and write a title. Use this binding procedure to make tabbed books for other skills, too. (See page 62 for photographs on how to fold a spine.)

do's and don'ts

Antonyms (ant = against, nym = name)

An antonym is a word that means the opposite, or nearly the opposite, of another word. For example, if a synonym for *tired* is *sleepy*, then antonyms for *tired* might be *active*, *energetic*, or *hyperactive*. Another synonym for tired might be *overused*, and the antonym would be *fresh* or *new*. Teach students how to use a Thesaurus by making and using your own. Use a Foldable Journal (page 290) to make a giant classroom Thesaurus.

Common Antonyms

above	below	empty	full	moving	still
add	subtract	fast	slow	near	far
alike	different	finish	begin	odd	even
all	none	first	last	offense	defense
always	never	forget	remember	on	off
asked	told	found	lost	open	close
asleep	awake	give	take	part	whole
back	front	good	bad	pull	push
beautiful	ugly	happy	sad	question	answer
before	after	hard	soft	quick	slow
begin	end	he	she	quiet	loud,
best	worst	healthy	sick, ill		noisy
bottom	top	heavy	light	rich	poor
boy	girl	high	low	rough	smooth
bright	dull	his	hers	short	tall
build	destroy	in	out	start	stop
clean	dirty	large	small	strong	weak
cold	hot	leave	stay	tame	wild
dark	light	left	right	thick	thin
day	night	long	short	true	false
down	up	lost	found	under	over
dry	wet	lose	win	wide	narrow
early	late	many	few	yes	no
easy	hard	more		young	old

Matchbook Antonyms (right): Use small strips of paper to make tiny matchbooks. Write or paste words on the front tabs of the matchbooks and antonyms under the tabs. See if students can name an antonym for a selected word before raising the tab. Write alternate antonyms for the words under the tabs on the top (not glued) section. See page 292.

Compound Words

Two words combined to make a new word is called a compound word. Some compound words mean the same as the two words combined: *blueberry* means the *berry* is *blue* in color. Some compound words change the meaning of the word, for example *bullheaded*.

Compound words can be open, closed, or hyphenated. *Open compound words* have a space between the two words. *Closed compound* words have no space between the two words. *Hyphenated compound words* have a hyphen between the two words.

Note: Students might be surprised to discover that dictionaries are not always in agreement on which words are or are not written as compound words.

Foldable® Charts:

Make Foldable charts for classroom use out of poster board or chart paper. Use photocopy paper or lined paper to make smaller, individual student charts.

-Make a giant two-column chart to collect *simple* (*into*) and *complex* (*everywhere*) compound words.
-Make a giant three-column Foldable chart to collect *open*, *closed*, and *hyphenated* compound words.
-Make a chart of compound words that *are* and *are not* always capitalized.

Foldable® Chart (below):

Fold a sheet of poster board into fifths vertically and horizontally to form twenty-five equal sections (see page 308). Write a letter of the alphabet in each section, placing x and y in the same square. Write compound words encountered during reading, and/or collect examples of compound words found in RWP.

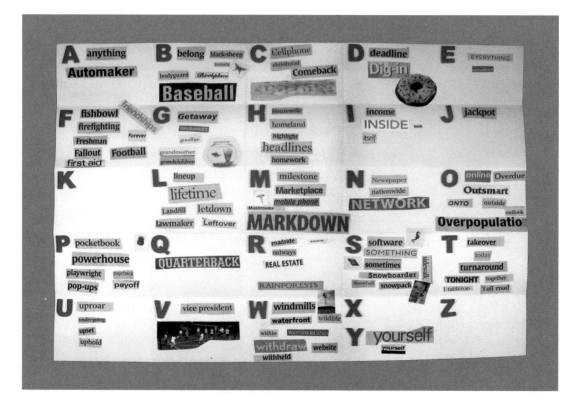

Dictionary Alternative: The compound words collected above could have been used to form a *Compound Word Dictionary*. Make a bound book dictionary using eight sheets of paper -- notebook paper, copy paper, chart paper, or poster board. See page 290 .

Compound Words

Four-Door Foldable®:
Use a dictionary to look up four of the following words, and list at least four compound words for each: air, back, ball, black, blue, butter, grand, out, over, sea, and sun.

Alternative (below): Collect examples of compound words that begin or end with any of the words listed above. Glue the compound words across the fold of each of the four sections to reinforce the fact that two separate words have been joined to form the compound words displayed.

Other words that could be used on the front tabs of the Foldable (left) include the following:

any	butter	good	play
back	check	grand	rain
ball	day	half	school
bath	door	head	sea
bed	down	home	side
bird	earth	house	snow
birth	every	land	some
black	eye	life	under
blood	fire	news	water
book	foot	out	wood
	for		work

Foldable® Pocket Chart Bulletin Board (right): Use one sheet of poster board to make this large bulletin board pocket chart and use it to collect compound word Foldables, VKV flashcards, and other compound word study aids. Teacher-generated print is featured on the pocket of this poster providing information on compound words.

Display Strip Alternative: Make another 1" fold along the bottom of a Foldable pocket chart and stapled 1/4" above the fold line to form a display strip for compound word VKV flashcards or sentence strips. See page 31 for an example of a pocket chart with a display strip.

Compound Words

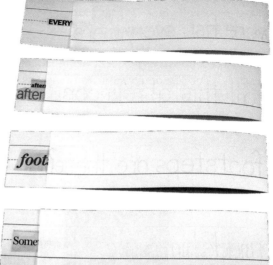

Compound Word Sentence Strips and Fold-Overs:
Write or glue a compound word to the left edge of a sentence strip. Roll the right edge around to cover the second (back) word, leaving the first word exposed. Read the first word. Open the tab, read the second word and read the words together as a compound word. Write a sentence using the compound word.

Foldable® Sentence Strips and VKVs:®
Use Foldable sentence-strip holders to sort and display single VKVs and sentence strips as illustrated above.

Compound Word Examples (right):
a. Use a sheet of 11" x 17" paper to make a large sentence strip holder, and display picture cards that form a compound word.

b. Write *bird* on one card and *house* on another card. Place the cards on a large holder that has been cut in half.

c. When the holders are pushed together they form the word *birdhouse*.

Extension: Ask students to define each word. Write the definitions on the back of the word cards. Display the definitions on the sentence strips, read them, and see if students can determine the meaning of the compound word they represent.

Make several compound word VKV flashcards. With practice, most students will be able to transfer what they learn about compound words using these VKV flashcards to other situations in which they read or write their own compound words. It is not necessary to make flashcards every time you discover a compound word. However, continue to make a few compound word VKV flashcards, and add them to the *Compound Word* section of your VKV Flashcard Box, page 16, throughout the school year.

Content Application: Help students find compound words in their spelling lists, social studies vocabulary terms, science text books, library books, poems, stories, and songs.

(VKV®) Flashcards: Closed Compound Word Ring

1. Fold a single flashcard in half.
2. Write half of a compound word to the left of the center fold so that the last letter of the word is very close to the middle fold. Write the second word on the right side of the card, with the first letter as close to the center fold as possible.
3. When open, each word should appear as a closed compound word. When folded in half, each word will appear to be separate.
4. Punch a hole ½" in from the short edge of the folded card and store the VKV flashcards on a large ring. Read the words individually.
5. Take the cards off the ring, open them and read them as compound words.

Picture Word Alternative (far right, above and below):

6. Fold each card so the words are to the inside. Place pictures of the words on the back of the flashcard.
7. Reverse all VKV flashcards so the pictures show. Read the words represented by the pictures, and read the pictures as compound words.

RWP Alternative (left & above): Combine words from RWP with pictures from classroom worksheets, photographs, and magazines to make this VKV. Punch holes in folded cards and store on a ring.

(VKV) Flashcards: Two-Tab Closed Compound Word

1. Close a double flashcard, then fold it in half.
2. Cut along the center fold line of one side to form two tabs.
3. Write half of a compound word under the first tab, and the other half under the second tab. The first word should stop at the cut line, and the second word should begin at the cut line. When both tabs are open the word appears as a closed compound word.
4. Open and close the tabs to view the words separately or joined to form a compound word.

Examples: *look, out* or *lookout*

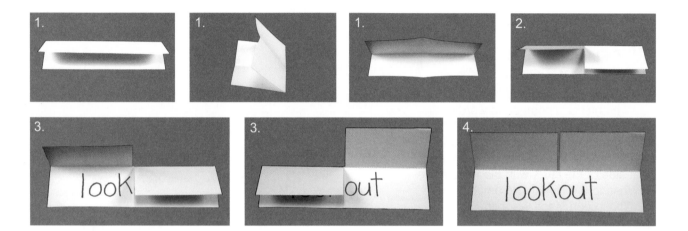

(VKV) Flashcards: Two-Tab Open Compound Words

Steps 1-2 Above.

3. Write the two words that form the open compound word under the tabs. Leave space between the words.
4. Have students illustrate each of the words on the front tabs of the VKV.
5. Open and close the tabs to view the words separately or as an open compound word.
6. Use the open compound word in a sentence, and write the sentence on the back of the flashcard.

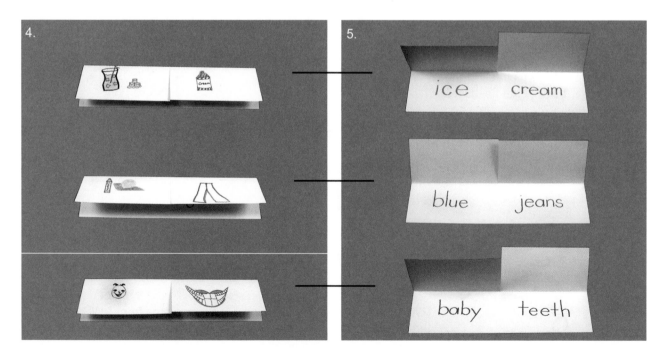

Compound Words VKV® Flashcard Instructions

VKV® Flashcards: Three Compound Words

1. Close a triple flashcard and fold it in half.
2. Cut off the upper left and bottom left sections of one half of the card.
3. Write the first half of a compound word on this single tab.
   Example: *blue*
4. Write nouns on the three flashcard sections to the right that will combine with the first word to form three compound words.
   Examples: *bird, berry, bell*
5. Open and close the two right tabs to form three compound words.
   Examples: *bluebird*
                    blueberry
                    bluebell

Below: Each of the VKV flashcards (a, b, and c) pictured below form three compound words that begin with the same word. Use the dictionary to determine if there are more than three compound words that begin with the featured word. If so, write the other words on the back of the flashcard.

Alternative: This VKV can be used for all three types of compound words.

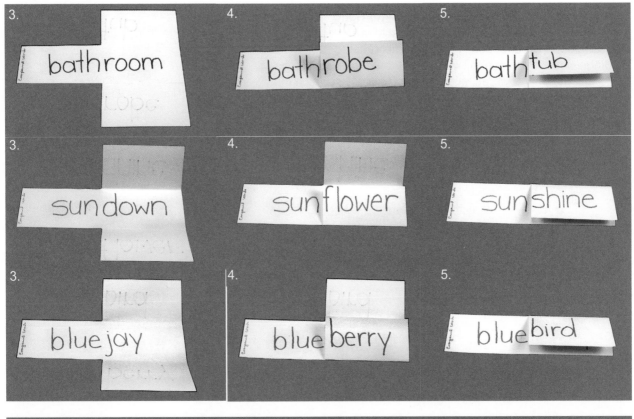

Compound Words

Some compound words are used more frequently than others. As students master basic sight words, add high-frequency compound words to their reading vocabulary and later to their spelling lists. Select from the examples listed below and add your own words.

Highlighting Compound Words: When students encounter compounds in a worksheet, magazine, or newspaper current event, have them use different colored crayons or highlighters to color the two words that form the compound word and then underline them as one word in a third color.

anybody	everybody	lookout	sometime
anyhow	everyday	maybe	sometimes
anymore	everyone	myself	somewhere
anyone	everything	nobody	today
anyplace	forever	outside	understand
anything	forget	overlook	upset
anyway	forgive	somebody	whenever
anywhere	goodbye	someday	wherever
cannot	however	somehow	whoever
comeback	inside	someone	without
evermore	into	something	yourself

VKV® (above): Two-tab closed compound word flashcard, see page 74.

Multi-Tab Vocabulary Foldable® (below and right):
Make a four-, six-, eight-, or ten-tab Foldable, and use it to collect compound words found in RWP or encountered during reading. Write any of the following under the tabs: sentences using the compound words, quotes from literature in which the word is used, definitions of the compound word and definitions of its individual words. See page 308.

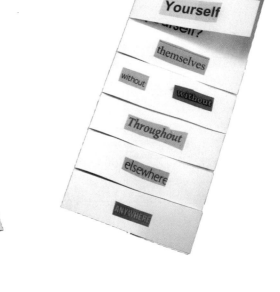

Compound Words   Closed

Make VKV Flashcards using words selected from this list and words collected from literature as well as other forms of print encountered in life situations.

airplane	classroom	hilltop	motorcycle
airport	cobweb	homework	mountaintop
anteater	cookbook	indoor	snowman
applesauce	cowboy	inside	starfish
armrest	crossover	into	strawberry
backbone	crosswalk	mouthwash	sunburn
backyard	cupboard	newspaper	sundown
baldheaded	cupcake	nighttime	sunflower
ballpark	daylight	notebook	sunlight
barefoot	daytime	notepaper	sunrise
barnyard	dishrag	oatmeal	sunset
baseball	dishwasher	pancake	sunshine
basketball	dodgeball	peanut	toothbrush
bathrobe	doorbell	peppermint	underground
bathroom	doorknob	playground	underwater
bathtub	dragonfly	popcorn	waterfall
bedroom	driveway	rainbow	wheelchair
birdbath	earring	raincoat	windmill
birdhouse	earthworm	roommate	
birdseed	eggshell	sailboat	
birthday	eyeball	sandbox	
birthplace	eyebrow	seacoast	
birthstone	fingernail	seashell	
blackbird	firefly	seaside	
blackboard	fireplace	setback	
blueberry	football	sidewalk	
bluebird	gingerbread	skateboard	
bookcase	goldfish	housework	
bookstore	grandfather	jellyfish	
butterfly	grandmother	keyboard	
buttonhole	grasshopper	kickoff	
campfire	greyhound	ladybug	
cheeseburger	hairbrush	mailbox	
	haircut	moonbeam	
	highchair	moonlight	

Three-Tab Foldable® (below):
Use a Foldable to collect pictures of compound words found on signs in your community. Use signs that will be seen frequently by students, and encourage students to look for them and read them in passing. See page 293.

Compound Word Open and Hyphenated

Make VKV Flashcards using words selected from this list, and words collected from literature as well as other forms of print encountered in life situations.

Open Compound Words

baby teeth
back seat
bad manners
ball game
black pepper
blue jeans
field trip
first aid
giant panda
grass snake
green bean
green light
hot cake
ice cream
nursery rhyme
nursery school
post office
super size
video game

Hyphenated Words

hide-and-seek
jack-in-the-box
jack-o-lantern

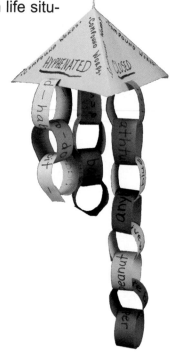

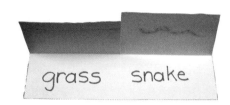

VKV® (above and below): Two-tab open compound word flashcards, see page 74.

Foldable® Pyramid Mobile (above): Use a pyramid Foldable to make a mobile to display examples of the three types of compound words. The compound words in this photo have been written on paper strips and connected to form word chains. See page 294.

Foldable® Compound Word Review (right): Have each student collect examples of open, closed, or hyphenated compound words collected from RWP. Cut the words in half and glue the first word under the left side and and second word under the right side of a shutterfold.

Alternative: Cut the front tabs so they can be opened and closed to form word strips. Students manipulate the tabs to read the words individually or as compound words.

Make several consonant VKV flashcards for initial, medial, and ending consonants. With practice, most students will be able to transfer what they learn about initial, medial, and final consonants from using these VKV flashcards to other situations in which they read or write words containing consonants. It is not necessary to make flashcards for all the words you use when studying consonants; however, continue to make a few consonant VKV flashcards, and add them to the *Consonants* section of your VKV Flashcard Box, page 16, throughout the school year.

Consonant Graphemes: Anyone who watches Wheel of Fortune™ or plays Scrabble™, knows that some consonants are more commonly used to form words than others. The following is a list of consonant graphemes listed from most to least commonly used: r, t, n, s, l, c, d, p, m, b f, v, g, h, k, w, th, sh, ng, ch, x, z, j, qu, wh, y.

VKV® Flashcards: Initial or Final Consonants

1. Fold a double flashcard into thirds.
2. Cut along the fold lines of the top strip. DO NOT cut the bottom strip.
3. Cut off the top left tab to focus on the initial consonants of CVC words. Cut off the top right tab to focus on final consonants in CVC words.
4. Write a CVC word so that one letter is in each of the three flashcard sections. In the example to the right, the medial and ending letters will be under the tabs.
5. If the initial consonant is showing, sound the consonant. Open the middle tab and sound the vowel. Open the last tab and sound the final consonant. Read the resulting word. Or, students might first sound the initial and ending consonants, and then add the medial vowel sound.

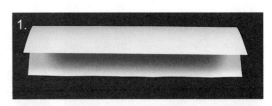

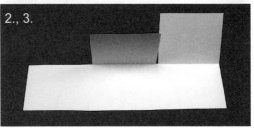

Alternate Activities:

Sort VKV Flashcards by initial consonants.

Sort VKV Flashcards by final consonants.

Sort VKV Flashcards by medial vowel sounds.
        See vowel section, pages 220 to 263.

VKV® Examples (below):
a. Focus on initial consonant /g/ and rime et.
b. Focus on final consonant /n/ and rime en.

VKV® Flashcards: Initial and Final Consonants

1. Fold a triple flashcard in half.
2. Cut off the top and bottom sections of one half of the card. Do not cut the middle section. Turn the single middle remaining tab to the left to focus on an initial consonant (See example a). Turn to the right to focus on a final consonant. (See example b).
3. In example *a*, write an initial consonant on the single flashcard section to the left, and write three *word families, or rimes* (see phonograms pages 143), on the three sections to the right.
4. Open and close the right tabs to form three words with the same initial consonant.
5. Reverse the procedure, as seen in example *b*, for three words with the same final consonant.

Left: Three words with different initial consonants are made with this VKV:
> time
> dime
> lime

Right: Three words that name shapes are formed with the same initial consonant:
> cube
> cone
> can

VKV® Flashcard: **Consonant Accordion**

1. Fold a sheet of copy paper into an eight-section accordion. See photographs 1-5 below.
2. Cut a 3" strip off the right side of the top seven sections leaving the bottom eighth section whole.
3. Glue the accordion sections together using clothespins to hold them in place until the glue dries.
4. Write a word family on the extended tab so that its first letter is next to the accordion fold.
5. Select and write five initial consonants on the accordion strips aligning the consonants next to the edge of the accordion section as illustrated in the photographs below.
6. Flip the accordion sections to form new words with different initial consonants.

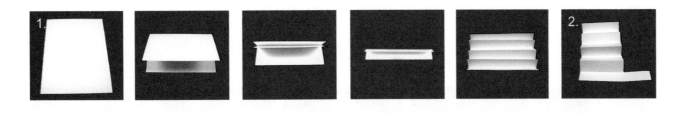

Extra Hands (right):
Clothespins are helpful when gluing multiple sections together at the same time.

Below: Half sheets of copy paper (4¼" x 8½", hamburger size) are large enough for CVC or CVCC words.

3.

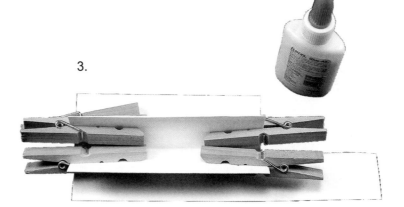

4.

Note From Dinah: The VKVs on this page are my one-paper versions of the stapled word family cards used in classrooms for decades. See examples of these great "old classics" on page 230.

Five Word Accordion (below):

VKV Flashcards: Consonant Steps

1. Fold a triple flashcard into fourths.
2. Cut off two of the top fourths, one of the middle fourths, and none of the last section of fourths.
3. Write a two-letter word that begins with a consonant on the top step.
Write a three-letter word that starts with the same consonant on the middle step. Write a four-letter word that begins with this consonant on the bottom step.
4. Fold and refold the three sections forward and backward, vertically and horizontally, to alternately view the words or the letters that form the words. See photos below.

Examples

Initial Consonant Word Steps:
> do
> dig
> dive

Final Consonant Steps:
> at
> hat
> sent

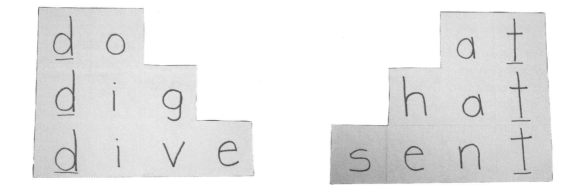

VKV Flashcards: Initial and Final Consonant Flips

1. Write a CVC word or a CVVC word in the middle of a single flashcard.
2. Fold the left edge of the card around to cover all letters except the final consonant. Open the card.
3. Fold the right edge around to cover all letters except the initial consonant. Open the card.
4. Open and close the tabs to review the initial and final consonants forming the word. Add the medial vowel sound to the CVC or CVVC word.

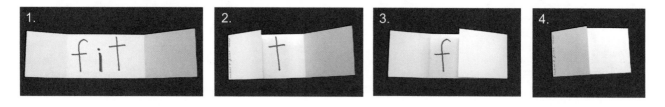

Consonants VKV® Flashcard Instructions

VKV® Flashcards: Consonants and Phonograms

1. Use a sheet of 8½" x 11" paper to make a shutterfold.
2. Fold the shutterfold into fourths.
3. Cut along the fold lines of the two small tabs, do not cut the back section of the shutterfold.
4. Write words or glue words so that initial consonants, blends, or digraphs are on the left side, and word families are on the right side of each of the four sections.
5. Open each tabbed section and write a sentence using the featured word under the tab.
6. If students find any of the words used in the activity in RWP, they are encouraged to cut and glue the words onto the manipulative.

VKV® Flashcards: Shutterfold Initial and Final Consonants

1. Use single flashcards, or sentence strips cut in half, and write a word that begins with a given consonant on the left and a word that ends with the same consonant on the right (a).
2. Collect examples of words that begin and end with the featured consonant, and write or glue them under the tabs (b).

Uncommon Final Consonants (below): Students will discover that some consonants are not commonly found at the end of English words. In the examples below, students will not find words that end in a sounded /h/ nor in a /j/.

Multi-Tab Foldable®:

Make three-, four-, or other multi-tabbed Foldables to use when studying consonants.

Determine which consonant will be featured. Place pictures of words that begin with the consonant on the front tabs of the Foldable. On one section of the open tab, write the name of the picture or find the word in RWP and glue it in place. On the other section of the open tab, have students write simple sentences that contain the word or dictate sentences to be written.

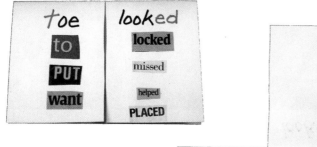

Same or Similar Sounds: Use a two-tab Foldable to collect examples of words with sounds that are the same or similar. Example: /t/ and /ed/ sounds

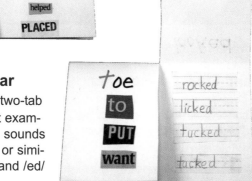

Two-tab Foldables® or Foldable® Charts

Make and use two-tab Foldables to collect words that begin and end with a given consonant. Notice the use of photographs on the front tabs and other examples of RWP under the tabs. See page 291.

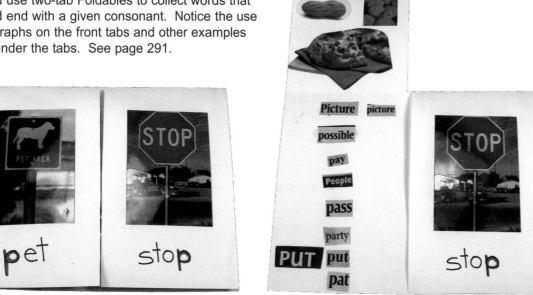

Bound Book Foldable®:

Make a Bound Book Foldable using six sheets of paper (student or classroom sized) and use it to make a 24 page reference book that features the twenty-one consonants: b, c, d, f, g, h, j, k, l, m, n, p, q, r, s, t, v, w, x, y, z.

Note: Use seven sheets of paper to make a 28-page bound book to feature the 26 letters of the alphabet.

Examples of Other Reference Books:

> Initial Consonant Animal Book.
> Initial Consonant Insect Book.
> Initial Consonant Geography Book.
> Initial Consonant Math Book.
> Initial Consonants that are Always Capitalized -- Proper Nouns.

Tactile Consonants:

Glue grits or coarse cornmeal onto any Foldable or VKV flashcard to make tactile consonants. See other tactile ideas and photographs on page 215.

Instructions for Dying Grits or Cornmeal*

Materials Needed:

> 2 cups of grits or coarse ground white corn meal
> one gallon zip-style bag, a stack of old newspapers, paper towels
> 4 oz. rubbing alcohol
> food coloring

1. Pour the alcohol into the bag. Make sure the bag does not leak before proceeding.
2. Add about ½ ounce of food coloring. (More or less can be added to adjust the color.)
3. Add grits or cornmeal to the bag, seal, and shake to distribute alcohol and color throughout.
4. When the grits or cornmeal is uniformly colored, empty the contents of the bag onto a thick section of old newsprint that has been covered with paper towels.
5. The alcohol will evaporate rapidly and the cornmeal or grits will be ready to use in a few hours.

Note: The examples below were made using grits that had been dyed yellow.

Check your school's policy on the use of toxic materials in the classroom before doing this activity with students. If rubbing alcohol is considered a toxic material, it cannot be used while students are in the classroom. Even if alcohol is not listed as a toxic material, dye the cornmeal after school hours at least one day before it is to be used in the classroom so students are not exposed to the smell of the evaporating rubbing alcohol.

Four-Door Foldable® Display Case and Consonant Cards:

Make 26 Foldable display cases to collect student-made or class-made consonant cards. These display cases can also be used to collect physical objects that start with the consonant featured. See page 137 in the "Letters" section of this book to see another photograph.

Two-Pocket Foldable® and Consonant Cards (not pictured):

Make thirteen two-pocket Foldables and glue them side by side to form a 26-page pocket book. Write one letter of the alphabet on each pocket, and use them to collect consonant cards. As students collect and sort cards, it becomes obvious that the empty pockets for the letters a, e, i, o, and u indicate they are not consonants.

Two-Tab or Three-Tab Foldables®:

Use any of the two- or three-tab Foldables featured on pages 292-293, or use two- or three-column charts or pocket Foldables for the following activities:

/r/	and	/r/ spelled wr- (wrist)
/t/	and	/t/ spelled -ed (hooked)
/n/	and	/n/ spelled -en (frozen) and /n/ spelled kn- (knock)
/s/	and	/s/ spelled /z/ (his)
/l/	and	/l/ spelled -le (able)
/f/	and	/f/ spelled ph- (phone)
/g/	and	/j/
hard c /k/	and	soft c /s/
hard g /g/	and	soft g /j/

/k/ spelled as /k/, as hard /c/, and as /ck/
y as a consonant and y as a vowel

j and g, Two-Tab Foldable® (below):
Photographed closed below left, and open below right.
Examples:
g = /j/ (giant, gym, gems, page, large)
j = /j/ (jump, jay, just, jam, jot, major)

Consonants Initial Consonant Word List

D = word is found in *Dolch 220 Word List*
F = word is found in *Fry's First Three Hundred Instant Words*.
See Appendix Two, Research Citations, pages 286-288.

b (initial)	c (initial *k* sound)	c (initial *s* sound)	d (initial)	f (initial)	g (initial *g* sound)
back F	cab	celery	dab	face F	gab
bad	cake	cell	dad	fact	gag
bag	call D F	cement	daddy	fad	gallon
bake	came D F	cent	date	fat F	game
ball F	can D F	center	day F	fall D F	gang
ban	cap	cereal	dear F	family	garden
banana	car	Cinderella	dent	far D F	gas
band	carry F	city	desk	farm	gate
bar	cat	circle	dew	fast D F	gave D F
bat	cave	circus	did D F	feel	gay
be D F	coat F	cycle	dig	feed	geese
bear	cob	cylinder	dim	fell	get D F
because D F	coin		dime	fever	gift
bed F	cold D F		din	fib	gill
bee	color F		dine	file	girl F
been D F	come D F		dish	fill	give D F
before D F	cone		disk	fin	go D F
best D F	cook		dive	find D F	goes D F
better D F	cool		do D F	fine F	goal
bid	cop		doctor	fire F	goat
big D F	corn		doe	first D F	goes D
bike	cost		does D F	fit	going D
big F	cot		dog F	five D F	gold
bill	could D F		done D	fix	golf
book F	cow		door F	fly F	good D F
both D F	cub		dot	food F	got D F
box F	cube		dove	for D F	gulf
boy F	cuff		down D F	fort	gull
bug	cup		duck	fossil	gum
bull	curb		dust	found D F	gun
bun	curl		dug	four D F	gust
bus	cure		dull	from F	gut
but D F	cut D F			full D F	gutter
buy F	cute			funny D F	
by D F				fur	

D = word is found in *Dolch 220 Word List*
F = word is found in *Fry's First Three Hundred Instant Words*.
See Appendix Two, Research Citations, pages 286-288.

g (*j* sound)	**h** (initial)	**j** (initial)	**k** (initial)	**l** (initial)	**m** (initial)
gel	had D F	jab	kangaroo	lake	mad
gem	hair	jade	keen	last F	made D F
gent	ham	jail	keep D F	lava	magnet
gene	hand F	jam	kennel	law	make D F
general	happy F	jar	kettle	lead	man F
gentle	hard F	jaw	key	leap	many D F
gentleman	has D F	jazz	kick	leave F	market
gentlemen	hat F	jell	kid	left F	may D F
geography	have D F	jelly	kill	lens	me D F
gerbil	head F	jet	kiln	let D F	men F
giant	hear F	jetty	kilo	letter F	met
giraffe	he D F	jewel	kin	lever	mice
gym	help D F	jig	kind D F	life	might F
	her D F	job	king	light D	mom
	here D F	jog	kingdom	like D F	money F
	high F	join	kiss	limit	month
	hill	joint	kit	little D F	moon
	him D F	joke	kitten	live D F	more F
	his D F	joy	kitty	long D F	morning F
	hold D F	jump D F	kiwi	look D F	most F
	home F	jungle	koala	lost	mother F
	hope F	junk food		love F	much D F
	house F	just D F		low	must D F
	hot D	jut		lunar	my D F
	how D F			lung	myself D F
	hurt D				

Foldable® Half Book (left):
Make a half-book using a bright color of 8½" x 11" paper. Cut the outline of a consonant from a contrasting color of the same sized paper. To make a kinesthetic letter, fold the letter in half and glue only half of it within the half-book as illustrated. Use the large letter booklet to collect words that begin and/or end with the featured consonant.

D = word is found in *Dolch 220 Word List*
F = word is found in *Fry's First Three Hundred Instant Words.*
See Appendix Two, Research Citations, pages 286-288.

n (initial)	**p** (initial)	**q** (initial)	**r** (initial)	**s** (initial)	**t** (initial)
nag	pan	The consonant *q* is always followed by *u*.	rain	safe	table
nail	part F		ran D F	said D F	tail
name F	park	quack	rap	same F	take D F
nanny	party	quail	rat	sat F	talk
nap	pat	quake	read D F	save	tar
near F	peak	quart	really	saw D F	tea
neck	peer	quarter	red D F	say D F	tell D F
need	penny	queen	rent	second F	ten D F
neighbor	people F	quick	rest	see D F	test
nest	pick D	quiet	ride D F	seem F	tide
never D F	pig		right D F	send	time
new D F	pill		rock	senses	to D F
newt	pint		round D F	set F	today D F
next F	pit		run D F	seven D F	together D
nice	point		rust	she F	ton
night F	pole			show F	too D F
nine	pop			sing D F	took F
no D F	port			sit D F	town F
nose	post			six D F	turkey
not D F	potato			so D F	turn F
now D F	power			some D F	turtle
number	pull D			soon D F	two F
nut	put D F			such F	
				sure F	

VKV® Flashcard Flip (right): Use this simple VKV to help students focus on initial consonants studied. Fold a card leaving a tab on the left side. Write or glue words so that the initial consonant of each word is on the exposed tab and it is visible when the card is closed. When open, words can be viewed and read. Have students exchange their flashcard flips with other students.

Clip It Closed: A clothespin or a paper clip may be used to keep VKV cards closed when viewing initial consonants or consonant blends.

D = word is found in *Dolch 220 Word List*
F = word is found in *Fry's First Three Hundred Instant Words*.
See Appendix Two, Research Citations, pages 286-288.

V (initial)	W (initial)	X (initial)	Y (initial)	Z (initial/medial)
valley	walk D F	X-ray	yak	zap
vane	wall	xylem	yam	zeal
vast	want D F	xylophone	yank	zebra
vegetable	warm D F		yard	zero
vent	was D F		yarn	zest
verb	wash D F		yawn	zigzag
very D F	water F		yea	zillion
vest	way F		year F	zinnia
vine	we F		yell	zip
visit	well		yellow D F	zipper
vision	were F		yelp	zippy
vocabulary	will F		yes D F	zone
voice	win		yet	zoo
volcano	wish F		yield	zoom
volume	with F		yogurt	zucchini
vote	we D		yolk	
vowel	week		you D F	
vulture	well D		your F	
	went D		yours D	
	were D		yo-yo	
	will D			
	wish D			
	with D F			
	woman F			
	work D F			
	would D			

Top-Pocket Foldable® (right):
Use this Foldable to feature a consonant. Write or glue four words that contain the featured consonant (initial, medial, or final) on the four tabs. Define the words under the tabs or use them in sentences. Write or illustrate the featured letter in the middle section. Collect and store quarter-sheet word cards or short stories written on half sheets of paper in the top pocket. See page 310. Use 11" x 17" bond (photocopy) or index weight paper (80#, 110#) to make the fold pictured.

D = word is found in *Dolch 220 Word List*
F = word is found in *Fry's First Three Hundred Instant Words.*
See Appendix Two, Research Citations, pages 286-288.

b	**c**	**d**	**f**	**ff**	**g**	**k**
(final consonant)	(hard c sound)	(final consonant)	(final consonant)	(final consonants)	(final consonant)	(final consonant)
bib	citric	and D F	beef	bluff	bag	ask D
blab	comic	around D	chef	buff	beg	back F
cab	cubic	bad	chief	cliff	big D F	black D F
club	fabric	bed	deaf	cuff	bug	blank
cob	garlic	cold D F	elf	fluff	dig	book F
crab	magic	could D F	goof	gruff	dog F	chalk
crib	medic	dad	grief	huff	drag	cook
curb	metric	did D F	if D F	miff	dug	creek
drab	mimic	end F	leaf	off	fig	drink D
fib	music	find D F	loaf	puff	flag	ink
flab	picnic	found D F	myself D	riff	fog	leak
grab	plastic	friend F	of D F	ruff	frog	lick
knob	public	good D F	reef	sheriff	hog	link
lab	rustic	had D F	roof	staff	hug	look D F
mob	topic	hand F	scarf	stiff	lag	mark
nab	tropic	hold D	self	stuff	leg	park
rib	zinc	kind D F	shelf	tiff	log	peek
rob		old D F	surf		long D F	pick D
rub		read D F	turf		pig	pink
scab		red D F	wolf		rag	pork
scrub		round D			rig	rank
shrub		said D F			ring	rock
slab		should F			rug	sank
stab		stand F			sag	shark
tab		would D F			sing	sink
tub					smog	sock
verb					snug	talk
					song	thank D
					sprig	think D F
					tag	walk D
					thing	week
					wag	work D F
					wing	
					wrong	

**Add or Change Final Consonants VKV®
(left):** Determine if students can change or add final consonants to make new words. Photo example left: bad, bag, ban, bat.
Other Examples: for, fork, fort; fib, fig, fin, fit; park, part, pard; pin, pink, pint; rib, rid, rig, rim, rip; see, seed, seek, seem; sob, sod, son; tab, tad, tag, tan, tap; win, wind, wing, wink. See page 80.

D = word is found in *Dolch 220 Word List*
F = word is found in *Fry's First Three Hundred Instant Words.*
See Appendix Two, Research Citations, pages 286-288.

l (final consonant)	**ll** (final consonant)	**m** (final consonant)	**n** (final consonant)	**p** (final consonant)	**r** (final consonant- *r* controlled vowels)	**s** (final consonant)
bail	all D F	am D F	again F	cap	another F	as D F
camel	ball F	bum	an D F	cop	better D F	atlas
capital	bell	calm	ban	cup	color F	bus
coal	bill	clam	been D F	dip	dear F	days
cool	call D F	cream	bin	drip	ear F	does D
coral	chill	dim	brown D	drop	far D F	gas
fail	doll	dream	can D F	gap	her D	has D F
feel	drill	drum	clean D	grip	for D F	his D F
final	dull	farm	down D F	help D	mother F	is D F
floral	fall D F	from D F	fan	hop	near F	its
foal	fell	gum	fun	jump D	or D F	plus
fool	fill	gym	green D	keep D	our D F	pus
fuel	full D	ham	hen	map	over D F	this D F
girl F	hall	him D F	in D F	mop	under D F	us D F
hail	hill	hum	man F	nap	year F	was D F
hotel	ill	jam	men F	nip	your F	yes D F
jail	jell	mom	nun	pup		
jewel	mall	palm	on D F	rap		
local	pull D	plum	open D F	rip		
motel	quill	poem	own D F	sap		
nasal	roll	ram	pen	shop		
pail	sell	rim	pin	sip		
peel	shall D F	seem F	ran D F	sleep D		
pool	small D F	storm	run D F	stop D		
pupil	spell	sum	seen	tap		
sail	spill	swam	seven D	tip		
school F	still	swim	soon D F	top		
spool	tall	team	sun	trip		
steal	tell D F	them D F	ten D	up D F		
stool	toll	trim	than F	whip		
tail	wall	warm D	then D F	zap		
tool	well D	yam	upon D F	zip		
total	will D F		when D F			
until F	yell					

Two-Column Foldable® Chart:
Display words that reinforce skills as they are encountered when reading literature or found in RWP.

D = word is found in *Dolch 220 Word List*
F = word is found in *Fry's First Three Hundred Instant Words.*
See Appendix Two, Research Citations, pages 286-288.

ss
(final consonant)
across
address
bass
bless
bliss
boss
class
cross
dress
floss
fuss
glass
gloss
grass
guess
hiss
kiss
lass
less
loss
mess
miss
moss
pass
press
surpass
toss

t
(final consonant)
about D F
at D F
best D F
bit
but D F
cat
cut D F
eat D F
first D F
fit
get D F
got D F
hat
hot D
hurt D
it D F
just D F
last F
left F
let D
light D
most F
must D F
next F
night F
not D F
out D F
present F
put D F
sit D
start D
that D F
want D F
what D F

tt
(final consonant)
batt
butt
mitt
mutt
putt

x
(final consonant)
box F
fax
fix
flax
flex
fox
lax
lox
mix
six D
tax
wax

z
(final consonant)
blitz
quartz
quiz
showbiz
topaz
waltz
whiz

zz
(final consonant)
buzz
fuzz
fizz
frizz
fuzz
jazz
razz

Focus on a Sound or Letter (above): Cut a giant letter and glue it onto a sheet of 8½" x 11" colored copy paper. Have students collect examples of the featured letter and/or sound from RWP or write their own examples. In the example above, **z** is found in initial, medial, and final position.

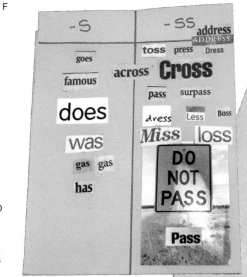

Two-Column Foldable® Chart (right): It is not uncommon to make a chart, table, or graph and find it is not large enough to collect all the words students want to display. When this happens, glue another sheet of paper to the bottom (or side) of the Foldable as illustrated to the right. Notice the use of photographs and words from RWP within the chart.

D = word is found in *Dolch 220 Word List*
F = word is found in *Fry's First Three Hundred Instant Words.*
See Appendix Two, Research Citations, pages 286-288.

b/bb
(medial consonant)

baby
blubber
bubble
cabin
fable
habit
labor
number
ribbon
robber
slumber
sober
table
tubby
timber

c/cc
(medial consonant)

bacon
became
because
cactus
circle
decay
factor
picture
raccoon
second

c
(soft *c* sound)

dice
face
ice
nice
peace
pencil
place
race
rice
since
space
twice

d/dd
(medial consonant)

daddy
hidden
hundred
medicine
middle
model
modern
radar
ready
video

dg
(medial, sounds like *j*)

fudged
hedged
ledges
pledging
ridges
wedged

f
(medial consonant)

fifty
infant
infect
left
lift
loft
refer
referee
reflex
reform
safety
sift
soft

ff
(medial consonant)

differ
difficult
buffalo
buffer
buffet
difficult
fluffy
puffin
stuffy
suffer
traffic

g/gg
(medial consonant)

ago
giggle
legal
saga
squiggle
sugar
wagon
wiggle
yogurt

g
(soft, sounds like *j*)

age
energy
legend
mileage
region
religion
sage
vegetable
veggie
village

h
(medial consonant)

ahead
behavior
behind
behold
overhead
overheat
rehearse
reheat
unhappy
unhealthy
upheaval

j
(medial consonant)

adjective
banjo
majesty
major
majority
object
project
reject
rejoice
rejoin
unjust

D = word is found in *Dolch 220 Word List*
F = word is found in *Fry's First Three Hundred Instant Words.*
See Appendix Two, Research Citations, pages 286-288.

k

(medial consonant)

ba<u>k</u>er
bro<u>k</u>en
hi<u>k</u>ing
ma<u>k</u>er
mar<u>k</u>et
mon<u>k</u>ey
nic<u>k</u>el
para<u>k</u>eet
sna<u>k</u>es
spea<u>k</u>er
stri<u>k</u>ing
ta<u>k</u>en
truc<u>k</u>er
tur<u>k</u>ey

l/ll

(medial consonant)

ba<u>ll</u>oon
ca<u>ll</u>er
co<u>ll</u>ar
co<u>ll</u>ect
do<u>ll</u>ar
fe<u>ll</u>ow
fo<u>ll</u>ow
ga<u>l</u>axy
ga<u>ll</u>on
o<u>l</u>d
pu<u>ll</u>ey
ru<u>l</u>er
so<u>l</u>id
va<u>ll</u>ey
ye<u>ll</u>ow F

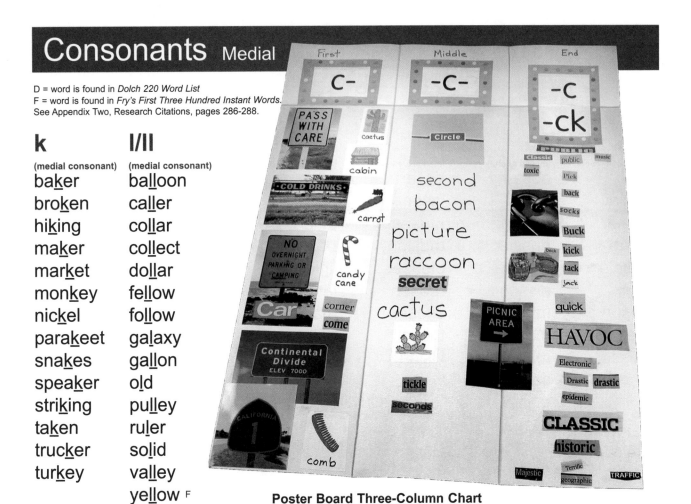

Poster Board Three-Column Chart

m/mm

(medial consonant)

co<u>m</u>ic
co<u>mm</u>a
co<u>mm</u>on
di<u>mm</u>er
gli<u>mm</u>er
ha<u>mm</u>er
hu<u>m</u>id
ma<u>mm</u>al
ma<u>mm</u>oth
nu<u>m</u>ber
si<u>mm</u>er
su<u>mm</u>er
te<u>m</u>per
ti<u>m</u>er
ti<u>m</u>id
tu<u>mm</u>y

n/nn

(medial consonant)

a<u>n</u>imal
ba<u>n</u>ana
bu<u>nn</u>y
cou<u>n</u>try
fu<u>nn</u>y F
ha<u>n</u>dle
ha<u>n</u>dy
ho<u>n</u>ey
mo<u>n</u>ey
mo<u>n</u>th
mi<u>n</u>eral
pe<u>nn</u>y
ru<u>nn</u>er
su<u>nn</u>y
wi<u>nn</u>er

p/pp

(medial consonant)

a<u>pp</u>le
gu<u>pp</u>y
ha<u>pp</u>en
ha<u>pp</u>y F
ma<u>p</u>le
o<u>p</u>en
pa<u>p</u>er
peo<u>p</u>le
pu<u>pp</u>y
pur<u>p</u>le
ra<u>p</u>id
re<u>p</u>tile
sna<u>pp</u>y
u<u>pp</u>er
zi<u>pp</u>er

qu

(kw sound)

ac<u>qu</u>ire
e<u>qu</u>al
e<u>qu</u>ation
e<u>qu</u>ator
li<u>qu</u>id
re<u>qu</u>est
re<u>qu</u>ire

(Also see *squ-* words.)

s<u>qu</u>are
s<u>qu</u>ash
s<u>qu</u>id
s<u>qu</u>iggly

r/rr

(medial consonant/
r-controlled vowels)

ca<u>r</u>pet
ca<u>rr</u>ot
ca<u>rr</u>y F
ci<u>r</u>cle
co<u>r</u>al
co<u>rr</u>al
fi<u>r</u>st
fo<u>r</u>est
ma<u>r</u>ine
pa<u>r</u>ent
pa<u>rr</u>ot
pu<u>r</u>ple
sto<u>r</u>y
te<u>rr</u>or
ze<u>r</u>o

Double Letters Shutterfold:
8½" x 11" shutterfold with four tabs to divide four words with double letters.

D = word is found in *Dolch 220 Word List*
F = word is found in *Fry's First Three Hundred Instant Words.*
See Appendix Two, Research Citations, pages 286-288.

s
(medial consonant)
al**s**o
ca**s**tle
her**s**elf
in**s**ide
mu**s**cle
mu**s**ic
per**s**on
que**s**tion
whi**s**tle

ss
(medial z sound)
de**ss**ert

ss
(medial sound)
bo**ss**y
fo**ss**il
flo**ss**ing
ha**ss**le
hi**ss**ing
le**ss**on
mi**ss**ing
mo**ss**y
mi**ss**ion
se**ss**ion
ta**ss**el
ti**ss**ue
to**ss**ing

s
(medial z sound)
de**s**ert
la**s**er
mu**s**eum
mu**s**ic
plea**s**e
rea**s**on
sea**s**on
tho**s**e
vi**s**ion
vi**s**it

t/tt
(medial consonant)
af**t**er
a**tt**ack
a**tt**ic
be**tt**er F
li**tt**le F
le**tt**er F
ma**tt**er
na**t**ure
pota**t**o
pre**t**zel
se**tt**ler
wa**t**er
win**t**er

Medial Consonant VKV®(below):
See instructions at the bottom of this page.

v
(medial consonant)
ca**v**ity
ci**v**ic
cle**v**er
di**v**er
fa**v**orite
fe**v**er
la**v**a
le**v**er
o**v**al
o**v**er
ri**v**er
se**v**en

w
(medial consonant)
al**w**ays
a**w**ay
co**w**er
for**w**ard
high**w**ay
je**w**el
plo**w**ing
po**w**er
re**w**ork
sho**w**er
to**w**er
un**w**ind

x
(medial consonant)
bo**x**es
fa**x**ing
fi**x**ing
fo**x**es
ne**x**t
si**x**th
si**x**teen
si**x**ty
ta**x**es
ta**x**i
te**x**t
wa**x**ing

z/zz
(medial consonant)
bli**zz**ard
bu**zz**ard
cra**z**y
di**zz**y
fi**zz**y
ha**z**y
ha**z**ard
la**z**y
li**z**ard
pi**zz**a
ra**z**or
wi**z**ard

3.

2.

1.

VKV® Flashcard: Medial Consonants (above right)
The VKV flashcard pictured above right can be used to bring attention to medial consonants.
1. Write a word in the middle of a single flashcard.
2. Fold the left and right edges over to cover all letters except the medial consonants featured.
3. With the tabs closed, observe the medial consonant/consonants. Open the left tab and then the right tab quickly while saying the word.

Make several consonant blend and digraph VKV flashcards for initial, medial, and ending sounds. It is not necessary to make flashcards for all the words used when studying consonant clusters; however, continue to make a few consonant blend and digraph VKV flashcards, and add them to the *Consonant Blends* and *Digraphs* section of your VKV Flashcard Box, see page 16, throughout the school year.

⬭VKV⬭ Flashcard: Consonant Blends and Digraphs #1

1. Fold a double flashcard in half to make a cutting line. Unfold.
2. Cut along the top fold line to form two tabs. Do not cut the back section.
3. Write the initial blend or digraph of a selected word under the first tab aligning the last consonant close to the middle fold line.
4. Write the remaining letters of the word under the second tab aligning the first letter close to the middle fold line.
5. Open and close the tabs to analyze the initial consonants and the vocabulary word they help form.

Alternate VKV®: Complete this same activity for words with affixes. See page 52.

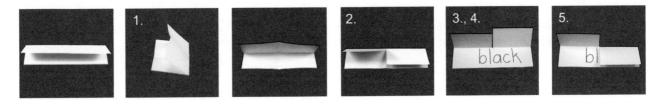

⬭VKV⬭ Flashcards: Consonant Blends and Digraphs #2

1. Fold a triple flashcard in half.
2. Cut along the fold line of the top and bottom strip. DO NOT cut the middle strip.
3. Cut off the top left and bottom left tabs, and write an initial consonant, a blend, or digraph on the remaining left center strip.
4. Select three word families that form words when added to the consonant, and write them on the three right sections.
5. Open and close the right tabs to form three words with the featured initial consonant/s.

Alternate VKV®: Reverse the VKV to focus on three different blends/digraphs and one phonogram.

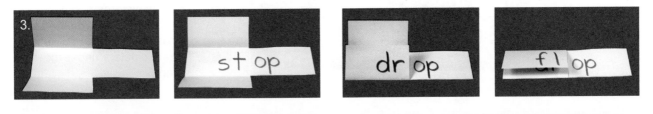

Two-Pocket Foldable®:
Find words that begin and end with consonant blends or digraphs, write them on word cards, or quarter sheets of paper, and store them in the appropriate pockets of a Foldable.

Foldable® Pocket Book (right):
As pictured, when multiple two-pocket Foldables are glued together side by side they form a multi-pocket book that can be used to collect digraph word cards and VKVs. See pages 31 and 291 for instructions on how to glue Foldables side by side to make them "grow."

Two-Tab Foldable® or Two-Column Foldable® Chart:
Find and record examples of words where the first consonants are silent -- **k**nowledge, **w**rap.

Picture Frame Foldable®:
Draw a picture of a queen or draw a picture of another **qu**- word in the frame. Find and collect words where **qu** sounds like **kw**, as in **quiet** or **queen**, and write or glue them inside the Foldable.

Bound Book Foldable® Journal:
Use four sheets of paper to make a bound-book Foldable and use it to collect **s** clusters -- **st**, **sp**, **sn**, **sm**, **sl**, **sc**, **sk**, **sw**, **spl**, **str**, **spr**, **scr**, **squ**. **Variation:** Use seven sheets of paper to make a Foldable book with fourteen pockets and use them to collect word cards and VKVs for the clusters listed.

Use two sheets of paper to make a bound-book Foldable and use it to collect **l** clusters -- **bl**, **cl**, **gl**, **pl**, **sl**. **Variation:** Use two sheets of paper to make a Foldable book with four pockets.

Use three sheets of paper to make a bound-book Foldable and use it to collect **r** clusters -- **br**, **cr**, **dr**, **fr**, **gr**, **pr**, **tr**, **wr**. **Variation:** Use four sheets of paper to make a Foldable book with eight pockets.

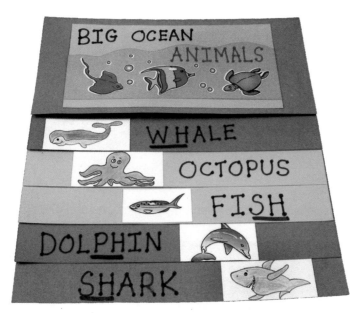

Layered Foldable® Content Focus (left):
Foldables and VKVs can feature science, math, or social studies vocabulary terms while integrating phonics skills.

The Foldable to the left was used with a Kindergarten ocean unit. Note that four of the animals' names contain consonant clusters. Draw pictures and write sentences or stories that contain the featured consonant clusters under the tabs.

D = word is found in *Dolch 220 Word List*
F = word is found in *Fry's First Three Hundred Instant Words*.
See Appendix Two, Research Citations, pages 286-288.

bl
(blend)

black D F
blade
blame
blank
blast
bleed
blender
bless
blind
blister
bloat
blood
block
blossom
blouse
blown
blue D
blueberry
bluff
blunt

br
(blend)

braid
brain
brake
brand
brave
bread
break
breath
breeze
bride
bridge
bright
brine
bring D F
brisk
broccoli
bronze
brook
brother
brought
brow
brown D F

ch
(digraph)

chalk
change
chart
check
cheerful
cheese
cherry
chess
chest
chew
chick
chicken
child
children
chin
chip
chocolate
choice
choose
chop
church

ch
(hard c sound)

character
chord
chorus
chrome
chronic
chrysalis
lichen

-ch
(final blend)

bench
branch
church
crunch
each F
lunch
much D F
peach
ranch
reach
such F
teach
touch

-ck
(hard c sound)

back F
black D F
block
brick
duck
flock
knock
lack
lick
lock
luck
pick D
quick
rack
rock
sack
shock
sock
stack
stick
stuck
tack
thick
tick
tock
track
trick
truck

Quarter-Sheet Study Cards:
Use quarter sheets of paper from the classroom publishing center (see page 13) to collect words and pictures of words that begin with consonant blends and digraphs studied.

Pop-Up Book:
Use to feature blends and digraphs. Glue multiple pop-up pages side by side to make a pop-up book. See page 299.

D = word is found in *Dolch 220 Word List*
F = word is found in *Fry's First Three Hundred Instant Words*.
See Appendix Two, Research Citations, pages 286-288.

cl
(initial blend)
clad
claim
clam
clap
class
classroom
claw
clean D F
clear
cliff
climb
close F
clothes F
cloud
clown
club
clue
clump

cr
(initial blend)
crab
cracker
craft
crane
crayon
cream
creek
cricket
crimson
crooked
crop
cross
crowd
crown
cruel
crust

-ct
(final blend)
act
detect
duct
eject
elect
fact
neglect
pact
react
reject
respect
select

dw
(initial blend)
dwarf
dwelling
dwindle

dr
(initial blend)
draft
drag
dragon
drain
drama
draw D
drawbridge
dream
dress F
drew
drift
drill
drink D
drip
drive
drizzle
drop
drove
drown
drug
drugstore
drum
dry

fl
(initial blend)
flag
flame
flamingo
flannel
flash
flat
flavor
flea
fledgling
fleece
flesh
flex
flight
fling
flint
flood
floss
flow
flower
flush
fly D F

Envelope Foldable® (below):
This Foldable can be used to feature four beginning and/or ending blends or digraphs.
Write the blends to be studied on the front tabs.
Under the tabs, list examples of words or find words in RWP that begin and/or end with the featured blends or digraphs. See page 297.

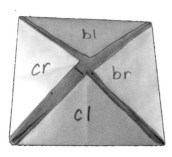

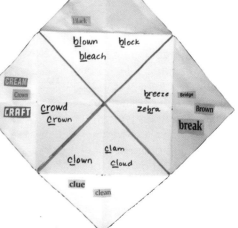

D = word is found in *Dolch 220 Word List*
F = word is found in *Fry's First Three Hundred Instant Words.*
See Appendix Two, Research Citations, pages 286-288.

fr-
(initial blend)

fraction
fragile
frame
free
freedom
freeze
fresh
friction
friend F
frog
from D F
frost
frown
frozen
fry

-ft
(final blend)

craft
draft
gift
left F
lift
loft
raft
rift
shift
sift
soft

gh-
(digraph: gh sound g)

gherkin
ghetto
ghost
ghostwriter

-gh
(digraph: gh sounds like f)

cough
enough
laugh D
rough
tough

-gh
(silent)

bright
eight D
fight
flight
high F
light D
might F
night
right D F
sigh
sight
slight
straight
thigh
thought
through
tight
weight

gl-
(initial blend)

glad
glade
glance
gland
glare
glass
glaze
gleam
glen
glide
glider
glimmer
globe
glory
gloss
glow
glue
glum

gr-
(initial blend)

grab
grade
graduate
grain
grant
graph
grasp
grass
gravel
grease
great
green D F
grid
gross
ground
group
grow D F
grub

kn-
(sounds like n)

knee
kneel
knew
knife
knight
knit
knob
knock
knot
know D F
knuckle

**Three-Tab Foldable®
(right):** Make this three-tab Foldable to feature three words beginning with the same blend or words that begin with three different blends -- *gr, fr, pr.* Draw or glue a picture word on the front tabs of the Foldable. Under the tabs, write or glue examples of other words that begin with the same blend, and write sentences or a short paragraph using the words. See page 293.

Consonants Blends and Digraphs Word List

D = word is found in *Dolch 220 Word List*
F = word is found in *Fry's First Three Hundred Instant Words*.
See Appendix Two, Research Citations, pages 286-288.

kr-
(initial blend)

krill
krypton

-ld
(final blend)

bold
cold D F
could D F
field
fold
gold
held
hold D
mold
old D F
should F
told
would D F

-lk
(final blend)

bulk
elk
hulk
stalk
sulk
talk
walk D
whelk

-lm
(final blend)

balm
calm
palm

-lp
(final blend)

gulp
help D F
pulp
scalp
yelp

-lt
(final blend)

belt
built
colt
felt
kilt
malt
melt
quilt
salt

-mp
(final blend)

bump
camp
chomp
damp
dump
jump D F
lamp
lump
pump
ramp
stamp

-nc(e)
(final blend)

chance
dance
fence
glance
prance
since

-nch
(final blend)

bench
bunch
cinch
clench
crunch
drench
inch
lunch
munch
pinch
wrench

-nd
(final blend)

and D F
around D
end F
find D F
found D F
friend F
grind
ground
hand F
kind D F
land
lend
mend
mind
pound
rind
round D
sand
send
sound
stand F
wind

-ng
(phoneme)

bring
cling
ding dong
fling
gang
hang
king
long D F
ping pong
rang
ring
rung
sang
sing
song
sting
string
strong
thing
wing
wrong

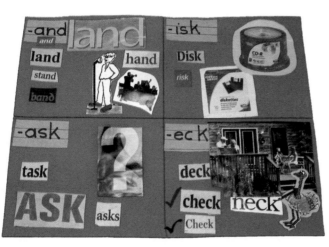

Folded Book (left): Fold a sheet of 8½" x 11" paper into fourths in order to collect words and pictures for final blends or digraphs -- *and*, *isk*, *ask*, and *eck*. When finished, write four different blends or digraphs on the back, and continue to collect and write words on both sides. This single sheet of paper can be used for over a week, and numerous grades can be taken. See page 289.

Have students select a given number of words from this Foldable for use in a writing or spelling activity.

D = word is found in *Dolch 220 Word List*
F = word is found in *Fry's First Three Hundred Instant Words.*
See Appendix Two, Research Citations, pages 286-288.

-nk
(final blend)
bank
blank
blink
bunk
drank
drink D
dunk
honk
ink
junk
link
mink
pink
plank
rink
sank
sink
skunk
tank
thank D F
think D F
trunk
wink

-nt
(final blend)
bent
cent
dent
flint
front
hint
lint
mint
pant
pint
present F
print
punt
sent
student
tent
vent
want D F
went D

ph
(digraph)
pharmacy
phase
phone
phonics
photo
photocopy
photograph

pl-
(initial blend)
place
plain
plane
planet
plant
plastic
play D F
please D F
pledge
plesiosaur
plot
plow
plum
plus

pr-
(initial blend)
prairie
praise
prance
prank
prawn
present F
pretty D F
price
pride
primary
prince
princess
principle
print
problem
product
proud
prune

-pt
(final blend)
kept
leapt
slept
wept

-rd
(final blend-
r controlled vowels)
bird
card
ford
hard
heard
herd
lard
lord
word
yard

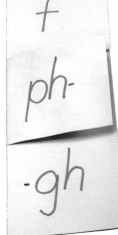

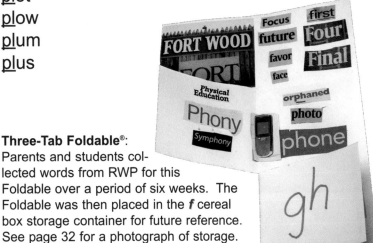

Three-Tab Foldable®:
Parents and students collected words from RWP for this Foldable over a period of six weeks. The Foldable was then placed in the *f* cereal box storage container for future reference. See page 32 for a photograph of storage.

Consonants Blends and Digraphs Word List

D = word is found in *Dolch 220 Word List*
F = word is found in *Fry's First Three Hundred Instant Words*.
See Appendix Two, Research Citations, pages 286-288.

qu-
(initial blend)
queen
quest
question
quick
quiet
quill
quilt
quit
quote

-rk
(final blend)
jerk
lurk
work D F

-rt
(final blend/
r controlled vowels)
art
cart
chart
dart
dirt
heart
hurt D
mart
part
port
shirt
short
skirt
smart
start D
tart
wart

sc-
(initial blend, hard sound)
scab
scale
scalp
scan
scar
scare
scarlet
score
scuba

sh-
(c, x, and s can sound like *sh*)
anxious
ocean
sugar

sh-
(digraph)
shade
shadow
shake
shall D F
shape
share
shark
she D F
shelf
shell
shield
shin
shine
ship
should F
show F

-sh
(digraph)
brush
crush
finish
push
rush
wash D
wish D F

sk-
(initial blend)
skate
skeleton
sketch
ski
skillet
skin
skirt
skull
skunk
sky

-sk
(final blend)
ask D F
desk
disk
dusk
task
tusk
whisk

sl-
(initial blend)
slam
slant
slash
sleep D F
sleet
slice
slick
slide
slim
slip
sliver
slow D

Two-Pocket Foldable® (above):
Make this Foldable to collect quarter-sheet study cards of words or pictures illustrating words that contain the featured blend or diagram.

Once numerous study cards are made, mix up the cards, and use the pockets for sorting. See page 291.

D = word is found in *Dolch 220 Word List*
F = word is found in *Fry's First Three Hundred Instant Words.*
See Appendix Two, Research Citations, pages 286-288.

sm-	sn-	sp-	st-	-st	sw-
(initial blend)	(initial blend)	(initial blend)	(initial blend)	(final blend)	(initial blend)
small D F	snack	spa	stamp	best D F	swallow
smart	snail	space	stand D	cost	swamp
smell	snake	spam	staple	crust	swan
smelly	snap	spank	star	dust	swarm
smile	sneakers	spark	start D F	fast D F	swat
smog	sneeze	sparkle	state	first D F	sway
smoke	sniff	speak	stay	just D F	sweat
smooth	snip	spear	steam	last F	sweater
smug	snooze	speed	stem	list	sweep
	snore	spell	stew	lost	sweet
	snorkel	spice	stomp	most F	swell
	snow	spin	stone	must D F	swim
		spine	stop D F	nest	swimmer
	-sp	sport	store	past	swing
	(final blend)	spot	storm	post	swish
	clasp	spun	story	rest	swollen
	crisp	spur	study	test	
	lisp	spy	stun	vest	
	wasp		stunt	west	
				zest	

The car goes **fast**

He wears a **vest**

I took a Test

The fossil is a **cast**

This pizza is the best

My dog is lost

Put ice in the Chest

I will be last

Multi-Tab Foldable® (far left):
Fold a sheet of paper like a hotdog, leaving about one third of the right side uncovered. Write or glue words so that only the final consonant blends or digraphs are visible when the left tabs are closed. Fold and cut as many tabs as needed. With tabs closed, students observe the final letters. Students open the tabs, read the word, and then use the word within a sentence. See page 308.

Variation (left): Under the tabs, write sentences that end in the featured words.

D = word is found in *Dolch 220 Word List*
F = word is found in *Fry's First Three Hundred Instant Words.*
See Appendix Two, Research Citations, pages 286-288.

th
(digraph)
(voiced as in *this*)

than F
that D F
the D F
their D F
them D F
then D F
there D F
these D F
they D F
this D F
those D

th
(digraph,
voiceless as in *thin*)

thank D F
thermometer
thick
thin
thing F
think D F
third F
thirty
thumb
thunder

-th

bath
both D F
fourth
math
month
moth
mouth
path
tooth
truth
with D F
worth

tr
(initial blend)

trace
tracks
train
travel
tree F
tribe
triceratops
trouble
truck
true
trunk
try D

tw
(initial blend)

tweezers
twelve
twenty
twice
twig
twilight
twin
twinkle
twirl
twister

wh
(digraph *w*)

whale
what D F
wheat
wheel
when D F
where D F
which D F
whiff
while F
whip
whisper
whistle
white D F
whittle
why D F

wh
(digraph *hw*)

who D F
whoop
whooping
 crane

wr
(*r* sound)

wrap
wreath
wreck
wren
wrench
wrestle
wrinkle
wrist
write D F
wrong

Two Sounds and Two-Tab Foldable®: Staple quarter sheets behind the tabs and use them to collect examples of **wh** and **hw** words. See photographs and instructions on page 67.

D = word is found in *Dolch 220 Word List*
F = word is found in *Fry's First Three Hundred Instant Words*.
See Appendix Two, Research Citations, pages 286-288.

-tch
(digraph)

catch
crutch
ditch
fetch
hatch
itch
latch
match
patch
pitch
sketch
stitch
stretch
watch
witch

sch-
(initial blend/
(hard sound)

schedule
scholastic
school F

shr-
(initial blend)

shrank
shrill
shrimp
shrink
shrub
shrubbery
shrunk

scr-
(initial blend)

scratch
scream
screen
screw
scribble

sph-
(initial blend)

sphere
sphinx

spl-
(initial blend)

splash
splinter

Foldable® Chart: Make a two-column chart to collect words and pictures of words that contain two featured digraphs. Notice that the photograph at the top of the chart features words with both *str-* and *thr-* blends.

Same Word, But Different:
When using RWP (real world print) ESL/ELL students are encouraged to find the same word written in different fonts and in different case letters. For example the word *spring* was found written in all capital letters, and in lower case letters with a capital *S*. See page 26 of Introduction.

spr-
(initial blend)

sprain
spray
spring
sprinkler
sprout
spruce

squ-
(initial blend)

square
squash
squat
squeeze
squid
squirrel

str-
(initial blend)

straight
strange
strap
straw
stream
street
stress
strong

thr-
(initial blend)

thread
three D F
threshold
throat
throne
through
throughout
throw

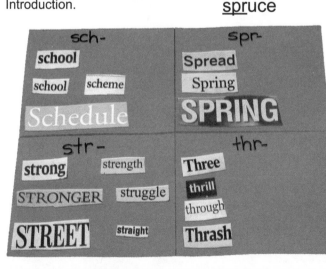

Folded Book and Oral Language Practice:
Use one sheet of paper to make a four-section Foldable and use it to collect examples of words that begin with four blends or digraphs. See page 289.

Extension: Have students select one word from their Foldable and use it in their daily writing, or have someone select a word for the student and see how quickly the student can orally use it in a sentence or a story.

D = word is found in *Dolch 220 Word List*
F = word is found in *Fry's First Three Hundred Instant Words*.
See Appendix Two, Research Citations, pages 286-288.

Silent b

(silent b in consonant digraph -mb)

bomb
climb
comb
crumb
debt
doubt
dumb
lamb
limb
numb
plumb
plumber
thumb
tomb

Silent c

(silent c)

muscle
scene
scenic
scent
science
scissors

Silent c

(silent c in -ck words)

back F
black D F
clock
dock
duck
flock
lock
luck
pick D
quick
stack
stick
stuck
tick
track
trick
truck

Silent g

(silent g in consonant digraph -gn)

design
gnarl
gnat
gnaw
gnome
gnu
reign
resign
sign

Silent -gh

(silent gh)

bright
eight D
fight
flight
high F
light D
might F
night
right D F
sigh
sight
slight
straight
thigh
thought
through
tight
weight

Silent h

(silent h)

exhibit
ghost
herb
honest
rhyme
rhythm
school
shepherd
spaghetti
vehicle

Foldable® Journal (left): Make a bound book Foldable to collect words that contain silent letters. Use these words in short stories. See page 290.

Three-Tab Foldable® (right): Make a three-tab Foldable and use it to feature three words with silent letters. See page 293.

D = word is found in *Dolch 220 Word List*
F = word is found in *Fry's First Three Hundred Instant Words.*
See Appendix Two, Research Citations, pages 286-288.

Silent k

(silent **k** in consonant digraph *-kn*)

doorknob
knee
kneel
knew
knight
knife
knit
knob
knock
knot
know
knuckle

Silent l

(silent *l* and silent *l* in consonant digraphs *-lk* and *-lf*))

calf
calm
could
folk
half
salmon
should
stalk
talk
walk
would
yolk

(*l* can be silent or voiced)

almond

Silent n

(silent *n* in consonant digraph *-mn*)

autumn
column
hymn

Silent p

cupboard
empty
pneumonia
raspberry
receipt

Silent Medial or Ending Consonants (below): Glue or write a word with silent letters inside a double flashcard. Cut the top section of the card so that silent letters in the word will be hidden under the remaining tab. Cut the cards to graphically demonstrate how some letters are used to spell words, but are not heard when the word is read or spoken. See contractions, page 110 for cutting suggestions.

li̅ t   **li̅ght**

Silent s

island
isle

Silent t

castle
Christmas
depot
fasten
listen
stretch
whistle
wrestle

Silent Initial Consonants Flipovers (below): Write or glue a word onto the right end of a single flashcard. Fold the left edge of the strip around to cover silent initial consonants.

rite   write

hole   whole

Silent u

bodyguard
guard
guess
guest
guide
lifeguard

Silent w

(silent *w*, silent *w* before *r*)

answer
sword
two
whole
whose
wrap
wreath
write
wrong

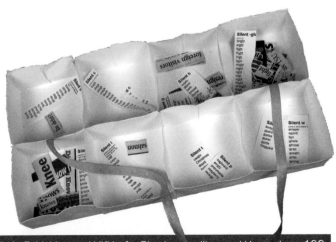

Sorting RWP (right): Eight display boxes were glued together to make the RWP collection tray pictured right. Notice the word list on this page was photocopied, cut, and placed in the boxes to guide students in their word search. See pages 254-255 for illustrated folding instructions.

Make several VKV flashcards that demonstrate how contractions are formed. With practice, most students will be able to transfer what they learn about forming contractions from using these VKV flashcards to other situations in which they read or write contractions. It is not necessary to make flashcards for all the contractions listed within this section; however, continue to make a few new contraction VKV flashcards and add them to the *Contractions* section of your VKV Flashcard Box, see page 16, throughout the school year.

VKV® Flashcards: Contractions

1. Write two words that form a contraction under the tab of a double flashcard.
2. With the card open, draw lines to indicate which letters will be omitted. In the example below, draw lines on the tab above the word that indicate the width of the o. Use a ruler to help align and sketch these cutting lines.
3. Cut the top strip away to expose the letters that will remain in the contraction. Leave the top strip intact over the letter/letters that are to be omitted.
4. Fold the tab down covering the letter/letters to be omitted, and draw an apostrophe on the front of the tab.
5. Open and close the tab to see the two words become a contraction, and the contraction revert back to two words.
Note: The contraction tabs will vary in size and position, and must be cut based upon the words written inside the double flashcard.

Flashcards: Contractions, continued

Example: Since the letters wi- need to be covered by a tab, sketch light lines indicating the width of these letters, and use the lines as a guide when cutting away sections of the top half to form a tab. Cut along the sketch lines. Cut away the left and right top sections. Draw an apostrophe on the front of the remaining tab to take the place of the letters the single tab will cover.

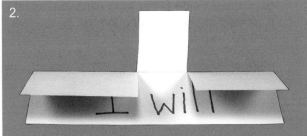

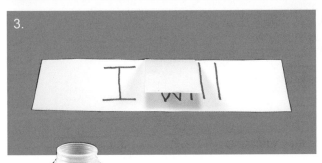

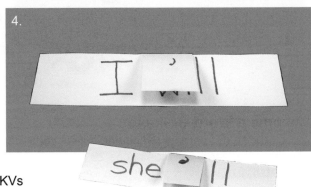

Right: Make contraction VKVs throughout the school term. When a memorable phrase containing a contraction is encountered in literature, make a VKV for the contraction, and record the phrase on the back.

Storage Option (above and right): Cut and decorate a half-gallon milk jug, leaving the handle to make an easy-to-carry storage container for VKV flashcards.

VKV® Flashcards: Contraction Rings

1. Fold a single flashcard in half.
2. Write a word or word pair on one side and a contraction using the word, or a contraction formed by the word pair, on the other side of the card.
3. Punch a hole along the short edge of the folded card and store the VKV flashcards on a large ring or in the VKV Flashcard Box, page 16.
4. Look at the left side of the word cards on the ring, and try to determine a contraction that could be formed using each word. Turn the card to check your answer.

1., 2.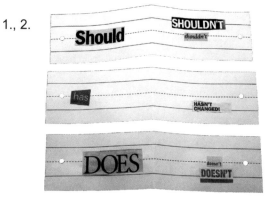

3.

Become a Word Collector:

Ask students and parents to find and collect contractions they encounter in RWP. Store the words until needed. (See storage ideas pages 28 and 30.) When ready to use, pour the words onto a piece of poster board to make access and selection easier. Teach students the importance of keeping the words turned so that the RWP (in this example, contractions) are easily read and identified. Remind parents and students who collect RWP to always arrange and store the cut words so that they face upwards, and can be read.

Foldable® Contractions Table:

This folded table can be made out of butcher paper and used to illustrate how word pairs are written as contractions. Encourage students to collect examples of contractions they encounter in RWP and glue them onto the table. See page 308.

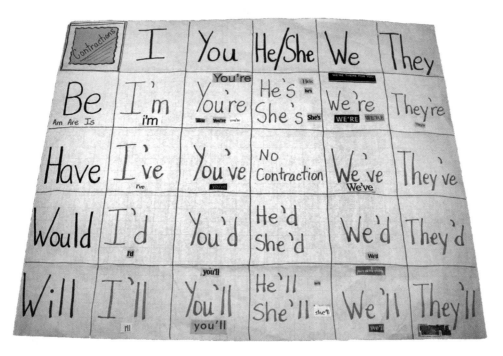

Foldable® Sentence Strip Holder:

Make and use two small sentence-strip holders (8½" x 11" paper) or one large holder (11" x 17" paper) to match word pairs and contractions. Display a word pair on one small holder and the contraction formed from the word pair on another, or together on a large holder as illustrated below. If necessary, trim the cards used with this activity so they will fit inside the sentence strip holder for easy storage. See page 306.

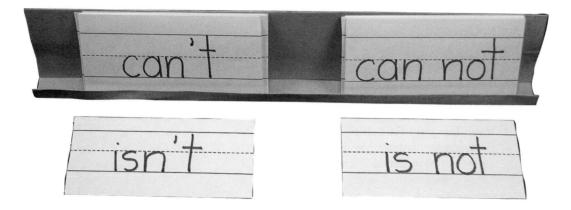

Contractions

Not

are not	aren't
cannot	can't
could not	couldn't
did not	didn't
do not	don't
does not	doesn't
have not	haven't
has not	hasn't
had not	hadn't
is not	isn't
might not	mightn't
must not	mustn't
need not	needn't
should not	shouldn't
was not	wasn't
were not	weren't
will not	won't
would not	wouldn't

Be

I am	I'm
you are	you're
he is	he's
she is	she's
it is	it's
we are	we're
they are	they're

Have

I have	I've
you have	you've
we have	we've
they have	they've
could have	could've
might have	might've
should have	should've
there have	there've
who have	who've
would have	would've

Would

I would	I'd
you would	you'd
he would	he'd
she would	she'd
we would	we'd
they would	they'd
it would	it'd
who would	who'd

Will

I will	I'll
you will	you'll
he will	he'll
she will	she'll
it will	it'll
we will	we'll
they will	they'll
who will	who'll

Other Contractions

I had	I'd
he had	he'd
let us	let's
there is	there's
that is	that's
that has	that's
what is	what's
what has	what's
where is	where's
where has	where's
who is	who's
who has	who's

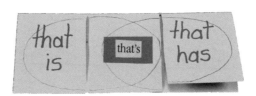

Venn-Diagram Foldable®: Make this Foldable for contractions that are written the same but have different meanings:

    that's: that is and that has,
    who's: who is and who has,
    where's: where is and where has,
    what's: what is and what has,
    I'd: I had and I would,
    he'd: he had and he would.

Contractions Foldables®

Multi-Tab Foldable® (right):

Make a multi-tabbed Foldable for contractions. Write or glue examples of contractions on the front tabs. Under the tabs do any of the following activities: students write sentences using the contractions, the teacher writes copy under the tabs for the students to read, or the class dictates copy for the teacher to type on a computer, print, and glue under the tabs. See page 308.

Bound Book Foldable® (below):

This Foldable journal can be used to collect examples of contractions and to provide practice using contractions in print. Student-generated copy, teacher-generated copy, and text from RWP can be placed within the journal. See page 290.

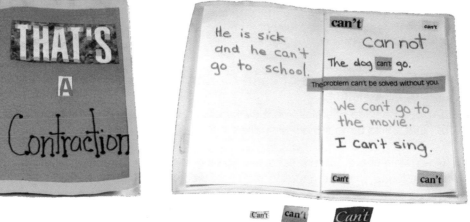

Pocket Foldable® and Contraction Cards (below):

Use a two-pocket Foldable to collect contraction study cards. This classroom manipulative or individual student study aid can be used to collect and sort word pairs and contractions, and it makes a handy reference source when students need to know how to spell and write a difficult contraction.

Dictionary Skills Quick Activities

1. Review the sequence and position of the letters of the alphabet.
Have students use a dictionary to find each letter of the alphabet and to illustrate the alphabet sequence used to organize a dictionary.

Procedure: With the dictionary closed, see if students can open the dictionary to a letter called out by the teacher or a classmate. To do this, students must know the order of the alphabet, and judge the approximate position of the letter they are trying to locate within the dictionary. Begin this activity by opening the dictionary to the middle and see which letters are found to the left and right of the center. Then, open the dictionary randomly in the front section and the back section, reviewing which letters are found in the first and second half of the alphabet. With practice, students will realize that some letters have more words than others. They will use this information when they search for words.

2. Teach and/or review alphabetizing.
Have students alphabetize words by first letters.
Have students alphabetize words by second letters.
Make books that require alphabetizing: student dictionaries, student telephone books*, student e-mail address books*, or an alphabetized autograph book.
*These can be made without giving personal information. Make the books, enter student names in alphabetical order, and leave blank spaces for their telephone number or e-mail address, or have non-functioning or made-up e-mail addresses.

3. Note the guide words on the top of each dictionary page.
Foldable Chart: Guide Word Activity
Write two guide words from the page of a classroom dictionary at the top of chart, and have students list a given number of words that would be found on this page.

Variation: Make a two-column chart. Write a pair of guide words in one column and list a given number of words that are and are not found on these pages in the second column. Have students try to determine which words should not be in the list based upon the given guide words. Write the words that would be found under the guide words and cross-out the words that do not belong.

Foldable® Pockets and Bound Two-Tab Books (above). Use the Foldables pictured to help teach guide words. Consider joining www.enchantedlearning.com for a small yearly fee to obtain access to an elementary dictionary with illustrations that can be printed. See examples from this dictionary in the pocket Foldable above left.

4. Use the dictionary to define words.
When trying to find the meaning of a word, use the dictionary to read two or more definitions and select the one that fits best.

Use the dictionary to find specific definitions for words for which students have only vague ideas of meanings. These words often occur in content areas -- science, math, and social sciences. Examples: air, plains, goods and services, addend, etc.

Use the dictionary to find alternative words that have the same meaning.
Example: *pretty* might be replaced with *attractive* or *pleasing*.
Note that several meanings are often listed for one word. Write the word, list two or three meanings in order of dictionary entry, and underline the most common meaning. Write a sentence for each definition.

Present a given number of words. Have students write what they think each word means, then look the words up in the dictionary to see if their definition is close to any of the dictionary definitions. Students then write the dictionary definition that is closest to their definition.

Use a dictionary with pictures, and note how the illustrations help explain the words. Have students write two words, illustrate them, and then write a definition for each.

5. Have students use the dictionary to determine correct spelling.
Students write a word the way they think it is spelled, and then they write the dictionary spelling next to the word. Use this same process for abbreviations, plurals, and correct use of capital letters.

6. Use the dictionary to aid pronunciation.
Divide the class into teams. Have a student from each team look up an unknown word and pronounce it as quickly as possible, trying to beat the other team. The first student to say the word correctly wins the round. Keep score.

7. Use the dictionary to divide two- and three-syllable words into syllables.
Show students how words are divided automatically when writing a long sentence or paragraph when using a computer. See syllables pages 190-198.

8. Use the dictionary to determine parts of speech.

9. Use dictionary definitions to determine synonyms and antonyms.

10. Use the dictionary to find multiple words that have the same prefix or initial root word, or compound words that begin with the same word.

Collecting Pictures in Alphabet Pockets: Make and use an alphabet Foldable pocket book to collect pictures to be added to the pictionary. Use thirteen sheets of 11" x 17" or 12" x 18" paper to make a 26-pocket booklet. Do not glue the edges of the pockets closed. Instead leave them open so oversized pictures, coloring sheets, photographs, and more will fit inside the collection pockets. See photograph on page 149.

Bound Book Foldable® (below): Giant Floor Pictionary
Use eight sheets of chart paper to make the 32-page Foldable bound book that is being used as an animal pictionary. Write one letter of the alphabet on each page, and glue pictures of animals inside on the appropriate pages to form a giant, floor pictionary. See page 290 for bound book instructions.

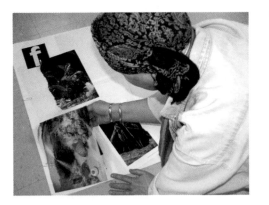

Use pictionaries to...

    ...teach and/or review initial letters and letter clusters
    ...teach and/or review A,B,C order
    ...provide practice in determining if a letter comes before or after another letter
    ...strengthen oral vocabulary and students' ability to recall terms
    ...define words using illustrations and/or simple text
    ...find synonyms for given words
    ...find antonyms for given words.

Use a pictionary or a dictionary to reinforce any of the skills discussed in this book:
-find examples of words with a given prefix
-find compound words that begin with the same word: bathrobe, bathtub, bathroom
-find words that have a given vowel sound
-find homonyms for words
-find words with a given number of syllables
-find words with silent letters
-find compound words, and more

Poster Board Bound Book Pictionary (left):
Use eight sheets of poster board to make this large, sturdy pictionary.
See page 290.

Two-Pocket Foldable®: Divided Alphabet

Use this Foldable to collect word cards and to sort the words on the cards as to their position within the alphabet -- first or second half. Write terms on quarter sheets of paper, and look the words up in the dictionary. Read aloud each dictionary definition, have students help you summarize it, and record the summary on the word cards. Young students might be asked to draw pictures to illustrate the word. Place the word or word/picture cards in the appropriate pockets.

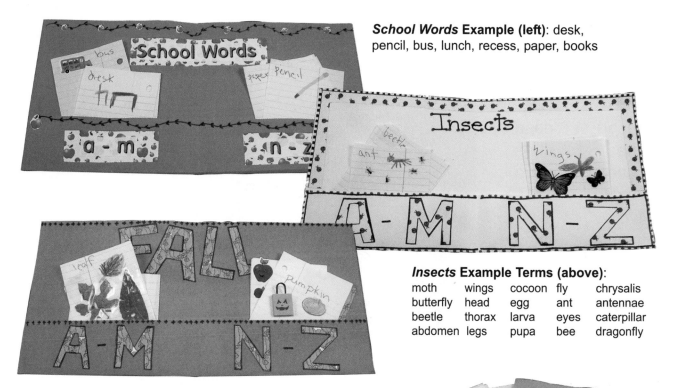

School Words **Example (left):** desk, pencil, bus, lunch, recess, paper, books

Insects **Example Terms (above):**

moth	wings	cocoon	fly	chrysalis
butterfly	head	egg	ant	antennae
beetle	thorax	larva	eyes	caterpillar
abdomen	legs	pupa	bee	dragonfly

Above: Real leaves were placed on the *leaf* word card using 2" clear tape.

Two-Column Foldable® Chart (below):
Use the dictionary to identify words given in a list as names of things that are:
-in the ocean or desert
-of the past or present
-hard or soft
-hot or cold
-dry or wet
-living or nonliving
-plants or animals

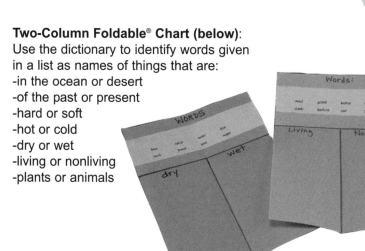

Word Lists (Above): Eight words were written on a computer, photocopied, and pasted to form six sets of the same list on a single page. Eight pages were printed and cut to provide lists for 24 students. The lists were then glued onto Foldables.

Make several VKV flashcards and use them to teach heteronyms. With practice, most students will be able to transfer what they learn about heteronyms from using these VKV flashcards to other situations in which they read or write heteronyms. It is not necessary to make flashcards for all the heteronyms listed in this section; however, do make VKV flashcards for heteronyms encountered in reading and writing. Store the cards in the *Heteronym* section of the VKV Flashcard Box, page 16.

Words that have the same spelling, but different meaning and pronunciation are called heteronyms. Example: desert (arid land) and desert (leave).

bow	bow
desert	desert
does	does
dove	dove
lead	lead
live	live
minute	minute
sow	sow
tear	tear
wind	wind

Four-Tab Foldable® Bound Book: See page 68 for instructions and photographs.

VKV® Flashcards: Heteronym Rings

1. Fold a single flashcard in half.
2. Write heteronyms to the left and right of the fold. You might wish to include a dictionary pronunciation guide with the words.
3. Punch a hole ½" in from the short edge of the folded card and store the VKV flashcards on a large ring.
4. Read the words individually noting different pronunciations.

Extension:

5. Place pictures of the words on the back of the flashcard, or write sentences using each word on the back.
6. Reverse all VKV flashcards so that the pictures or sentences are showing. Repeat step 4.

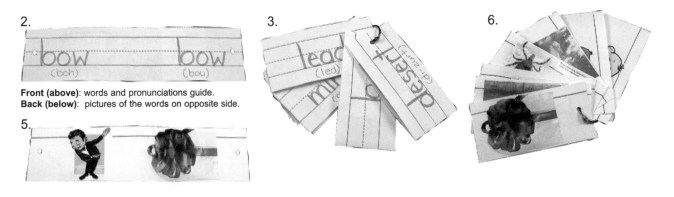

2.
(bow (boh) bow (bou))
Front (above): words and pronunciations guide.
Back (below): pictures of the words on opposite side.

5.

3.

6.

Heteronyms Foldables®

Top-Pocket Foldable® (right): Label and illustrate heteronyms on the two front tabs of the Foldable. See page 310 for instructions, and page 142 for another photo example.

Left: Write four heteronyms on the four front inside tabs of the top-pocket. Have students compose and write sentences using the featured heteronyms. Collect examples of other heteronyms on quarter sheets or single strips, and store them in the pocket.

Right: The word *sow* is written on a front tab. Pictures of the animal called a *sow* and seeds to *sow* are pictured under the tab.

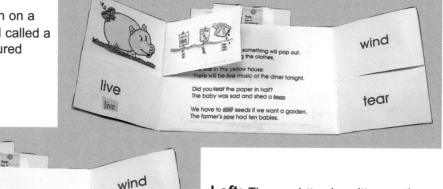

Left: The word *live* is written on the front tab. Pictures of a place to *live* and a *live* performance are pictured under the tab.

Right: The word *wind* is written on a front tab. Pictures of *wind* and something that one needs to *wind* are pictured under the tab.

Below: The word *tear* is written on a front tab. Pictures of a *tear* from the eye and something like paper that one might *tear* are pictured under the tab.

Quarter Sheets:
Use quarter sheets and/or VKVs to collect examples of heteronyms. Store them in the top-pocket.

Homographs are words that have the same spelling, but differ in meaning and origin. *Sow* (seeds) and *sow* (female swine) are examples of words that are spelled the same but have different meanings and pronunciations. When homographs are spelled the same but pronounced differently, they are called heteronyms. See page 120.

arms	-body parts -weapon	last	-the end -to endure
ball	-round object -formal dance	palm	-inside of the hand -kind of tree
bat	-club -flying mammal -wink	ring	-circle -bell sound -jewelry
crow	-sound of a rooster -a black bird	tick	-sound -an arachnid
date	-a specific time -a day, month, and year -a fruit -a meeting	top	-spinning toy -highest point -shirt
ear	-body part -ear of corn	wave	-hand motion -wind driven water
fly	-insect -move with wings	well	-healthy, satisfactory -hole dug for water
hide	-keep out of sight -animal skin	will	-document -is going to -wish, determination
jam	-fruit preserve -push or press	yard	-space around a house -measurement, 36 inches
key	-used to lock and unlock -part of a piano or computer keyboard		

Make several VKV flashcards and use them to teach homographs. With practice, most students will be able to transfer what they learn about homographs from using these VKV flashcards to other situations in which they read or write homographs. It is not necessary to make flashcards for all the homographs listed on the previous page; however, do make VKV flashcards for homographs encountered in reading and writing. Store the cards in the *Homographs* section of your VKV Flashcard Box, page 16.

(VKV®) Flashcards: Three-Word Homographs

1. Fold a triple flashcard in half.
2. Cut along the fold line of the top and bottom strip. DO NOT cut the middle strip.
3. Cut off the top left and bottom left tabs, and write a word on the remaining center strip. With the right tabs open, write and/or illustrate a homograph for the word in the center section.
4. Raise the bottom tab, and write and/or illustrate another homograph for the word.
5. Close the final tab and write another homograph, or leave this tab blank if only two homographs are known.
6. Open and close the right tabs to reveal the homographs.
7. Self check your knowledge of homographs. See how many homographs you can recall for the given word before looking under the tabs.

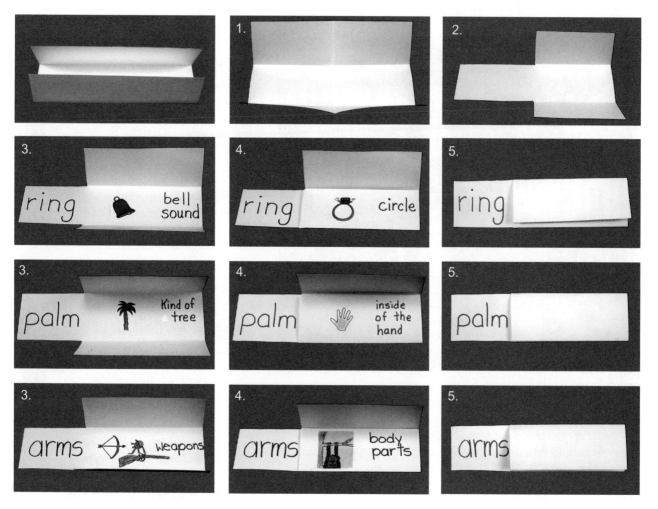

Homographs VKV® Flashcard Instructions

VKV® Flashcards: Two-Word Homographs

1. Fold a double flashcard into thirds.
2. Cut along the fold lines on top side only.
3. Cut off the top left tab.
4. Write a word on the left tab.
5. Write and/or illustrate homographs for the word under the two tabs.
6. Check your knowledge of homographs by trying to determine the homographs before opening and closing the tabs.

Two-Tab Foldable® Books (below): Homographs or Homophones
Make two-tab Foldables, fold them in half, and glue them side by side to make bound books. Use the book to collect examples of homographs or homophones found in RWP, encountered while reading books and stories, and used in writing. Write sentences or paragraphs using the homographs or homophones under the tabs. See page 68 for instructions and other examples.

Display, Collect, and Store (above):
Use a sheet of poster board to make a large pocket chart to display information on homographs and to collect Foldables, VKVs, and quarter-sheet cards relating to homographs. Note that metal nuts (nuts and bolts) have been glued to the pocket chart. See page 309.

Homophones Foldables®

Words that sound the same but are spelled differently and have different meanings are homophones. Examples: *here, hear*
break, brake
buy, by, bye.

Animal Names and their Homophones:

ant	aunt
bear	bare
bee	be
deer	dear
doe	dough
ewe	you
flea	flee
fowl	foul
gnu	new, knew
hare	hair
horse	hoarse
moose	mousse
tapir	taper
tern	turn
tick	tic

Foldable® Two-Tab Bound Book:
See page 68 for instructions and photographs illustrating how to bind this book. Pages inside the book are pictured below.

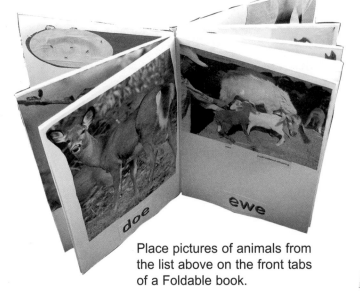

Place pictures of animals from the list above on the front tabs of a Foldable book.

Write and illustrate the homophone for each animal name under the tabs. On this example, a small mirror (blue frame) was glued under the right tab to illustrate "you."

Homophones Word List

Homophones are words that sound the same, but are usually spelled differently and have very different meanings:

air	cent	leak	pole	seam	their
heir	scent	leek	poll	seem	there
					they're
ant	close	made	rain	sew	
aunt	clothes	maid	reign	so	threw
			rein	sow	through
bail	die	mail			
bale	dye	male	rap	sight	to
			wrap	site	too
be	eye	meat			two
bee	I	meet	read	soar	
			reed	sore	toe
beat	fir	night			tow
beet	fur	knight	read	stair	
			red	stare	vary
berry	flower	none			very
bury	flour	nun	right	stake	
			rite	steak	weed
blew	hall	one	write		we'd
blue	haul	won		steal	
			road	steel	would
board	hear	our	rode		wood
bored	here	hour	rowed	sum	
				some	you
brake	hi	pail	role		ewe
break	high	pale	roll	sun	
				son	
buy	him	pain	rose		
by	hymn	pane	rows	tea	
bye				tee	
	in	peace	sail		
cell	inn	piece	sale	team	
sell				teem	
	knot	peal	sea		
	not	peel	see		

⬭VKV⬭ Flashcards: Two-Word Homophones

1. Fold a single flashcard in half.
2. Write homophones to the left and right of the fold.
3. Punch a hole ½" in from the short edge of the folded card and store the VKV flashcards on a large ring.
4. Read the words individually, noting that they have the same pronunciation.

Extension:

5. On the back of each card write the words toward the inside of the fold. Place pictures of the words on either side of the words, or write a sentence using each word.
6. Reverse all VKV flashcards so that the pictures or sentences are showing. Repeat step 4.

Words Only

Words and Pictures

⬭VKV⬭ Flashcards: Homophones #2

1. Fold a double flashcard strip in half. Cut along the top fold line only. Do not cut through the back.
2. Draw or glue pictures of homophones on the front tabs and write the words under the tabs.
3. Read the words individually, noting that they have the same pronunciation.

Letters of the Alphabet

Making Letter Cards:
- Cut letters out of fine sandpaper.
- Glue colored grits or sand onto letter flashcards to make them tactile.
- Use dots of colored glue on or around letter flashcards to make them tactile.
- Outline letters with colored glue. Allow to dry. Place a clean sheet of paper over the raised letters and make letter rubbings.
- Print sets of letters using different fonts on your computer.
- Collect examples of letters from commercial print.
- Make a set of stenciled letters.
- Use die cuts to make a set of cut-out letters.

Above: Use gummed stickers to make sets of letter cards.

Students Use Letter Cards to:
-say the names of the letters as each card is drawn.
-sequence a given number of letters in alphabetical order.
-find letter cards that match the letters in a given word.
-sort letters of different colors.
-sort letters by different fonts.
-sort letters by font size -- large, medium, small.
-sort letters by height -- tall (b, d, f, h, k, l, t) and short
      (a, c, e, i, m, n, o, r, s, u, v, w, x, z).
-sort letters written with tails (g, j, p, q, y) and without tails.
-sort capital letters and lowercase letters.
-pair capital letters with corresponding lowercase letters.
-sort letters written with circles (a, b, d, g, o, p, q) and without circles.
-sort letters written with and without sticks.
-sort letters with lines (f, t) and without lines.
-sort letters with the same capital and lowercase forms
      (Cc, Kk, Mm, Pp, Ss, Vv, Ww, Xx, Zz).

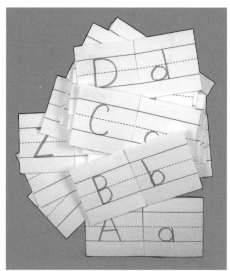

Shutterfold Letter Cards (right & below):
Cut 26 sentence strips in half and use them to make 26 small shutterfolds that will be used as single flashcards. On the front tabs, write a capital letter on one side and a lower case letter on the other side until a flashcard is made for each letter of the alphabet. Find examples of words that begin with capital and lower case letters in RWP and glue and/or write them under the appropriate tabs.

Letters of the Alphabet

Half Book Foldable® for Sandpaper Letters (below):
Cut 26 sheets of 8½" x 11" paper in half to form fifty-two 4¼" x 5½" pieces (index weight paper works best for long-term use). Fold these in half like hamburgers. Cut upper case and lower case letters out of light-weight sandpaper and glue the letters to the front tabs of the small "booklets." Use quarter sheets of lined paper stapled to the inside of the booklets to collect examples of words that always begin with a capital letter, for example *Halloween* and *Hawaii*, and examples of words that usually begin with a lower case letter -- *how*, *have*.

Glue Dots (below): Add drops of food coloring to a small bottle of white glue to make colored glue. Add cream of tartar or corn starch if you want thicker glue. Outline letters or words with glue dots and allow to dry to 24-hours.

Place a sheet of scratch paper over the glue dots and rub with a paperless crayon. Connect the dots and say the name of the letter or the word.

Writing in Colored Grits (right):
Dye enough white grits or cornmeal to cover the bottom of a tub to a thickness of one-inch.

Use the grits as a medium for finger writing letters, spelling words, or key vocabulary terms. Students can call out words for each other and take turns writing them in the colorful sand-like material.

Recipe for dyed grits, page 85.

Letters of the Alphabet

Shutterfold Letters:

Use 11" x 17" paper to make letter shutter-folds. Write, stencil, photocopy, or use a letter press to make capital and lower case letters for the left and right sides of the shutterfolds. Collect pictures and/or words under the tabs.

Extension: This activity is perfect for collecting proper nouns under the capital letter and common nouns under the lower case letter.

Include student names and photographs under the capital letter or proper noun tab.

Use student art and photographs of objects named by common nouns and found in the classroom and the school. You can also use magazine pictures or computer clip art.

Picture Frame Foldables®:

These booklets are used to feature or bring attention to whatever is pictured within the frame. Above, a photograph was taken of a local hospital sign and used to teach the letter /h/.

Inside the booklet, pictures and words were collected by a class over a period of five days, and then the book was stored in the H cereal box so it could be used and referenced throughout the year. Encourage students to continue to add words, sentences, and pictures to stored Foldables.

Letters of the Alphabet

Accordion Foldable® Pockets

Accordion Foldable® Alphabet Pockets:
Poster board can be used to make a large alphabet pocket chart for the primary classroom.

> **Materials Needed**:
> - 7 sheets of poster board
> - 2" clear tape
> - Large alphabet letter cards
> - Alphabet stickers
> - Pictures and words for each letter
>   (collected over a period of time)

1. Fold a 4" pocket along the long edge of each sheet of poster board.
2. Accordion fold each poster board into four equal sections.
3. Tape the ends of the poster board together leaving a ¼" space between the sheets. (See letter D connected by tape to E in the photograph. Note space.) This space will allow easy folding and storage.
4. Glue the large alphabet letter cards onto the top of the accordion sections, and place the alphabet stickers on the pockets.
5. Add pictures and RWP to the front of the alphabet pockets.
6. Use the pockets to collect vocabulary word cards and to alphabetize words.

Letters of the Alphabet

Billboard Foldable®: The top photograph (a) shows the alphabet billboard Foldable with all tabs closed. The bottom photograph (f) shows it with the tabs open. Notice how the letters are replaced by pictures when the tabs are opened (photographs b, c, d, e). Sight words, vocabulary terms, and/or spelling words are collected under the tabs.

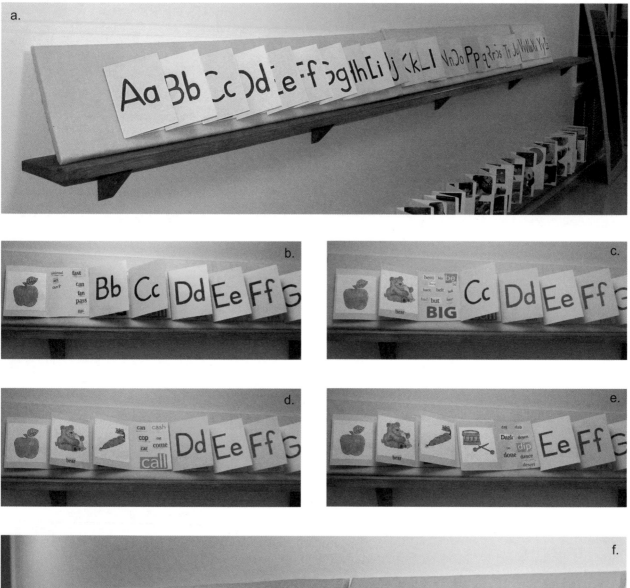

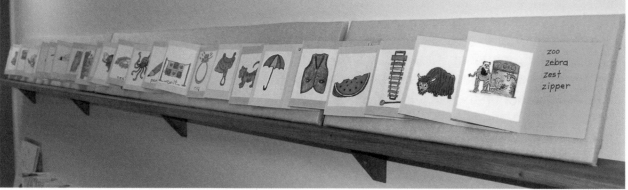

Letters of the Alphabet

Foldable® Matchbooks as Bulletin Boards: Make any of the following giant Foldable letter charts using matchbooks and have students:

-read every other letter.
-read only the vowels.
-read only the consonants.
-read one of the words written under a given tab.
-name the pictures under a given tab.
-cover some letters with sticky notes and ask students to read the letters not covered.
-read the *fifth* or *twentieth* letter (use ordinal numbers).
-read the letter that comes after *j*.
-read the letter that comes before *w*.

Collecting Pictures (left and above): This alphabet board features "Plants We Eat." Students glue pictures of fruits, vegetables, and nuts under the appropriate tabs.

A top-pocket Foldable, made using a piece of poster board is also pictured. It can be used to collect large pictures, student worksheets, internet articles, and more. See page 310.

Collecting Words (right): Matchbook alphabet boards can be used to collect words encountered while studying a topic or theme. For example, under the *A* matchbook tab of this insect bulletin board the words *ant*, *antenna*, and *abdomen* might be found.

Quarter-Sheet Flashcards (below): Use a tiny piece of double sided tape along the top edge to attach quarter sheets of terms and/or pictures under the large matchbook tabs. Flashcards can be removed when the unit is complete, and the matchbook board can be used for another unit of study. When finished, staple the "old" cards together along the top edge, through the double sided tape, and keep them for review and continued vocabulary immersion.

Letters of the Alphabet

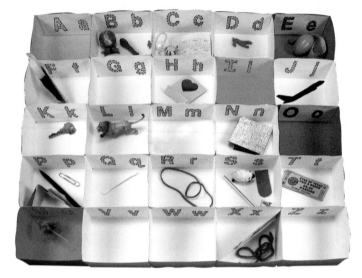

Display Boxes for Objects (left):

Use twenty-five sheets of 8½" x 11" paper to make twenty-five display boxes. Use clothespins to aid in gluing them together to form a five-by-five box grid. See photographs on page 254.

Label the boxes with the letters of the alphabet, placing Xx and Yy in the same box.

Use the boxes to collect examples of physical objects with names that begin with the letters of the alphabet.

Note: In the example to the left, the consonant boxes are white and the vowel boxes are color coded.

Display Boxes for Letters

(right): Use the alphabet display boxes described above to collect examples of words from RWP that begin with the letters of the alphabet. Or, have students cut out examples of the individual letters from RWP and sort them into the boxes. See page 254.

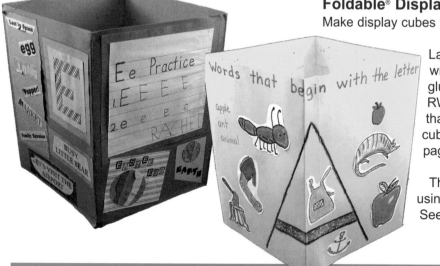

Foldable® Display Cubes (below left):

Make display cubes to feature letters of the alphabet.

Lay the display cubes flat. Practice writing letters on the four sides, glue examples of letters found in RWP, and glue pictures of words that begin with the letters. These cubes can be folded to form a four-page book and stored flat.

The cubes pictured were made using two sheets of 11" x 17" paper. See page 296.

Letters of the Alphabet

Accordion A-B-C Foldable®
(right): Accordion books can be made to feature one letter. The letter **Cc** example to the right had pages for the following: RWP capital **C**, RWP lower case **c**, pictures of words that begin with the letter **c**, words that begin with the letter **c**, and words that have the letter **c** as a medial or final letter. See page 300.

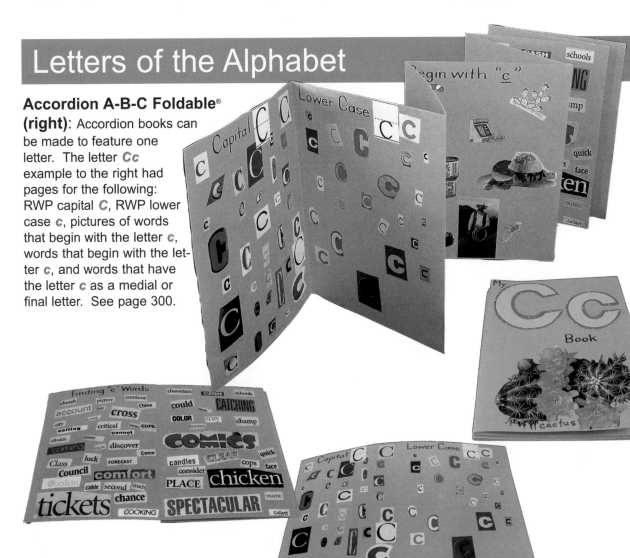

A B C D E F G H I J K L M N O P Q R S T U V W X Y Z
1 2 3 4 5 6 7 8 9 10 11 12 13 14 15 16 17 18 19 20 21 22 23 24 25 26

Two-Tab Foldable® Book (below): Make 13 two-tab Foldables using 8½" x 11" paper and glue them side by side to make a 26-page booklet. Number the front tabs -- 1 to 26. Sequentially write the letters of the alphabet under the appropriate tabs -- **Aa** under the "1" tab and **Zz** under the "26" tab. Students guess what letter will be under the "2" tab or under the "15" tab and then look under the tab to check their response. See page 291.

Multi-Pocket Foldable® Book (above and below): Glue 13 two-pocket Foldables together, side by side with the help of clothespins, to form a 26-pocket booklet. Sequentially label the pockets with the letters of the alphabet and use them to collect letter and word cards. See page 291.

Envelope Fold (below): Feature a letter inside an envelope fold, and four picture words that begin with the letter on the front of the four tabs. Write words or glue under the four tabs of the Foldable. See page 297.

Letters of the Alphabet

Four-Door Displays for Sequencing: Use 8½" x 11" paper to make 26 four-door display cases, one for each letter of the alphabet (see page 303). Label and use to collect physical objects, letter flashcards, or word cards that begin with the letters of the alphabet.

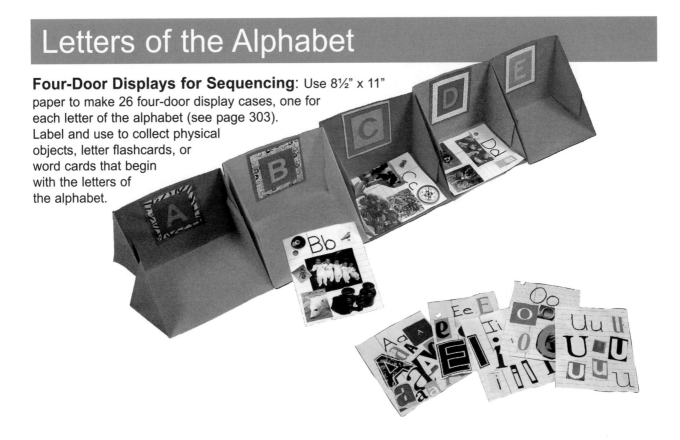

Folded Table or Chart (below): Fold a sheet of poster board into a 6-column x 5-row grid. Label as illustrated with the letters of the alphabet. Collect and glue examples of letters found in RWP. Turn this into a game by having students place markers on designated letters. For example, a student might be asked to place a red marker on a large letter J and a blue marker on the letter F. Encourage students to develop their own letter identification games. See page 308.

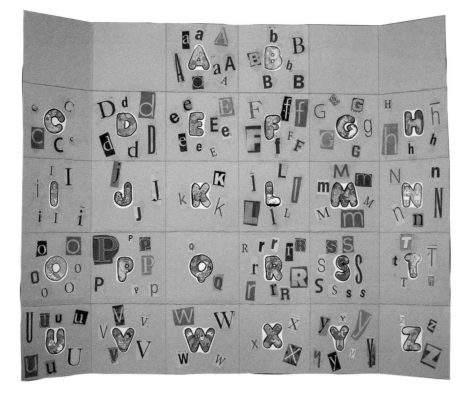

Letters of the Alphabet

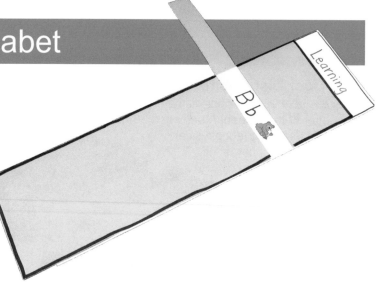

Window Card (right): Fold a brightly-colored sheet of 11" x 17" or 12" x 18" paper like a hotdog. Place the fold to the left. Cut a 1" strip in one end of the top section to form a window 3" below the top edge. Cut sheets of white 11" x 17" paper in half to make 5½" x 11" cards. Place a card inside the colored section. With the window tab open, move the card as you write letters of the alphabet or vocabulary words on the exposed section. Write letters or words to fill the card. Students move the card up and down to expose different letters or words in the window and they read what is visible.

A-B-C Bound Book (below): Make this bound book using eight sheets of art paper or 11" x 17" copy paper. See page 290. Use it to collect examples of letters from world print and to practice writing letters.

Top-Pocket Foldable® (below): Use one sheet of 11" x 17" copy paper or 12" x 18" art paper to make this top-pocket Foldable and use it to study the letters of the alphabet. When possible, place pictures and physical objects on the tabs. In the *S* example below, *seeds* (top left), *sand* (bottom left), and *salt* (top right) have been placed on the inside tabs using 2" clear tape. A gummed *seal* has been placed on the bottom right tab. See pages 121 and 310.

Hand-y Reminder (left): Show students how their hands can help them remember which direction the circles of the letters b and d, and p and q point. I see students placing their hands below the desk to check their letter formation during spelling tests and writing activities.

Moon Extension: When observing a waxing moon, notice that it is filling in the circle of the letter *b* (think brighter), and a waning moon fills in the circle of the letter *d* (think dimmer). This poem will help you identify a waxing and waning moon.

*b for **brighter** full moon grows,*
*d for **dimmer** full moon goes.*
                                    -Dinah Zike

Individualize a Four-Door: Instead of using letters (pictured above) take digital photos of a student's hands forming these four letters, print them, cut, and glue them to the front tabs of a four-door Foldable. Students can collect words that contain these consonants and write them under the appropriate tabs. See page 299.

Letter Book Jackets (below): Use thirteen sheets of 8½" x 11" paper cut in half along the hotdog axis (long) to make 26 book jackets. Collect examples of letters cut from RWP, examples of words that begin with the letters, and pictures of words that begin with the letters. Students may also practice writing the featured letters within the book jackets, or use stamps or stencils to form the letters. Three dog biscuit boxes have been cut and painted to form the book shelves pictured. Students can take turns alphabetizing the books jackets within this miniature library. See page 307.

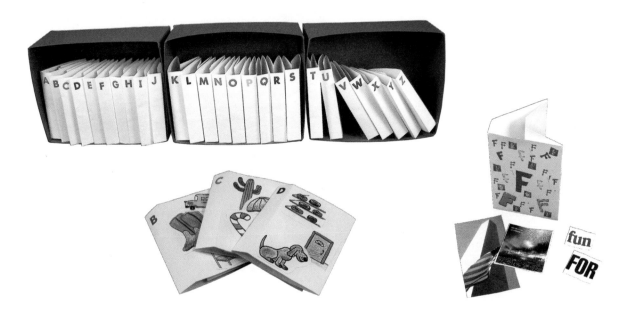

Letters of the Alphabet

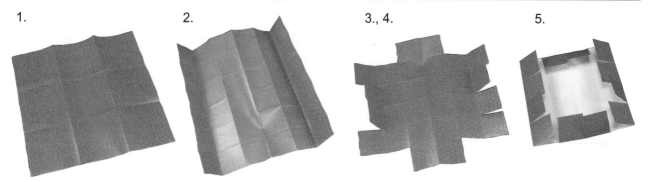

1.   2.   3., 4.   5.

Twelve-Letter Coverup Foldable® Card:

1. Begin with a square of paper such as scrapbook paper (12" x 12"), or cut a sheet of 12" x 17" paper to form a square.
2. Fold the paper into thirds and then in half along both axes to form a 6-column x 6-row grid.
3. Cut off the top two left and right squares, and the bottom two left and right squares.
4. Cut along the fold lines of the outer row of squares.
5. Fold the tabs forward to make a square as pictured.
6. Write 12 letters being studied under the tabs of the Coverup. (The same letter can be used multiple times depending on how many letters students know or need to review.)
7. With all tabs open, call out letters for students to find. If a student has the letter called, they cover it by closing the tab. (Call numerous words with the same letter if a limited number of letters are on the card.)
8. The student who covers all tabs first wins. Check the student's card by reviewing the words called.

6., 7.

8.

Coverup Foldable® Cards: Make coverup cards to review consonant blends, digraphs, sight words, synonyms, antonyms, contractions, and science or math vocabulary terms and definitions.

Tutor: Use as a one-on-one activity for students who need extra help mastering a skill.

Eight-Letter Coverup Foldable® Card: Fold the square into a 5-column x 5-row grid to make an eight-item coverup card.

Letters of the Alphabet

Label the tabs of the Foldable using stickers, stencils, stamps, computer generated print, or hand written letters.

Top-Tab Foldable®: Alphabet Wrap Around

Needed: 26 sheets of multicolored paper (any size) arranged in a pleasing color sequence.

1. Make a cutting template by folding a sheet of same-sized paper into a 10 column x 8 row grid. Label the outer ring of squares with letters as illustrated.
2. Put the template over the first sheet of color paper. Use clothespins to keep them together while cutting. Begin by cutting out the "z" square on the template while also cutting the sheet of paper under the template.
3. Place another sheet of paper behind the template, secure, and cut away the "y" square.
4. Continue to place clean sheets of paper behind the template, and cut not only the next letter square, but also the extra exposed paper that shows when each new sheet of paper is placed behind the template.
5. Stack the sheets of cut paper and place them on top of a whole sheet of paper. See the tabs forming.
6. Continue to cut new sheets of paper until all tabs have been cut.
7. Staple the 26 sheets of paper together on the left side (shown) or bind with rings.
8. Add a cover for the book. See the black cover on the example above.

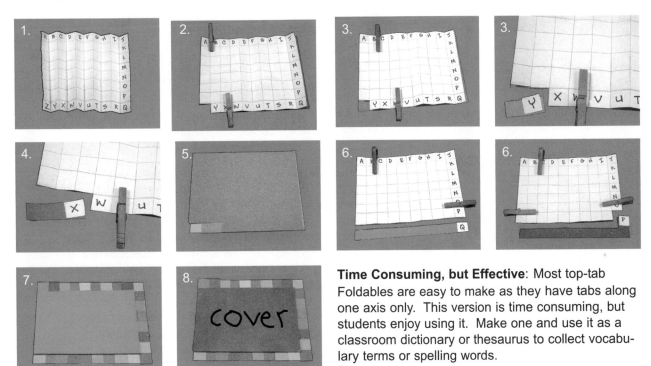

Time Consuming, but Effective: Most top-tab Foldables are easy to make as they have tabs along one axis only. This version is time consuming, but students enjoy using it. Make one and use it as a classroom dictionary or thesaurus to collect vocabulary terms or spelling words.

Letters of the Alphabet

Alphabet Top Pockets: Use sheets of 8½" x 11" paper to make top-pocket Foldables for the letters of the alphabet. Place capital letters on the left front tabs, and lower case letters on the right front tabs. To introduce or reinforce proper nouns and common nouns while teaching the letters of the alphabet, collect words and picture words that are capitalized under the left tab, and words that are not capitalized under the right tab. See page 310 for complete direction, and see page 121 for another example.

Above: On the inside center section, collect examples of capital and lower case letters from RWP (real world print). Use ink stamps, gummed stickers, and student writing to provide more examples of printed letters.

Above: Continue to collect examples of words that begin with the featured initial consonants, either capital or lower case, inside the left and right sections of the Foldable, as seen in the photograph above right.

Letter Cards (left): Give each student a quarter sheet of paper. Provide numerous forms of RWP for students to use to find one word that begins with the featured consonant in either its capital or lower case form. Have students glue their word to the top edge of their word card. Draw pictures to illustrate the words, or have students dictate sentences using the words, and record them on the letter cards. When all glue is completely dry, collect the cards and store them inside the top pocket. Use these vocabulary extension cards for sorting activities, alphabetizing, syllable practice, phonics lessons, and lessons on capitalization.

Phonograms contain a **vowel grapheme followed by a consonant grapheme.** Examples of *Phonograms* include the following: *-an, -ay, -ill, -ip,-ot, and -un.* See pages 156 to 175 for Foldables, VKVs, and word lists for other rhyming word families, or rimes.

VKV® Flashcard: **Four-Words, One Rime**

Use this VKV Foldable to show how different initial consonant sounds can be added before a phonogram to make new words. (See pages 156 to 159, Rhyming Word Families.)

1. Close up a triple flashcard and fold into thirds.
2. Open it again and cut along the fold lines on the top and bottom sections. Do not cut the middle section.
3. Cut off the top left and right sections. Cut off the bottom left and right sections.
4. Write a phonogram on the far right tab.
5. Write an initial consonant, blend or digraph (so that it will be completely covered by the other three tabs) before the phonogram in order to form a word.
6. Fold the other three tabs over and write consonants, blends, or digraphs on these tabs to form three more words.
7. Open and close the tabs and read the words formed. See example at bottom of page.

Note: This VKV is also discussed on page 157.

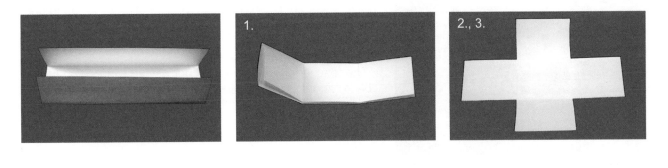

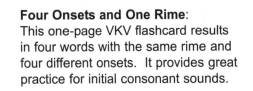

Four Onsets and One Rime:
This one-page VKV flashcard results in four words with the same rime and four different onsets. It provides great practice for initial consonant sounds.

One Onset with Four Rimes: Write one consonant, blend, or digraph on the left extended tab and four different rimes on the tabs to the right.
Example: initial consonant *k* -- k*in*, k*id*, k*it*, k*iss*.

Pictures & Picture Words

Pictures and picture words can be used to strengthen oral vocabulary. When a written word naming the picture is included, a correspondence between the word and the object represented in the picture is made.

Picture Word Twist and Turn (left): Cut a large cardboard box into equal sections. Paint the sections and allow them to dry thoroughly before proceeding.

Use 2" clear tape to connect the sections edge to edge. Place the tape on the front and back of each joint. Leave ½" space between the taped sections to form a hinge that will allow the sections to fold like an accordion and store.

Glue pictures to the twister board and allow glue to dry. Cover the pictures with 2" clear tape to protect them during use. Pictures might be arranged by themes or units. For example, the twister board to the left has pictures of animals from around the world.

Use both sides of the twister board for two different sets of picture words. One board can provide practice for up to one hundred picture words.

Play: "Calling" and "Twisting"
The teacher or a student calls out a word pictured on the board and tells a selected student what action they should take. For example, the student might be told to place their right foot on the picture of a *beach*, left hand on the picture of a *wave*, left foot on a *dune*, and right hand on a *gull*. Students take turns "calling" and "twisting."

Clear Vinyl Twist and Turn (right): Place quarter-sheet flashcards or VKVs under a two yard length of thick, clear vinyl. Play as outlined above. Clear vinyl can be purchased in most fabric departments.

This is a fast way to individualize practice, and get young students involved in helping each other learn vocabulary terms. Students like the novelty of stepping on their flashcards.

VKV® Flashcard: Rebus VKV®

1. Write a simple sentence in the middle of a triple flashcard, omitting one word (usually a noun). Lightly sketch lines on the top and bottom tabs above and below the picture word to indicate it's width.

2. Draw or glue a picture of the omitted word onto the flashcard. Cut along the sketched lines. Cut off the top and bottom tabs over the sentence, leaving the tabs over and under the picture word.

3. Close each tab over the picture word, and draw or glue pictures on these two tabs to form three complete sentences. See example at bottom of page.

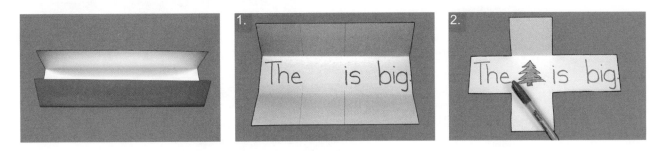

Above: If the three pictures in the example above were of a tree, a dog, and a pig, the three sentences would be: The tree is big. The dog is big. The pig is big.

Variation: To vary the VKV, encourage students to add an adjective (describing word) before the noun as they read the VKV. Examples: The green tree is big. The mean dog is big. The wild pig is big.

I go to the store.

I go to the car.

I go to the zoo.

Rebus Activities: Vary the tab position on this VKV to feature different sentence parts. For example, the tabs might be cut so that the first word of a sentence is changed. Pictures of students could be used on the tabs to represent the pronouns -- I, we, they.

Half Book Cards: Notice the way this flash-card is designed. Either the top half or the bottom half can be used as a study aid in a pocket chart or on a sentence strip. These color flashcards feature pictures on the top half and words on the bottom. See page 289.

closed

open

Quarter-Sheet Letter and Picture Cards: Use quarter sheets of paper to make letter flashcards. Collect pictures, letters, and words that begin with each of the letters and glue them to the flashcards. Use the flashcards in Pocket Foldables, Display Cases, Top-Pocket Foldables, Pocket Charts, and on Sentence Strips. Glue them into Foldable Journals and other projects.

Note From Dinah: Quarter sheets of lined paper have been part of my publishing center for 30 years.

I encourage their use because they are:
- less expensive than index cards.
- easily handled by students.
- psychologically advantageous as they are only a portion of a piece of paper.
- a perfect fit inside Foldables and Foldable projects -- pockets, display cases, shutterfolds, and on sentence strip holders.
- small in size allowing all students to contribute something to a bulletin board or class project.

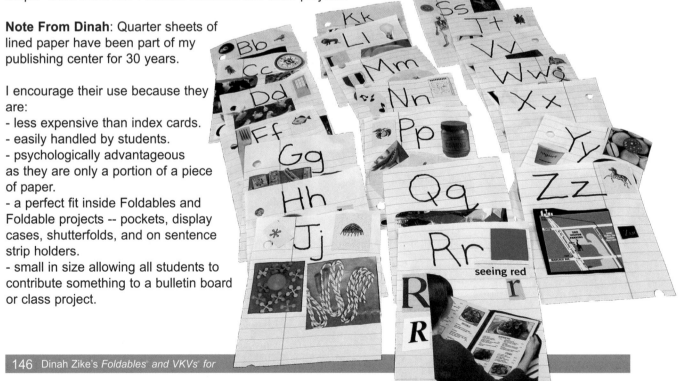

Picture Accordion Foldable®: Use 26 sheets of paper to make an accordion alphabet picture line. See page 300 for instructions. Every primary classroom has a picture vocabulary wall or poster. I like to use my accordion Foldable for this. Other uses: when closed it can be read like a "book;" it can be stretched down a hallway; or taken outside for letter identification activities.

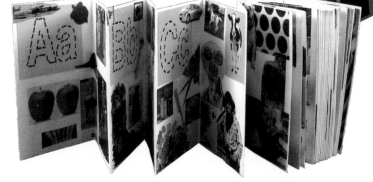

Add Pockets: See an example of an accordion Foldable with pockets on page 131.

Giant Pyramids Foldable® (below): Use sheets of poster board to make giant pyramids. See page 294. Velcro™ or paper clips can be used to hold the pyramids together for display, thus allowing them to be folded and stored for future use. Use the three sides of the pyramids to collect pictures of things being studied. For example, use the three sides of the pyramid to collect pictures of any of the following:

-red, yellow, blue
-circle, square, triangle
-large, medium, and small
-morning, noon, night
-breakfast, lunch, dinner
-beginning, middle, ending
-first, next, last
-threes in fairy tales or literature
-past, present, future
-science water cycle terms: evaporation, condensation, precipitation, and more.

Pictures & Picture Words

Hidden Pictures and Oral Vocabulary:

Object: Students open tabs in numeric order to gradually expose parts of a hidden picture. The first tab to be opened should expose the least obvious part of the picture. Students sequentially open more tabs to determine what picture is hidden under the tabs.

1. Make an envelope fold, see page 297.
(The examples on this page used 8½" x 11" colored paper.)
2. Glue or draw a picture inside the envelope fold.
3. Close the tabs to cover the picture. Determine which section of the picture might be the least obvious. Label the tab over the least obvious part of the picture "1." Continue numbering the tabs from least to most obvious.

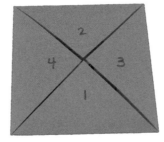
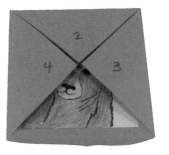

Observe and Analyze (above): When students open tab #1, guide them to observe it is a picture of an animal with a special mouth, nose, and fur. Students might guess that it is picture of a dog or a monkey. Open tab #2 and note the small ears. What animal has a nose, mouth, and fur like this, and small ears? Some students will identify the picture correctly as a bear. If a student does not, they proceed to tab #3. Students can play this simple oral vocabulary game with each other.

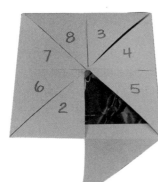

Eight-Tab Hidden Picture: Cut each of the four envelope folds in half along the existing fold lines. Number the tabs as described above. Use coloring book pictures, magazine pictures, and original student art.

Visual Literacy: This activity is a good introduction to perspective and visual literacy in general. These are skills we need to foster in young students as they live in rich and constantly changing visual environment.

Pictures & Picture Words

Picture Pocket-Book Foldable® (above): Use 13 sheets of 11" x 17" index weight (80#) paper to make the multi-pocket Foldable pictured above. Glue the pockets together side by side, but DO NOT glue the ends of the pockets closed. (In the upper right photograph, you will see that some pictures collected in the pockets are larger than the pockets and stick out of the Foldable.) Sequentially label the pockets with the letters of the alphabet. Labels can be written by the teacher or students, or gummed stickers can be used. Collect pictures, sort them, and store them in the pockets. This storage activity provides student practice using initial consonants and introduces alphabetizing. Use the pictures collected for any of the Foldable and VKV activities in this book. (See page 291 for instructions on making a multi-pocket book.)

Picture Accordion Foldable® (below): The accordion pictured below was made using 26-half sheets of 8½" x 11" index weight paper. To integrate RWP from the community, photographs of street signs were used as the sequential alphabet labels for the accordion sections, but anything could be used for the alphabet including pictures of words beginning with the letters, computer generated letters, stickers, stamps. Have students and parents search for examples of upper case and lower case letters in RWP and pictures of words that illustrate each letter. As a class, collect, sort, and glue the letters and/or pictures into the booklet.

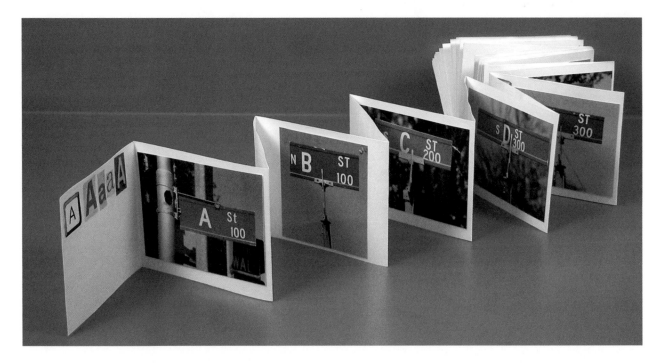

Prefixes are letter clusters that are added before a root or base word. Prefixes enhance or change the meaning of the base word they precede. When a prefix is added to the beginning of a word, the spelling of the root word does not change. The most common prefixes are *re-*, *un-*, and *dis-*.

The prefix *un-* usually means the "opposite of." When studying this prefix, discuss or review antonyms.
    Example: happy, *un*happy
There are some situations where *un-* cannot be used:
    Example: the opposite of *good* is *bad* not "ungood"
            the opposite of *win* is *lose* not "unwin"

Older students might notice that sometimes the letters *un-* at the beginning of a word are part of the base word and not a prefix.
    Examples: *uncle* and *under*

VKV® Flashcards: Three-Word Prefixes

1. Close a triple flashcard, then fold it in half.
2. Cut along the top and bottom fold lines. Do not cut through the middle section.
3. Cut off the top and bottom right sections leaving the middle tab.
4. Write a word on the extended right tab. Begin the first letter of the word near the fold line.
5. Open all tabs and write a prefix before the given word.
6. Close the bottom tab and write another prefix that changes the meaning of the word.
7. Close the top tab over the bottom tab. A word without a prefix should be visible.
8. On the back of the VKV, write sentences using the three terms, and observe how each prefix changes the meaning of the root word.

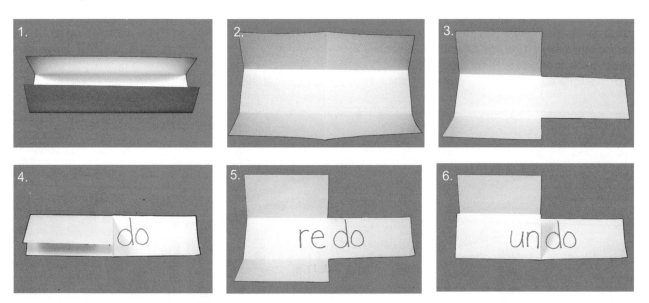

Examples: *cover, discover, recover*
            like, dislike, unlike
            cooked, uncooked, precooked
            told, retold, untold

Extension: Use these examples to demonstrate to students how prefixes change the meaning of the root word.

Make several VKV Foldable flashcards and use them to teach prefixes. With practice, most students will be able to transfer what they learn about prefixes from using these kinesthetic flashcards to other situations. It is not necessary to make flashcards for all the prefixes listed in this section; however, do make VKV Foldable flashcards for prefixes encountered in reading and writing throughout the year. Store the cards in the *Prefixes* section of your VKV Flashcard Box, page 16.

(VKV) Flashcard: Two-Word Prefixes

1. Fold a single flashcard so that half of the card is covered by a tab and half is exposed.
2. With the tab to the left, write a prefix on the front of the tab and write the base/root word to the right.
3. Under the tab, write the definition of the prefix.
4. Students read and define the word with and without the prefix, and then open the tab to check their understanding of the prefix used.

(VKV) Flashcards: Four-Word Prefixes

1. Close a triple flashcard, then fold it into thirds.
2. Cut along the fold lines of the top and bottom strips. Do NOT cut the middle strip.
3. Cut off the top left and bottom left tabs. Cut off the top right and bottom right tabs.
4. Write a prefix on the single left tab and a base to the right of the prefix in the middle of the flashcard.
5. Fold and write three different roots/bases on the other three tabs.
6. Read the four words formed.
7. Define the words based upon the meaning of the prefix. Write sentences using the words on the back.

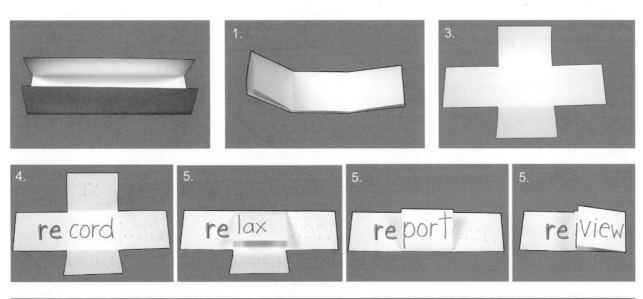

Tabbed Project Board: Use chart paper or bulletin board paper to make a giant tabbed bulletin board like the one pictured to the right and below. See page 305 for instructions.

Foldable® Bound Book (right):

Use a hotdog fold to make two-tab Foldables with 11" x 17" paper. Make multiple sections, depending on the number of prefixes to be featured. Always allow extra pages for future additions to the booklet.

Fold the two-tab sections in half, and glue them side by side to make bound books. Clothespins can be used to hold the sections together while the glue dries.

Use the book to collect examples of prefixes found in RWP, and encountered while reading literature, singing songs, reading signs, or completing worksheets on prefixes.

Under the tabs, write sentences or paragraphs using the words collected on the front tabs.

See page 68 for photographs and instructions on binding a Foldable book.

Foldable® Charts:

Make a three-column Foldable chart. Use it to record words with prefixes, write the meaning of each prefix, and the meaning of each word as they relate to the prefixes.

> **Example**:
>
> | Words with Prefixes | Meaning of Prefix | Meaning of Word |
> |---|---|---|
> | *dislike* | *opposite of* | *does not like* |
> | *nonsense* | *not* | *does not make sense* |

Foldable® Pocket Chart (right):

Use a sheet of 11" x 17" or 12" x 18" paper to make a pocket chart. Collect examples of words with and without prefixes found in world print or encountered during classroom work. Write or glue words onto the top part of the chart. See page 309.

Make VKV flashcards of words with and without prefixes and store them in the pockets. Use the flashcards for matching activities or have students sort them into the correct pockets as an assessment tool.

Trifold Foldable® or Three-Tab Foldable® (below):

Understanding the meaning of a prefix can help students decode new words encountered in reading and used in writing. Fold a trifold into thirds. Cut along the fold lines of the far right section as shown below to make three tabs. Write common prefixes to the left and base words on the right front tabs. Write the base words with the prefixes under the tabs. See the example below. Trifold instructions are on page 293.

Note: Some of the most common prefixes are *re-*, *un-*, *dis-*, and *non-*.

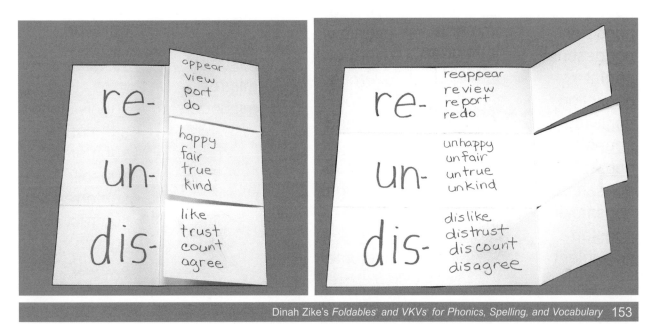

The twenty prefixes listed below have been found to account for 93% of suffix use in common language. Select ability appropriate words for student use.

1. un-
(not)

unbeaten
uncomfortable
undo
unequal
unfair
unfold
unforgettable
unhappy
unhurt
unkind
unload
unlucky
unnamed
unnoticed
unnecessary
unopened
unusual
untrue
unwilling
unwrap

6. non-
(not, opposite of)

nonaquatic
nondairy
nondescript
nonfat
nonfiction
nonliving
nonpoisonous
nonprofit
nonsense
nonsmoking
nonstop
nonviolent

2. re-
(back, again)

react
readmit
reappear
reattach
rebound
rebuild
recall
receipt
record
recycle
redecorate
redo
reduce
refill
reforest
relax
relay
report
return
review

7. in-, im-
(in, into)

immediate
immerse
immigrate
implant

incision
include
induce
infect
inhale
inside

3. in-, im-, ir-, ill-
(not, opposed to)

imbalance
immature
impassable
impolite
impossible

inaccurate
inactive
incorrect
independent
invisible

irregular
irreparable
irreplaceable
irresponsible

illegal
illiterate
illogical
illusion

8. over-
(too much, above, beyond)

overdue
overflow
overgrown
overhead
overjoy
overland
overlap
overload
overnight
overpass
overtake
overtime

4. dis-
(not, opposed to)
dis-
(reversal, opposite, away, not, free from)

disable
disagree
disappear
disappoint
disapprove
discontinue
discount
discourse
discover
dishonest
dislike
disinfect
distrust

9. mis-
(bad, wrongly)

misbehave
miscount
misprint
misread
misshapen
misspell
mistake
mistreat
mistrust
misunderstand

5. en-, em-
(cause to)

enable
enact
encase
enchanted
encircle
enclose
encounter
encourage
endanger
endure
enforce
engrave
enhance
enjoy
enlarge
enlist
enquire
enrage
enrich
enroll
entangle
entomb
entrust
envision

10. sub-
(under, less, beneath, lower)

subdivision
submarine
submerge
subsoil
subterranean
subtract
suburb
subway

Prefixes Twenty Most Common

Source: White, T.G.I, Sowell, V., and Yanagihara, A. (1999). Teaching elementary students to use word-part clues. *The Reading Teacher*, 42, 302-308.

11. pre-
(before)

preamble
precaution
precooked
prefix
prejudice
premolar
prepared
preschool
presell

16. super-
(above, over, more so than other related things, beyond)

superhero
superhuman
superman
supermarket
superior
supersize
superstar
superstore
superstructure
superwoman

12. inter-
(between, among)

interact
intercity
intercom
intermediate
intermission
international
Internet
interrupt
intersect
interstate
interview

17. semi-
(half, partial)

semiannual
semicircle
semicolon
semiconscious
semidarkness
semifinal
semiformal
semiprecious
semiprivate
semisweet

13. fore-
(before)

forecast
forefathers
foreground
forehand
forehead
forerunner
foresee
foreshadow
foretell
forewarn

18. anti-, ant-
(against)

antacid
Antarctic
antibacterial
antifreeze
antiseptic
antislavery
antismoking
antisocial
antiwar

14. de-
(opposite of, down)

debone
debug
debus
decaffeinated
declaw
defend
deflate
delay
deplane
descent

19. mid-
(middle)

midair
midday
midfield
midlife
midnight
midpoint
midrange
midsemester
midsize

15. trans-
(across)

transcontinental
transform
transit system
transport
transportation

20. under-
(too little, below, less than)

underage
underclothes
undercook
undercover
underdog
underfed
underfoot
undergo
underground
underline
underpass
undersea
understand

Four-Door Display Foldable® (left): Use a piece of 11" x 17" index weight or cover stock paper to make this collapsible display case. Make one for each prefix studied and use them to collect examples of words formed with each prefix. Words collected on quarter sheets and student writing on half sheets of lined paper can also be stored in the display. Use the displays for as long as needed and when finished, collapse the display and store it in the "Prefixes" cereal storage box. See page 303.

Note From Dinah: Use the displays again later in the year as a review. I have found that students are interested in seeing things they contributed to in the past and look upon them as "easy" due to their academic growth. It not only acts as a review, but it makes students "feel smart."

Important Definitions:

A *grapheme* is sound, letter, or letter combination that forms a *phoneme*.

Examples: /f/ in *f*at or /ff/ in cu*ff*
/ph/ in *ph*oto
/gh/ in tou*gh*

A *phonogram* is usually formed by a vowel grapheme and an ending consonant grapheme (*-ab, -an, -at*). Phonograms are often called *word families*, *rhyming word families*, or *rimes*. Sometimes a phonogram is a syllable in a multi-syllable word, making the larger word easier for a beginning reader to read and write.

Examples: cab-in   rot-ten
mat-ter   win-ter
man-ner   zip-per

VKV Flashcards: Phonogram Syllables

1. Write a two-syllable word in which a phonogram is one of the syllables on a single flashcard.
2. Fold the left flap of the flashcard over to cover the part of the word that is not part of the phonogram.
3. Open the folded card. Fold the opposite flap over to cover the phonogram.
4. Students can open and close the card in different directions to view the word's phonogram separate from and as part of the featured word. Some words are formed using two phonograms -- *hid-den, rot-ten*.

Note: This VKV helps students find and use phonograms they know as they analyze and read large words.

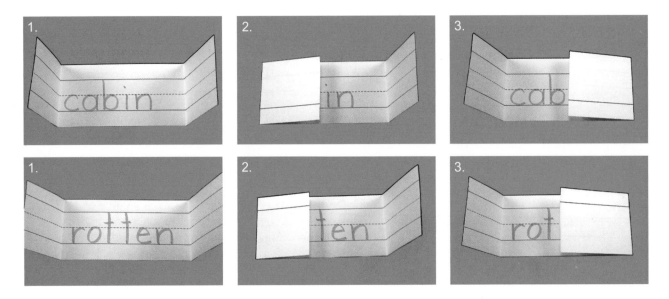

Research Note:

The thirty-seven most frequently used patterns (Wylie and Durrell, 1970) are listed below:

a   -ack, -ail, -ain, -ake, -ale, -ame, -an, -ank, -ap, -ash, -at, -ate, -aw, -ay
e   -eat, -ell, -est
i   -ice, -ick, -ide, -ight, -ill, -in, -ine, -ing, -ink, -ip, -it
o   -ock, -oke, -op, -ore, -ot
u   -uck, -ug, -ump, -unk

Make several VKV flashcards and use them to teach phonograms. With practice, most students will be able to transfer what they learn about phonograms from using these VKV flashcards to other situations in which they encounter phonograms. It is not necessary to make flashcards for all the phonograms listed in this section; however, do make VKV flashcards for phonograms encountered in reading and writing throughout the year. Store the cards in the *Phonograms*, or *Rimes*, section of your VKV Flashcard Box, page 16.

⬭VKV® Flashcards: Four-Word Phonograms

1. Close a triple flashcard, then fold it into thirds.
2. Cut along the two fold lines found on both the top and bottom strip. DO NOT cut the middle strip.
3. Cut off the top left and right tabs. Cut off the bottom left and right tabs, leaving the middle top and bottom tabs attached.
4. Write a phonogram (rime) on the middle extended tab to the far right.
5. Fold the bottom flap over, and write an initial consonant on it.
6. Do the same with the left flap.
7. Do the same with the top flap.
8. Open and close the tabs, and read the four words formed.

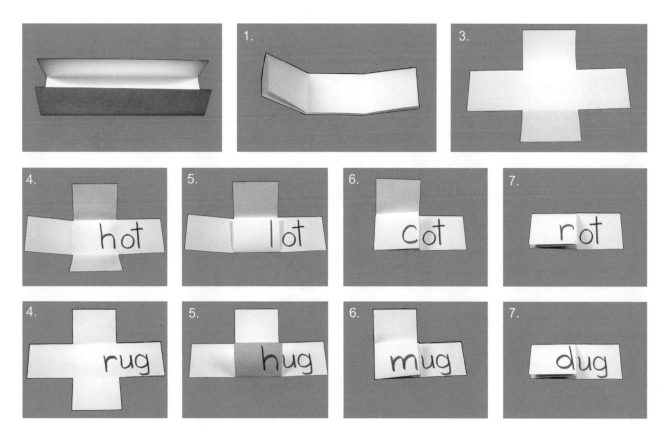

Reverse: Make the VKV above, but reverse the process. Write an onset (one initial consonant or consonant blend) on the extended left tab. Write four rimes on the right tabs. Read the four words formed. Write the words and analyze how they are similar and different.

Examples: *ran, rim, rot, rut*
             bat, bib, bus, ban

(VKV) Flashcards: Nine Word Phonogram

1. Close a triple flashcard, then fold it in half.
2. Cut along the center fold of both the top and bottom strip. DO NOT cut the middle strip.
3. Close all the tabs so that the flashcard is a single strip without tabs.
4. As you open the right tabs, write three phonograms (word families) on the top, bottom and middle.
5. Close all the tabs so that the flashcard is a single strip without tabs.
6. As you open the left tabs, write three initial consonants on the top, bottom and middle.
7. Open and close the tabs, and read the nine words formed.

Example: phonograms: -*an*, -*all*, -*at*
initial consonants: f, b, c

nine words formed:

fan, fall, fat	*went, west, wet*	*dint, did, dip*
ban, ball, bat	*bent, best, bet*	*lint, lid, lip*
can, call, cat	*vent, vest, vet*	*hint, hid, hip*

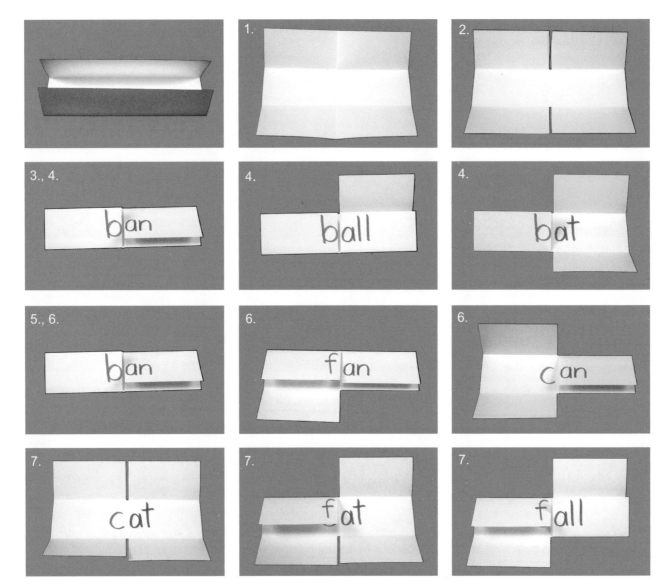

(VKV) Flashcards: 12 Word Phonogram (or 12 Syllable)

1. Close a triple flashcard, then fold it in half.
2. Fold the left half of the flashcard in half to form two smaller sections.
3. Cut along all folds along the top and bottom strips. DO NOT cut the middle strip.
4. Cut off the top and bottom small left tabs.
5. Fold the tabs so the flashcard is a single strip without tabs.
6. As you open the right tabs, write three phonograms (rimes) on the top, bottom and middle.
7. Fold all the tabs so that the flashcard is a single strip.
8. On the front of the left tab, write an initial consonant. Open the left tab, and write another consonant on the exposed left tab. Continue until four initial consonants have been written.
9. Open and close the tabs, and read the twelve words or syllables formed.

Example: phonograms/rimes: -an, -ed, -ut   -ot, -ill, -in
onsets: b, m, n, r   d, p, sp, t

twelve words formed:	ban	man	nan	ran		dot	pot	spot	tot
	bed	med	ned	red		dill	pill	spill	till
	but	mut	nut	rut		din	pin	spin	tin

rust	dust	bust	must		dress	less	bless	press		best	vest	pest	rest
rug	dug	bug	mug		drink	link	blink	prink		bent	went	pent	rent
rid	did	bid	mid		drop	lop	blop	prop		ban	van	pan	ran
gun	bun	sun	fun		bed	fed	ned	led		hat	pat	mat	tat
gill	bill	sill	fill		bib	fib	nib	lib		hop	pop	mop	top
gob	bob	sob	fob		bit	fit	nit	lit		hen	pen	men	ten
lug	pug	bug	mug		big	gig	pig	jig		din	sin	bin	fin
lad	pad	bad	mad		but	gut	put	jut		dell	sell	bell	fell
lass	pass	bass	mass		beg	get	pet	jet		dun	sun	bun	fun

Top-Tab Word Family Foldable®:
Use six sheets of 12" x 12" scrapbook paper or six sheets of 12" x 17" art paper to make this easy Foldable. Five sheets of paper will be used to make the inside sheets, and one sheet will be cut to make a cover. See page 298 for instructions.

The template for this example was folded into fifths forming a twenty-five square grid. Punch holes and use rings to bind this classroom book.
See page 141 for instructions for making a 26-tab alphabet book.

Note From Dinah: The teacher-generated print on the cover of the book is also being used to teach sequencing and steps. Notice that within the text the word families have been underlined and color coded to the tabs. The print inside the book on each phonogram page was student-generated print that was dictated to the teacher.

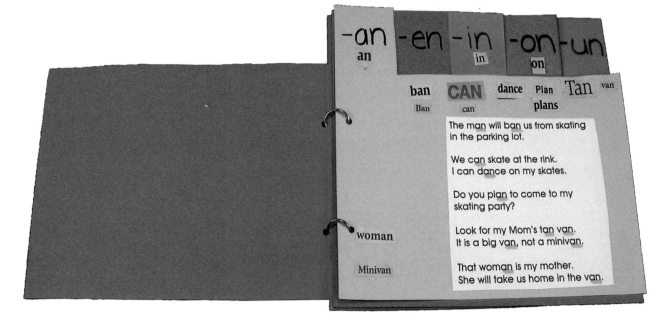

Foldable® Pyramid Mobile (right):

Cut off the top tip of a pyramid and push yarn through the cut from the inside to the outside. Use a large piece of tape (2" tape works best) placed around the yarn instead of tying a knot. A knot will eventually pull through the top of the pyramid, while the tape will adhere to the yarn and serve as a knot. Punch holes on each edge of the three sides and tie long pieces of yarn from these holes. Small fishing line weights or metal washers can be tied to the ends of the yarn to keep it straight (see photograph). Wrap word cards around the yarn and glue them in place. See page 294.

Sentence Strips or Word Strips (below): Use half
sheets of copy paper (4¼" x 5½") to make these multi-tabbed phonogram booklets. Collect words on the front tabs and use them in sentences under the tabs. Students can dictate sentences or a short story using the words to the teacher. The book can be read by the class and used as a study guide. When finished, place the book in a short /a/ cereal storage box for future reference. See page 306.

A phonogram is formed by a vowel grapheme and an ending consonant grapheme. Phonograms are often called *word families*, *rhyming word families*, or *rimes*.

-ab	-ack	-ad	-ag	-all	-am	-an	-ance
(initial consonants)	(initial consonants)	(initial consonants)	(initial consonants)	(initial consonants)	(initial consonants)	(initial consonants)	(initial consonants)
cab	back	bad	bag	ball	bam	ban	dance
dab	hack	cad	gag	call	cam	can	lance
gab	lack	dad	hag	fall	dam	Dan	(initial blends/ digraphs)
jab	pack	fad	lag	gall	ham	fan	chance
lab	rack	gad	nag	hall	jam	Jan	France
tab	sack	had	rag	mall	Pam	man	glance
(initial blends/ digraphs)	(initial blends/ digraphs)	lad	sag	tall	yam	pan	prance
blab	black	mad	tag	wall	(initial blends/ digraphs)	ran	stance
crab	knack	pad	wag	(initial blends/ digraphs)	cram	tan	trance
drab	quack	sad	(initial blends/ digraphs)	small	dram	van	
grab	stack	tad	brag	squall	pram	(initial blends/ digraphs)	-and
scab	track	(initial blends/ digraphs)	drag	stall	ram	bran	(initial consonants)
slab	-act	Brad	flag		scam	clan	band
stab	(initial consonants)	Chad	shag		slam	flan	hand
	act	clad	slag		spam	plan	land
	fact	glad	snag		wham	scan	sand
	pact	shad	stag			span	(initial blends/ digraphs)
	tact	-aft	swag			Stan	bland
	(initial blends/ digraphs)	(initial consonants)				than	brand
	tract	raft					gland
		(initial blends/ digraphs)					grand
		craft					stand
		draft					strand
		graft					
		shaft					

Word Families

| Sad | day |

Word Families

mad
glad
bad

Dad. Dad. Dad.

| | day |

ads

had

MEMO PAD

Two-Tab Foldable® with a Title: To add a title or main idea on a Foldable, fold one side longer than the other to form an extended tab much as you would when making a Foldable concept map. See page 302 for concept maps.

A phonogram is formed by a vowel grapheme and an ending consonant grapheme. Phonograms are often called *word families*, *rhyming word families*, or *rimes*.

-ang	-ank	-ap	-ar	-ash	-ass	-at	-atch
(initial consonants)	(initial blends)	(initial consonants)	(initial consonants)	(initial consonants)	(initial consonants)	(initial consonants)	(initial consonants)
bang	bank	cap	bar	bash	bass	bat	batch
fang	lank	gap	car	cash	lass	cat	catch
gang	rank	lap	far	dash	mass	fat	hatch
hang	sank	map	jar	gash	pass	hat	latch
pang	tank	nap	mar	hash	sass	mat	match
rang	yank	rap	par	lash	(initial blends/ digraphs)	pat	patch
sang	(initial blends/ digraphs)	sap	tar	mash	brass	rat	(initial blends/ digraphs)
(initial blends/ digraphs)	blank	tap	(initial blends/ digraphs)	rash	class	sat	scratch
clang	clank	(initial blends/ digraphs)	char	sash	glass	tat	thatch
slang	crank	chap	scar	(initial blends/ digraphs)	grass	vat	
sprang	drank	clap	spar	brash		(initial blends/ digraphs)	-ax
	flank	flap	star	clash	-ast	brat	(initial consonants)
	frank	scrap	war	crash	(initial consonants)	chat	ax
	plank	slap		flash	cast	flat	fax
	prank	snap		slash	fast	gnat	lax
	shank	strap		smash	last	scat	max
	shrank	trap		stash	mast	slat	pax
	spank	wrap		trash	past	spat	tax
	stank			thrash	vast	splat	wax
	thank				(initial blends/ digraphs)	that	(initial blends/ digraphs)
					blast		flax
							relax

Quarter-Sheet Cards: Students should feel ownership of their flashcards -- adding artwork, drawing arrows, underlining things they need to remember, writing sentences, and gluing words from RWP. It is not uncommon to find the same word numerous times in different forms of print on a single word card (different fonts, all caps, all lowercase, plural form, with affixes).

Rhyming Word Families Short Vowel Rimes

A phonogram is formed by a vowel grapheme and an ending consonant grapheme. Phonograms are often called *word families*, *rhyming word families*, or *rimes*.

-ed	-ell	-eg	-en	-end	-ent	-ess	-est
(initial consonants)	(initial consonants)	(initial consonants)	(initial consonants)	(initial consonants)	(initial consonants)	(initial consonants)	(initial consonants)
bed	bell	beg	den	bend	bent	less	best
fed	cell	keg	hen	end	cent	mess	jest
led	dell	leg	men	fend	dent	(initial blends/ digraphs)	lest
red	fell	peg	pen	lend	gent	bless	nest
Ted	hell		ten	mend	lent	chess	pest
wed	jell		(initial blends/ digraphs)	send	rent	dress	rest
(initial blends/ digraphs)	Nell		then	tend	sent	guess	test
bled	sell		when	vend	tent	press	vest
bred	tell		wren	(initial blends/ digraphs)	vent	stress	west
fled	well			blend	went		zest
shed	yell			trend	(initial blends/ digraphs)		(initial blends/ digraphs)
shred	(initial blends/ digraphs)				scent		blest
sled	dwell				spent		crest
sped	quell						quest
	shell						
	smell						
	spell						
	swell						

Word Window (below): Fold the top sheet of a half book in half. Cut into the fold to make a small window. Open the half book, and write a word or align a cut-out word behind the window so it is visible through the window when the book is closed. On the inside write words that relate to the word viewed through the window. Below, notice the use of a photograph from the community, teacher written words, and words collected from RWP. Teach older students how to cut their own windows to help them focus on a word, word family, and more. This word window is a small version of a picture frame book, found on page 303.

Rhyming Word Families Short Vowel Rimes

A phonogram is formed by a vowel grapheme and an ending consonant grapheme. Phonograms are often called *word families*, *rhyming word families*, or *rimes*.

-et	-ew	-ib	-ic	-ick	-id	-iff	-ift
(initial consonants)	(initial consonants)	(initial consonants)	(initial consonants)	(initial consonants)	(initial consonants)	(initial consonants)	(initial consonants)

-et (initial consonants)
bet
get
jet
let
met
net
pet
set
wet
yet
(initial blends/digraphs)
fret

-ew (initial consonants)
dew
few
hew
pew
(initial blends/digraphs)
blew
brew
chew
crew
drew
flew
knew
screw
slew
strew
threw

-ib (initial consonants)
bib
fib
rib
(initial blends/digraphs)
crib
glib

-ic (initial consonants)
comic
epic
logic
magic
manic
mimic
panic
sonic
toxic
(initial blends/digraphs)
tropic

-ick (initial consonants)
kick
lick
pick
sick
tick
wick
(initial blends/digraphs)
brick
chick
click
flick
quick
slick
stick
thick
trick

-id (initial consonants)
bid
did
hid
kid
lid
rid
(initial blends/digraphs)
grid
skid
slid

-iff (initial consonants)
jiff
(initial blends/digraphs)
cliff
skiff
sniff
stiff
whiff

-ift (initial consonants)
gift
lift
rift
(initial blends/digraphs)
drift
shift
swift
thrift

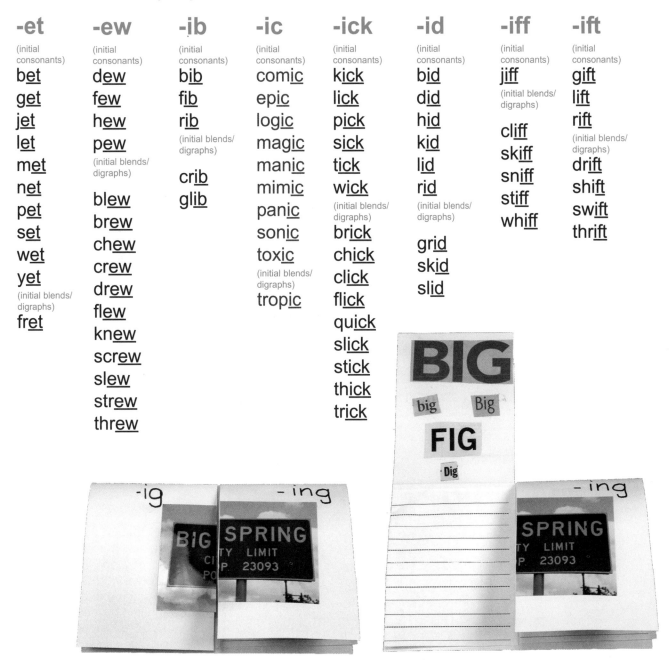

Two-Tab Foldable® (above): This photograph of a sign has been glued across the cut of a two-tab Foldable to illustrate two word families -- *-ig* and *-ing*. Collect examples of *-ig* and *-ing* words under the tabs. Notice that quarter sheets of lined paper can also be stapled or glued under the tabs.

A phonogram is formed by a vowel grapheme and an ending consonant grapheme. Phonograms are often called *word families*, *rhyming word families*, or *rimes*.

-ig	-ill	-ilt	-im	-in	-ing	-ink	-int
(initial consonants)	(initial consonants)	(initial consonants)	(initial consonants)	(initial consonants)	(initial consonants)	(initial consonants)	(initial consonants)
big	bill	jilt	dim	bin	bing	kink	hint
dig	Bill	kilt	him	din	ding	link	lint
fig	fill	tilt	rim	fin	king	mink	mint
gig	gill	wilt	vim	gin	ping	pink	tint
jig	hill	(initial blends/ digraphs)	(initial blends/ digraphs)	kin	ring	rink	(initial blends/ digraphs)
pig	ill	built	brim	pin	sing	sink	flint
rig	Jill	guilt	grim	sin	wing	wink	glint
wig	kill	quilt	prim	tin	zing	(initial blends/ digraphs)	print
(initial blends/ digraphs)	mill		slim	win	(initial blends/ digraphs)	blink	splint
brig	pill		swim	(initial blends/ digraphs)	bring	brink	sprint
sprig	rill		trim	chin	cling	chink	squint
swig	sill		whim	grin	fling	clink	
twig	till			shin	sling	drink	
	will			skin	spring	shrink	
	(initial blends/ digraphs)			spin	sting	think	
	chill			thin	swing		
	drill			twin	thing		
	frill				wring		
	grill						
	quill						
	skill						
	spill						
	thrill						

Trifold Foldable® (left):
Make and use a trifold to collect examples of words that end in three different word families, or rimes. A student recorder might be designated by the class to list these words on the Foldable. See page 293.

Photocopy the finished Foldable so each student has a copy of the words to study in class and/or at home. See "Introduction" page 27.

A phonogram is formed by a vowel grapheme and an ending consonant grapheme. Phonograms are often called *word families*, *rhyming word families*, or *rimes*.

-ip	-iss	-ist	-it	-ix	-ob	-ock	-od
(initial consonants)	(initial consonants)	(initial consonants)	(initial consonants)	(initial consonants)	(initial consonants)	(initial consonants)	(initial consonants)
dip	hiss	list	bit	fix	cob	dock	cod
hip	kiss	mist	fit	mix	gob	hock	God
lip	miss	(initial blends/ digraphs)	hit	six	job	jock	god
nip	(initial blends/ digraphs)	grist	kit		lob	lock	mod
rip	bliss	twist	lit		mob	mock	nod
sip		wrist	pit		rob	rock	pod
tip			sit		sob	sock	rod
zip			wit		(initial blends/ digraphs)	tock	sod
(initial blends/ digraphs)			(initial blends/ digraphs)		blob	(initial blends/ digraphs)	(initial blends/ digraphs)
blip			flit		knob	block	clod
chip			grit		snob	clock	plod
clip			knit			crock	prod
drip			quit			flock	shod
flip			skit			frock	trod
grip			slit			knock	
ship			spit			shock	
skip			split			smock	
slip						stock	
snip							
trip							
whip							

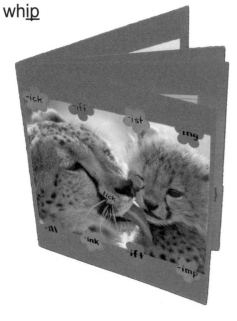

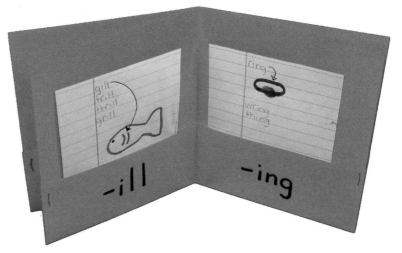

Two-Pocket Foldable® (above): Make and glue several two-pocket Foldables together to form this multi-pocket phonogram book. The example above was made using 8½" x 11" colored copy paper. See page 291.

Rhyming Word Families Short Vowel Rimes

A phonogram is formed by a vowel grapheme and an ending consonant grapheme. Phonograms are often called *word families*, *rhyming word families*, or *rimes*.

-og	-ong	-op	-oss	-ot	-ub	-uck	-ud
(initial consonants)	(initial consonants)	(initial consonants)	(initial consonants)	(initial consonants)	(initial consonants)	(initial consonants)	(initial consonants)
bog	bong	bop	boss	cot	cub	buck	bud
cog	dong	cop	loss	got	dub	duck	cud
fog	gong	hop	moss	hot	hub	huck	dud
hog	long	mop	toss	jot	pub	luck	mud
jog	song	pop	(initial blends/ digraphs)	lot	rub	muck	suds
log	tong	sop	floss	not	sub	puck	(initial blends/ digraphs)
tog	(initial blends/ digraphs)	top	gloss	pot	tub	suck	crud
(initial blends/ digraphs)	prong	(initial blends/ digraphs)		rot	(initial blends/ digraphs)	tuck	spud
blog	strong	chop	-ost	tot	club	(initial blends/ digraphs)	stud
clog	thong	crop	(initial consonants)	(initial blends/ digraphs)	flub	cluck	thud
flog	throng	drop	cost	blot	grub	pluck	
frog	wrong	flop	lost	clot	scrub	shuck	
grog		plop		knot	shrub	stuck	
slog		prop		plot	snub	struck	
smog		shop		shot	stub	truck	
		slop		slot			
		stop		spot			
				trot			

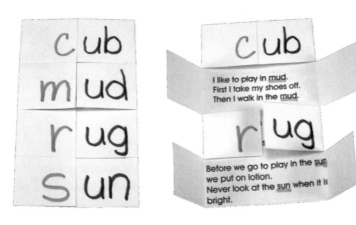

Shutterfold Word Families (left):
Make an 8½" x 11" shutterfold. Fold the closed shutterfold into fourths. Cut along the fold lines of the two small, top tabs. Do not cut through the middle, back section. Write rimes on the front right tabs and onsets (initial consonants or blends) on the front left. Open and close the tabs to view four initial onsets, four rimes, and the four words formed. Under the tabs, write or glue sentences using the words. See page 292.

Rhyming Word Families Short Vowel Rimes

A phonogram is formed by a vowel grapheme and an ending consonant grapheme. Phonograms are often called *word families*, *rhyming word families*, or *rimes*.

-uff	-ug	-ull	-um	-umb	-ump	-un	-unch
(initial consonants)	(initial consonants)	(initial consonants)	(initial consonants)	(initial consonants)	(initial consonants)	(initial consonants)	(initial consonants)
buff	bug	bull	bum	dumb	bump	bun	bunch
cuff	dug	full	gum	numb	dump	fun	hunch
muff	hug	pull	hum	(initial blends/ digraphs)	hump	gun	lunch
puff	jug	(initial consonants)	mum	crumb	jump	nun	munch
(initial blends/ digraphs)	lug	gull	rum	plumb	lump	pun	punch
bluff	mug	lull	sum	thumb	pump	run	(initial blends/ digraphs)
fluff	pug	mull	yum		rump	sun	brunch
gruff	rug	null	(initial blends/ digraphs)		(initial blends/ digraphs)	(initial blends/ digraphs)	crunch
scuff	tug	pull	chum		chump	shun	
snuff	(initial blends/ digraphs)	(initial blends/ digraphs)	drum		frump	spun	
stuff	chug	skull	glum		grump	stun	
	drug		plum		plump		
	plug		scum		slump		
	shrug		slum		stump		
	slug		strum		trump		
	smug						
	snug						
	thug						

Trifold Foldables® (right):
Fold a closed trifold into fourths. Cut along the fold lines of the right section to form four small tabs. Write an initial consonant on the large left section. Write four word families on top of the four tabs. Under the tabs, write the word formed and illustrate the words or glue pictures of the words. See page 293.

A phonogram is formed by a vowel grapheme and an ending consonant grapheme. Phonograms are often called *word families*, *rhyming word families*, or *rimes*.

-ung	-unk	-unt	-us	-ush	-ust	-ut
(initial consonants)	(initial consonants)	(initial consonants)	(initial consonants)	(initial consonants)	(initial consonants)	(initial consonants)
d**ung**	b**unk**	h**unt**	b**us**	g**ush**	b**ust**	b**ut**
h**ung**	d**unk**	p**unt**	p**us**	h**ush**	d**ust**	c**ut**
l**ung**	f**unk**	r**unt**	(initial blends/ digraphs)	l**ush**	g**ust**	g**ut**
r**ung**	h**unk**	(initial blends/ digraphs)	pl**us**	m**ush**	j**ust**	h**ut**
s**ung**	j**unk**	bl**unt**		r**ush**	l**ust**	j**ut**
(initial blends/ digraphs)	p**unk**	gr**unt**		(initial blends/ digraphs)	m**ust**	n**ut**
cl**ung**	s**unk**	st**unt**		bl**ush**	r**ust**	r**ut**
fl**ung**	(initial blends/ digraphs)			br**ush**	(initial blends/ digraphs)	(initial blends/ digraphs)
sl**ung**	ch**unk**			cr**ush**	cr**ust**	gl**ut**
spr**ung**	dr**unk**			fl**ush**	tr**ust**	sh**ut**
st**ung**	fl**unk**			pl**ush**	thr**ust**	sm**ut**
str**ung**	pl**unk**			sl**ush**		str**ut**
sw**ung**	shr**unk**			thr**ush**		
wr**ung**	sk**unk**					
	tr**unk**					

Word Family Pocket Booklets (above):
Glue multiple two-pocket Foldables together to form word family booklets. Make a booklet for each long vowel and/or short vowel and label the pockets with phonograms that begin with the featured vowel. See page 291.

The phonogram booklets pictured above are color coded to the vowels within the phonograms:

yellow = a   pink = i   orange = u
blue = e   green = o

A phonogram is formed by a vowel grapheme and an ending consonant grapheme. Phonograms are often called *word families*, *rhyming word families*, or *rimes*.

-ace	-aid	-ain	-ake	-ale	-ape	-aste
face	laid	lain	bake	bale	cape	baste
lace	maid	main	cake	dale	gape	haste
mace	paid	pain	fake	gale	nape	paste
pace	raid	rain	lake	hale	tape	taste
race	*(initial blends/ digraphs)*	vain	make	kale	*(initial blends/ digraphs)*	waste
(initial blends/ digraphs)	braid	wain	rake	male	drape	*(initial blends/ digraphs)*
brace	staid	*(initial blends/ digraphs)*	take	pale	grape	chaste
grace		brain	wake	sale	scrape	
place	**-ail**	chain	*(initial blends/ digraphs)*	tale	shape	**-ate**
space	bail	drain	brake	vale		date
trace	fail	grain	drake	*(initial blends/ digraphs)*	**-are**	fate
	hail	plain	flake	scale	bare	gate
-ade	jail	slain	quake	shale	care	hate
bade	mail	Spain	shake	stale	dare	late
fade	nail	sprain	snake	whale	fare	mate
jade	pail	stain	stake		hare	rate
made	rail	strain		**-ame**	mare	*(initial blends/ digraphs)*
wade	sail	train	**-ane**	came	rare	crate
(initial blends/ digraphs)	tail		bane	fame	ware	grate
blade	wail	**-aint**	cane	game	*(initial blends/ digraphs)*	plate
glade	*(initial blends/ digraphs)*	faint	lane	lame	flare	skate
grade	flail	paint	mane	name	glare	slate
shade	quail	saint	pane	same	share	spate
spade	snail	taint	sane	tame	snare	state
trade	trail	*(initial blends/ digraphs)*	vane	*((initial blends/ digraphs)*	stare	
		quaint	wane	blame		
-age	**-air**		*(initial blends/ digraphs)*	flame	**-ase**	
cage	fair	**-ait**	crane	frame	base	
page	hair	bait	plane	shame	case	
rage	pair	gait			vase	
sage	*(initial blends/ digraphs)*	wait			*(initial blends/ digraphs)*	
wage	chair	*(initial blends/ digraphs)*			chase	
(initial blends/ digraphs)	flair	strait				
stage	stair	trait				

A phonogram is formed by a vowel grapheme and an ending consonant grapheme. Phonograms are often called *word families*, *rhyming word families*, or *rimes*.

-ave
(initial consonants)

cave
gave
pave
rave
save
wave

(initial blends/ digraphs)

brave
crave
grave
shave
slave
stave

-aze

daze
faze
gaze
haze
maze
raze

(initial blends/ digraphs)

blaze
craze
glaze
graze

-ay
(initial consonants)

bay
day
gay
hay
jay
lay
may
nay
pay
ray
say
way

(initial blends/ digraphs)

bray
clay
fray
gray
play
pray
slay
spray
stay
stray
sway
tray

-ead
(initial consonants)

bead
lead
read

-eak
(initial consonants)

beak
leak
peak
teak
weak

(initial blends/ digraphs)

bleak
creak
sneak
speak
squeak
streak

-eal
(initial consonants)

deal
heal
meal
peal
real
seal
veal
zeal

(initial blends/ digraphs)

squeal
steal

-eam
(initial consonants)

beam
ream
seam
team

(initial blends/ digraphs)

cream
dream
gleam
scream
steam
stream

-ean
(initial consonants)

bean
dean
lean
mean

-ear
(initial consonants)

dear
fear
gear
hear
near
rear
tear
year

(initial blends/ digraphs)

clear
smear
spear

-eat
(initial consonants)

beat
feat
heat
meat
neat
peat
seat

(initial blends/ digraphs)

bleat
cheat
cleat
pleat
treat
wheat

-ee
(initial consonants)

bee
fee
knee
see
tee
wee

(initial blends)

flee
glee

-eed
(initial consonants)

deed
feed
heed
need
reed
seed
weed

(initial blends/ digraphs)

bleed
breed
creed
freed
greed
speed
steed

-eef
(initial consonants)

beef
reef

-eek
(initial consonants)

leek
meek
peek
seek
week

(initial blends/ digraphs)

cheek
creek
sleek

-eel
(initial consonants)

eel
feel
heel
keel
peel
reel

(initial blends/ digraphs)

kneel
steel
wheel

-eem
(initial consonants)

deem
seem
teem

-een
(initial consonants)

keen
seen
teen

(initial blends/ digraphs)

green
queen
screen
sheen

Rhyming Word Families Long Vowel Rimes

A phonogram is formed by a vowel grapheme and an ending consonant grapheme. Phonograms are often called *word families*, *rhyming word families*, or *rimes*.

-eep
(initial consonants)
beep
deep
keep
weep
(initial blends/ digraphs)
sheep
steep

-eer
(initial consonants)
beer
deer
jeer
peer
(initial blends/ digraphs)
cheer
queer
sneer
steer

-eet
beet
feet
meet
(initial blends/ digraphs)
fleet
greet
sheet
sleet
street
sweet

-ibe
(initial blends /digraphs)
bribe
scribe
tribe

-ice
(initial consonants)
dice
lice
mice
nice
rice
vice
(initial blends/ digraphs)
price
slice
spice
twice

-ide
(initial consonants)
hide
ride
side
tide
wide
(initial blends/ digraphs)
bride
chide
glide
pride
slide
snide
stride

-ie
(initial consonants)
die
fie
lie
pie
tie
vie

-ife
(initial consonants)
fife
life
rife
wife
(initial blends/ digraphs)
knife
strife

-ight
(initial consonants)
fight
light
might
night
right
sight
tight
(initial blends/ digraphs)
flight
knight
plight
slight

-ike
(initial consonants)
bike
hike
like
mike
pike
(initial blends/ digraphs)
spike
strike

-ile
(initial consonants)
bile
file
mile
pile
tile
(initial blends/ digraphs)
smile
while

-ime
(initial consonants)
dime
lime
mime
time
(initial blends/ digraphs)
chime
crime

-ine
(initial consonants)
dine
fine
line
mine
nine
pine
vine
wine

-ipe
(initial consonants)
pipe
ripe
wipe
(initial blends/ digraphs)
gripe
snipe
stripe
tripe

-ire
(initial consonants)
dire
fire
hire
mire
tire
wire
(initial blends/ digraphs)
squire

-ise
(initial consonants)
guise
rise
vise
wise

-ite
(initial consonants)
bite
cite
kite
lite
mite
rite
site
(initial blends/ digraphs)
quite
spite
white
write

-ive
(initial consonants)
dive
five
hive
jive
live
(initial blends/ digraphs)
chive
drive
strive
thrive

A phonogram is formed by a vowel grapheme and an ending consonant grapheme. Phonograms are often called *word families*, *rhyming word families*, or *rimes*.

-o
go
no
pro
so

-oach
(initial consonants)
coach
poach
roach

-oad
(initial consonants)
load
road
toad

-oak
(initial consonants)
oak
soak
(initial blends/digraphs)
cloak
croak

-oal
(initial consonants)
coal
foal
goal
(initial blends/digraphs)
shoal

-oam
(initial consonants)
foam
loam
roam

-oan
(initial consonants)
loan
moan
(initial blends/digraphs)
groan

-oat
(initial consonants)
boat
coat
goat
moat
(initial blends/digraphs)
bloat
float
gloat
throat

-obe
(initial consonants)
lobe
robe
(initial blends/digraphs)
globe
strobe

-ode
(initial consonants)
bode
lode
mode
rode

-oke
(initial consonants)
coke
joke
poke
woke
(initial blends/digraphs)
broke
choke
smoke
spoke
stoke
stroke

-old
(initial consonants)
bold
cold
fold
gold
hold
mold
old
sold
told
(initial blends/digraphs)
scold

-ole
(initial consonants)
hole
mole
pole
role
(initial blends/digraphs)
stole
whole

-ome
(initial consonants)
dome
home
(initial blends)
chrome
(common exceptions to long vowel pronunciation)
come
some

-one
(initial consonants)
bone
cone
lone
tone
zone
(initial blends/digraphs)
clone
drone
phone
prone
stone

-ope
(initial consonants)
cope
hope
lope
mope
nope
pope
rope
(initial blends/digraphs)
grope
scope
slope

-ore
(initial consonants)
bore
core
fore
gore
more
pore
sore
tore
wore
(initial blends/digraphs)
chore
score
shore
spore
store
swore

-ose
(initial consonants)
hose
nose
pose
rose
(initial blends/digraphs)
prose
those

-ost
(initial consonants)
host
most
post

-ote
(initial consonants)
dote
note
rote
tote
vote
(initial blends/digraphs)
quote
wrote

-ove
(initial consonants)
cove
dove (vb)
(initial blends/digraphs)
clove
drove
grove
stove
trove

-oze
(initial consonants)
doze
froze

-ow
(initial consonants)
low
row
tow
(initial blends/digraphs)
blow
flow
glow
know
show
slow

score

A phonogram is formed by a vowel grapheme and an ending consonant grapheme. Phonograms are often called *word families*, *rhyming word families*, or *rimes*.

-ube
(initial consonants)

c<u>ube</u>
l<u>ube</u>
r<u>ube</u>
t<u>ube</u>

-ude
(initial consonants)

d<u>ude</u>
n<u>ude</u>
r<u>ude</u>

(initial blends)

cr<u>ude</u>
pr<u>ude</u>

-uge
(initial consonants)

h<u>uge</u>

-uke
(initial consonants)

d<u>uke</u>
n<u>uke</u>

-ule
(initial consonants)

r<u>ule</u>

-ume
(initial consonants)

f<u>ume</u>
perf<u>ume</u>

(initial blends/ digraphs)

pl<u>ume</u>

-une
d<u>une</u>
t<u>une</u>

-use
(initial consonants)

f<u>use</u>
r<u>use</u>
<u>use</u>

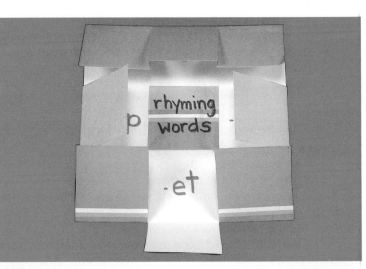

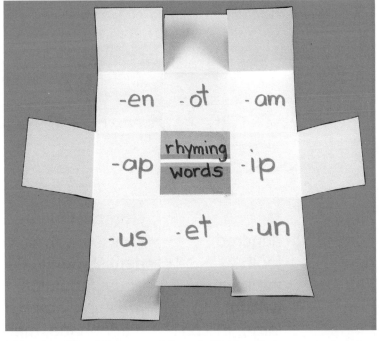

Rhyming Word Coverup (above): Make a Coverup card and write word families (rimes) under the tabs. With all tabs open, call out words. Have students fold the tabs of their card to cover word families they hear when the word is called. Students try to be the first to cover all the word families on their Coverup Card. See page 140 for instructions with photographs.

Note: When making numerous coverups, make sure the cards are not all the same. Just like Bingo cards, Coverups need to differ. Students begin with all tabs open, and close tabs to cover phonograms they hear in words read by the teacher or a classmate.

Primary students will study stem words more than root words; however, root words will begin to appear in first and second grade reading programs.

-Note that many dictionaries will tell the country and language origin of the word.
-Look at the stem/root word with and without prefixes and suffixes.
-Collect other words that look and sound like the stem/root word. Analyze the meaning of each word to determine if it was formed from the same root.
-Note that the root can be found at the beginning, middle, or ending of a word.

(VKV) Flashcards: Initial or Final Root Words or Stem Words

1. Close a triple flashcard, then fold it in half.
2. Cut along the fold line of the top and bottom strip. DO NOT cut the middle strip.
3. Cut off the top right and bottom right rectangles.
4. Write a root word on the single right tab, and write the meaning of the word to the left.
5. Write two different prefixes on the tabs to the left.
6. Read the the two different words formed.
7. Define the words based upon the meanings of the root word and the added prefixes. Write sentences using the words on the back of the VKV flashcard.

Note: Reverse this flashcard when the root word is at the beginning of the word instead of the end.

Root	Meaning	Common Words
cent	hundred	cent (penny 1/100), century, centimeter, percent
dent	tooth	dentist, dental floss, dentures
equ	the same	equal, equation
graph	writing	graphics, graph, telegraph
mega	large, million	megaphone, megabit
min	little	minute, miniature, minimum
nav	ship, sail	navigation, navy
port	carry	portable, report
scrib	write	scribble, scribe, script, description
therm	heat	thermostat, thermometer
vid, vis	see	video, visual, vision, visor
zo	animal	zoo, zoologist

Make several VKV flashcards and use them to teach root words. With practice, most students will be able to transfer what they learn about root words from using these VKV flashcards to other situations in which they encounter root words. It is not necessary to make flashcards for all the root words listed in this section; however, do make VKV flashcards for root words encountered in reading and writing throughout the year. Store the flashcards in the *Base/Root Word* section of your VKV Flashcard Box, page 16.

VKV Flashcards: Medial Root Words or Stem Words

1. Fold a double flashcard into thirds.
2. Cut along the fold lines of the top strip. DO NOT cut the bottom strip.
3. Cut off the top middle tab.
4. Write a root word in the middle of the flashcard on the exposed center section.
5. Write a prefix under the left tab. Write a suffix under the right tab.
6. Read the words formed. Determine how many words can be formed.

Examples: root word joy   school   cover
            en joy   preschool   discover
            en joy ment   preschooler   discovering

Note: Use this VKV flashcard to review affixes -- prefixes and suffixes.

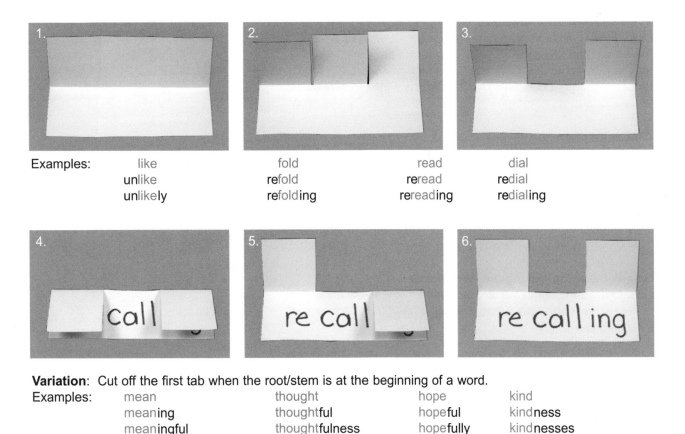

Examples: like   fold   read   dial
             unlike   refold   reread   redial
             unlikely   refolding   rereading   redialing

Variation: Cut off the first tab when the root/stem is at the beginning of a word.
Examples: mean   thought   hope   kind
             meaning   thoughtful   hopeful   kindness
             meaningful   thoughtfulness hopefully   kindnesses

Suffixes are letter clusters or syllables added to the end of base words. Sometimes a suffix is added directly to a word. For example -*s* is added directly to *boy* to form the word *boys*.

Examples: talk, talks, talked, talking

Sometimes adding a suffix changes the spelling of a word.

Examples: cry, cried; sip, sipped, sipping

Sometimes suffixes change the tense or meaning of a word.

Examples: I look at books. (present tense)
I looked at books. (past tense)

Some common suffixes used by beginning readers and writers include: -*s*, -*er*, -*est*, -*ed*, -*ing*, -*less*, -*ly*.

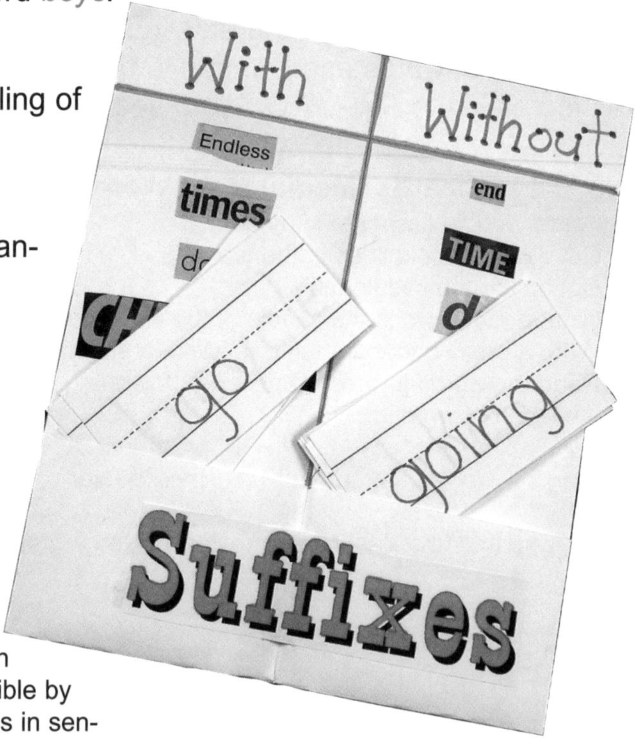

Three-Column Foldable® Chart:
Make a three-column chart. Use it to record a word in the left column. Record as many new words as possible by adding endings to the given word. Use the new words in sentences in the right column. Try using all the words in sentences to form a paragraph.

Example of new words:
Given Word: drive
New Words: drives, driving, driven, driver
Sentences:
I wish I could drive a car.
My mother drives a truck.
We are driving to school.
My mother has driven for a long time.
She is a good driver.

Simple Paragraph using the New Words:
I like to drive my car. One day as I was driving, I saw another driver I know. She drives a red car. She has driven this car for a long time.

Variation Using RWP (right): The folded chart to the right was made using 8½" x 11" paper. Find words with suffixes in RWP. Cut and glue the base word in the first column and the suffix in the second column. Use the word in a sentence in the last, largest column. Use several of the words to write a simple paragraph on the back, or use the words as a class to orally create stories.

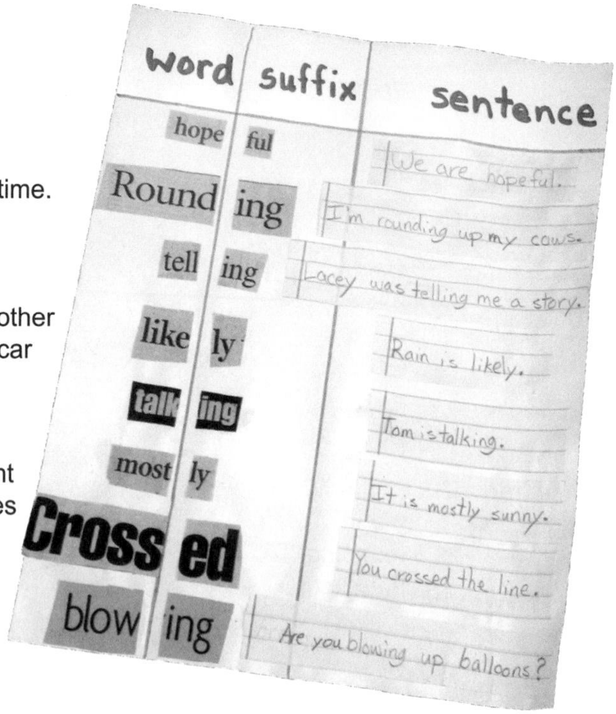

Suffixes are letter clusters or syllables added to the end of base words.

A word that ends in silent **e** usually keeps the **e** when adding a suffix beginning with a consonant.

Examples:
awe *n*   awesome *adj*
care *v*   careful *adj*
nine *n*   ninety *n*

A word that ends in silent **e** usually drops the **e** when adding a suffix beginning with a vowel.

Examples:
explore   explored   exploring
fine   finer   finest
ice   ices   icy

A word ending in **y** and following a consonant usually changes the **y** to **i** before a suffix is added unless the suffix begins with **i**.

Examples:
carry   carried   carrying
dry   dried   drying

A word ending in *ie* in which the **e** is silent -- change the *ie* to **y** before adding *-ing*.

Examples:
die   dying
lie   lying

The letter **k** is usually added to words ending in **c** before a suffix beginning with **e**, **i**, or **y**.

Examples:
mimic   mimicking

When adding a suffix to a one-syllable word ending with a single vowel and consonant, double the final consonant before adding a suffix that begins with a vowel.

Examples:
chop   chopped   chopping
drop   dropped   dropping

A word having more than one syllable, ending in one consonant and following one short vowel, usually doubles the final consonant before a suffix beginning with a vowel, provided the accent is on the last syllable.

Examples: forget   forgetting   commit, committed, committing

With words ending in a final consonant preceded by two vowels do not double the final consonant.

Examples: beat, beaten   need, needed   seed, seeded

RWP (above): Made using a quarter sheet of paper.

Accordion (left): Use an accordion Foldable to collect examples of words with one-letter, two-letter, three-letter or more suffixes. See page 300.

Make several VKV flashcards and use them to teach suffixes. With practice, most students will be able to transfer what they learn about suffixes from using these VKV flashcards to other situations in which they encounter suffixes. It is not necessary to make flashcards for all the suffixes listed in this section; however, do make VKV flashcards for suffixes encountered in reading throughout the year. Store the flashcards in the *Suffix* section of your VKV Flashcard Box, page 16.

VKV® Flashcard: Add a Suffix

1. Fold a single flashcard so that half of the card is covered by a tab and half is exposed.
2. With the tab to the right closed, write a word on the front left of the tab and write a suffix to the right.
3. On the back of the VKV, write the definition of the suffix.
4. Students open the right tab and read the word without the suffix. A picture might be used to help define the term. See photograph below.
5. Students close the right tab to read the word with the suffix. Encourage students to use the word in a sentence with and without the suffix.
6. Write examples of student sentences on the back of the VKV.

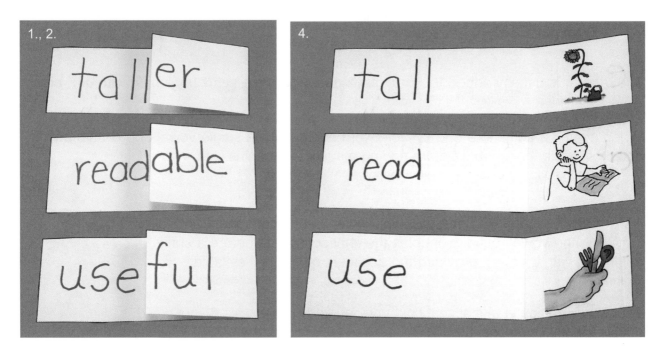

-er

bake	bak<u>er</u>
bank	bank<u>er</u>
boat	boat<u>er</u>
bowl	bowl<u>er</u>
camp	camp<u>er</u>
clean	clean<u>er</u>
climb	climb<u>er</u>
compute	comput<u>er</u>
dine	din<u>er</u>
dream	dream<u>er</u>
drive	driv<u>er</u>
farm	farm<u>er</u>
fight	fight<u>er</u>
garden	garden<u>er</u>
golf	golf<u>er</u>
hike	hik<u>er</u>
hunt	hunt<u>er</u>
kick	kick<u>er</u>
lead	lead<u>er</u>
learn	learn<u>er</u>
listen	listen<u>er</u>
mine	min<u>er</u>
mow	mow<u>er</u>
paint	paint<u>er</u>
pitch	pitch<u>er</u>
play	play<u>er</u>
preach	preach<u>er</u>
print	print<u>er</u>
ride	rid<u>er</u>
sail	sail<u>er</u>
sell	sell<u>er</u>
ski	ski<u>er</u>
spell	spell<u>er</u>
teach	teach<u>er</u>
trade	trad<u>er</u>
train	train<u>er</u>
walk	walk<u>er</u>

VKV® with RWP: Make the VKV pictured above using RWP to form two words -- base word, and base word with an affix. See instructions on the previous page.

Difficult to Spell: Since the following words sound like they end in *-er* they are difficult for beginning writers and ESL/ELL students to spell. Make VKVs for a few key *-or* words to expose students to the different spelling.

-or

act<u>or</u>
auth<u>or</u>
conduct<u>or</u>
doct<u>or</u>
debt<u>or</u>
edit<u>or</u>
profess<u>or</u>
sail<u>or</u>

VKV Flashcard: Accordion Suffixes

1. Fold a sheet of 8½" x 11" copy paper into an eight section accordion book.
2. Cut a three-inch strip off the right side of the top seven sections, leaving the bottom section whole.
3. Glue the sections together to form an accordion. See page 53 for instructions and photographs.
4. Write a suffix on the extended tab, so the first letter is close to the accordion folds..
5. Write words on the accordion strips so their ending letters are close to the suffix. See #4 and #5.
6. Fold and flip the accordion section to add the suffix to each of the words listed.

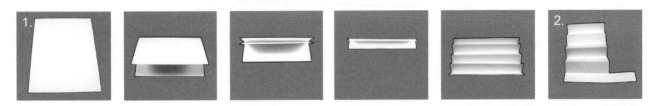

-ing

bowl<u>ing</u>
build<u>ing</u>
call<u>ing</u>
dwell<u>ing</u>
fight<u>ing</u>
fill<u>ing</u>
flavor<u>ing</u>
floor<u>ing</u>
go<u>ing</u>
jump<u>ing</u>
learn<u>ing</u>
mean<u>ing</u>
offer<u>ing</u>
open<u>ing</u>
paint<u>ing</u>
play<u>ing</u>
school<u>ing</u>
scout<u>ing</u>
season<u>ing</u>
see<u>ing</u>
sing<u>ing</u>
talk<u>ing</u>
tell<u>ing</u>
walk<u>ing</u>
work<u>ing</u>

The suffix -*ing* is most frequently used with verbs, but can also form nouns.

Examples: clothing (clothes)
bedding (linens)
building (a structure)
dwelling (a home, habitat)
painting (a painted picture)
seasoning (a condiment)

The suffix -s is added to nouns to indicate plural, or more than one.

-s

Words ending in **y** and following a vowel usually keep the **y** when a suffix is added.

bay	bay**s**
boy	boy**s**
cowboy	cowboy**s**
day	day**s**
donkey	donkey**s**
key	key**s**
monkey	monkey**s**
toy	toy**s**
tray	tray**s**
way	way**s**

Above: Using the Matchbook Foldable above, play a concentration game to match base words with and without a suffix. Use narrow strips of paper to make small matchbooks. See page 292.
Below (left): Three-Column Foldable Chart, see page 308 for details.
Below (right): Two-Tab Foldable where students write a simple story under the tabs. See page 291.

Words	+ s	Sentences
school	schools	I run the schools.
land	lands	I visited many lands.
pet	Pets	Sue has many pets.
kid	kids	How many kids do you have?
dog	Dogs	Arlene has three dogs!
star	Stars	How many stars can you see?

The twenty suffixes listed below have been found to account for 93% of suffix use in common language. Select ability appropriate words for student use.

1. -s, -es
(plurals)
books
boxes
boys
calls
colors
days
draws
ears
friends
girls
hands
homes
houses
mornings
mothers
names
nights
plays
presents
reads
rides
schools
tells
trees
trucks
years

6. -ion, -tion, -ation, -ition
act, process
action
addition
competition
condition
protection
subtraction

2. -ed
(past tense verbs)
asked
boxed
called
cleaned
colored
ended
helped
jumped
liked
looked
named
opened
played
thanked
wanted
wished

7. -ible, -able
(can be done)
adorable
comfortable
doable
laughable
likeable
readable
suitable
treatable
valuable

combustible
flexible
gullible
horrible
impossible
possible

3. -ing
(verb form = present participle)
bringing
calling
cleaning
coloring
cutting
drawing
eating
ending
finding
getting
giving
going
helping
knowing
looking
putting
seeing
standing
telling
thinking
wishing
working

8. -al, -ial
(having characteristics of)
commercial
financial
logical
magical
mechanical
musical
mystical
physical
practical
spherical
whimsical

4. -ly
(characteristic of)
friendly
kindly
likely
lively
lonely
loudly
lovely
motherly
nearly
quickly
softly
timely
unfriendly
warmly
yearly

9. -y
(characterized by)
bossy
cloudy
dreamy
dusty
foamy
frisky
frosty
fruity
fully
glassy
goody
grassy
greedy
showy
sleepy
tricky

5. -er, -or
(person connected with)
builder
buyer
caller
catcher
drinker
helper
jumper
opener
owner
reader
runner
singer
speaker
talker
teacher
trucker
washer
worker

actor
conductor
doctor
editor
professor

10. -ness
(state of, condition of)
darkness
goodness
happiness
kindness
likeness
wilderness

Source: White, T.G.I, Sowell, V., and Yanagihara, A. (1999). Teaching elementary students use word-part clues. *The Reading Teacher*, 42, 302-308.

11. -ity, -ty
(state of)

activity
community
honesty
loyalty
poverty
reality
security

16. -er
(comparative)

bigger
brighter
colder
faster
further
heavier
higher
hotter
longer
lighter
newer
nicer
older
prettier
quicker
quieter
shorter
slower
smaller
smarter
softer
taller
warmer

12. -ment
(action or process)

department
development
enjoyment
experiment
government
placement

17. -ive, -ative, -itive
(adjective form of a noun)

alternative
attentive
combative
conservative
defensive
destructive
digestive
passive
productive
talkative

13. -ic
(having characteristics of)

angelic
comic
fantastic
historic
poetic
public
robotic
terrific
tragic

18. -ful
(full of)

bashful
beautiful
colorful
faithful
forceful
forgetful
graceful
harmful
helpful
hopeful
mouthful
painful
peaceful
restful
stressful
successful
thankful
thoughtful
truthful
useful
willful
wishful
wonderful

14. -ous, -eous, -ious
(possessing the qualities of)

adventurous
dangerous
disastrous
fabulous
fictitious
marvelous
monstrous
nervous
joyous
religious
serious
wondrous

19. -less
(without)

colorless
doless
endless
fruitless
helpless
homeless
hopeless
mindless
nameless
sleepless
thankless
useless
waterless
wireless

15. -en
(made of, to make)

blacken
darken
fasten
frighten
lighten
shorten
soften
strengthen
sweeten
thicken
weaken
widen

20. -est
(comparative)

ablest
biggest
boldest
busiest
chalkiest
cleanest
clearest
cloudiest
coldest
earliest
fastest
finest
greatest
hottest
largest
meanest
nearest
nicest
oldest
smallest
wildest

Add -er or -or to a noun to change the meaning to *one who*.

VKV® Flashcards: Three-Suffix VKV®

1. Close a triple flashcard, then fold it in half.
2. Cut along the fold line of the top and bottom strip. DO NOT cut the middle strip.
3. Cut off the top left and bottom left rectangles.
4. Write a base word on the single remaining left tab.
5. Write three different suffixes on the right three tabs.
6. Read the three different words formed by flipping each tab closed.
7. Define the three words based upon the meaning of each suffix.
8. Write sentences using the words on the back of the VKV or have students illustrate.

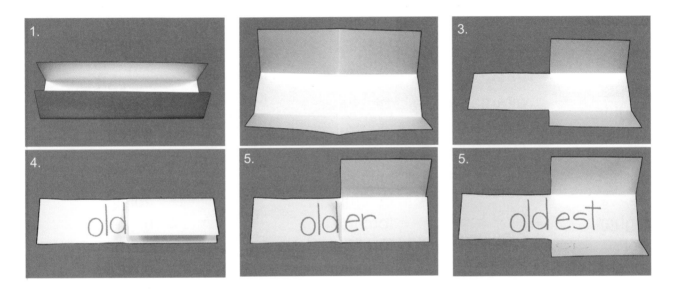

Six-Word Variation (below): Place the single tab to the right, and write a suffix on the tab. Write three base words on the left tabs. Open and close the left tabs and read the three words formed. Fold the suffix back and read the base words without the suffix. Students will read six words with this VKV, three with, and three without a suffix.

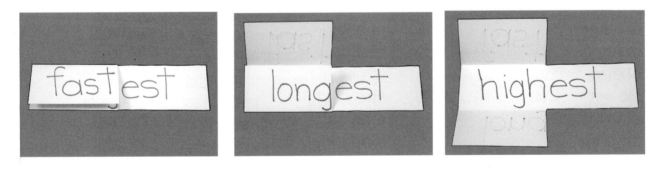

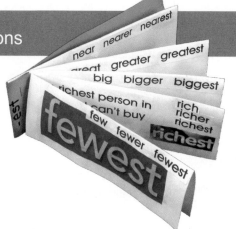

Adjective

Adjective	-er (comparative)	-est (superlative)
big	bigger	biggest
black	blacker	blackest
blue	bluer	bluest
bright	brighter	brightest
cool	cooler	coolest
cute	cuter	cutest
dry	drier	driest
fast	faster	fastest
high	higher	highest
hot	hotter	hottest
light	lighter	lightest
long	longer	longest
mean	meaner	meanest
neat	neater	neatest
nice	nicer	nicest
old	older	oldest
quick	quicker	quickest
quiet	quieter	quietest
short	shorter	shortest
slow	slower	slowest
storm	stormier	stormiest
sweet	sweeter	sweetest
tall	taller	tallest
thick	thicker	thickest
ugly	uglier	ugliest
warm	warmer	warmest
white	whiter	whitest
young	younger	youngest

Common Exceptions:

bad	worse	worst
good	better	best

Sentence Strip (above): Use half sheets of 8½" x 11" paper to make the Foldable pictured above. See page 306.

Four-Column Folded Chart (below): Use a sheet of 8½" x 11" paper to make this Foldable Chart, and use it to collect adjectives with *-er* and *-est* suffixes. See page 308.

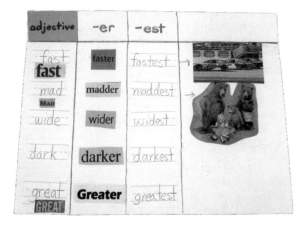

Adding *-y* or *-ly* changes a noun into an adjective.

Example: snow, snow**y**

-y

chalk**y**
cloud**y**
dream**y**
dust**y**
earth**y**
fish**y**
flower**y**
foam**y**
frisk**y**
frost**y**
fruit**y**
glass**y**
grass**y**
greed**y**
hand**y**
health**y**

itch**y**
leaf**y**
leather**y**
length**y**
luck**y**
might**y**
milk**y**
mold**y**
mood**y**
push**y**
scratch**y**
shadow**y**
sick**ly**
speed**y**
spook**y**
squeak**y**

stick**y**
sugar**y**
thirst**y**
thorn**y**
trust**y**
wind**y**

-ly words can also be adverbs:

-ly, -ily

angri**ly** adv
brief**ly** adv
clear**ly** adv
complete**ly** adv
eeri**ly** adv
gent**ly** adv
large**ly** adv
most**ly** adv
quick**ly** adv
rough**ly** adv
slow**ly** adv
soft**ly** adv
total**ly** adv

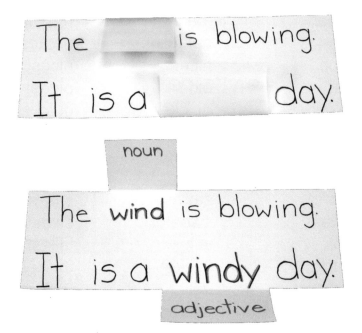

Shutterfold VKV® (above): Make a shutterfold using a sheet of 11" x 17" photocopy paper. Write a simple sentence under the top shutter using a noun that can be turned into an adjective by adding *-y*. Write a simple sentence under the bottom shutter using the adjective. Cut the top and bottom shutters away so that only a small section is left to cover the featured noun and adjective. Close the tabs and see if students can complete the sentences. Open the tabs to check responses.

Use Foldables and VKVs to add suffixes to sight words:

Verbs:

(add suffixes)

bring
call
carry
clean
draw
eat
fall
grow
help
jump
laugh
like
live
open
pick
play
pull
read
ride
run
talk
thank
think
try
use
walk
wash
went
were
wish
work

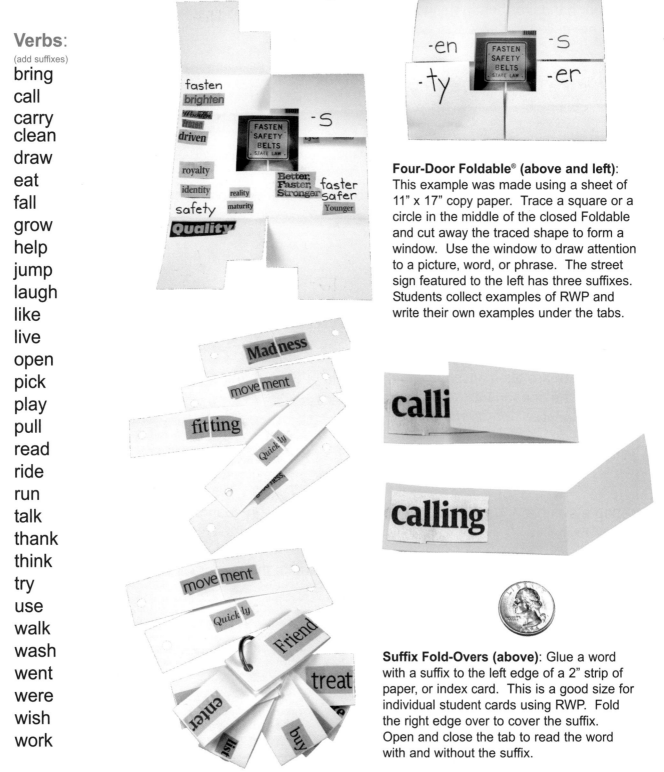

Four-Door Foldable® (above and left): This example was made using a sheet of 11" x 17" copy paper. Trace a square or a circle in the middle of the closed Foldable and cut away the traced shape to form a window. Use the window to draw attention to a picture, word, or phrase. The street sign featured to the left has three suffixes. Students collect examples of RWP and write their own examples under the tabs.

Suffix Fold-Overs (above): Glue a word with a suffix to the left edge of a 2" strip of paper, or index card. This is a good size for individual student cards using RWP. Fold the right edge over to cover the suffix. Open and close the tab to read the word with and without the suffix.

Small Suffix RWP Ring (above): Cut a quarter sheet of paper into fourths to make the single small suffix cards pictured. Fold them in half and position RWP across the fold so that the base word is on one side and the suffix on the other. Punch holes and store the cards on rings. Read the words on the ring with and without the suffixes.

Words have one or more parts that we can hear as we say them. We can tap a finger, clap our hands, or beat a rhythm stick to the single or multiple sounds of a word. These parts are called *syllables*.

There is one *vowel sound* in every *syllable*.
> **Examples**:   bun-ny, hel-lo, sum-mer

Two vowels can make one sound:
> **Examples**:   thir-teen, rai-sin.

Some vowels are silent. A word with two vowels, one voiced and one silent, can have one syllable.
> **Examples**:   bike, joke, like, wake

Sometimes *y* acts like a vowel in a syllable.
> **Examples**:   cy-cle, hap-py

Prefixes and suffixes are usually separate syllables.
> **Examples**:   re-lax, fourteenth

When there are two consonants in the middle of a word, the syllables are divided between the consonants.
> **Examples**:   dad-dy, mat-ter

When double consonants are part of a the root word, they are not divided.
> **Examples**:   will-ing, miss-ing

When a syllable ends with a vowel, the vowel has a long sound.
> **Examples**:   ho-tel, hip-po

When a syllable ends with a consonant, the vowel in the syllable is short.
> **Example**:   mag-net

Consonant blends and digraphs usually stay together in a syllable.
> **Examples**:   with-out, fish-er-man

Make several VKV flashcards and use them to teach syllables. With practice, most students will be able to transfer what they learn about syllables from using these VKV flashcards to other situations in which they need to use syllables to decipher a word during reading or in their writing. It is not necessary to make flashcards for all the words in the following syllable lists; however, do make VKV flashcards for syllabication of special words encountered in reading and writing throughout the year. Store the cards in the *Syllables* section of your VKV Flashcard Box, page 16.

(VKV) Flashcard: Syllables

1. Write one-syllable words on a single flashcard without any folds or tabs.
2. Fold a single flashcard in half and use it with two-syllable words. Fold a single flashcard into thirds and use it with three-syllable words, fold into fourths and use it with four-syllable words, and continue the process for words with more than four syllables.
3. To study VKVs with more than one syllable, fold the flashcard so only the first syllable shows. Slowly unfold the flashcard to sequentially reveal the next syllables.

Dictionary Integration:
Observe how syllables of words are indicated within the dictionary pronunciation guide. Note the dots dividing the syllables and compare them to the dots used on the folds of the VKV syllable cards.

On the Back:
-write a pronunciation guide for the word.
-write a sentence using the word.
-write a sentence and leave a blank for students to fill the word in orally.

Foldable® Syllables Charts:

Fold a sheet of copy paper or chart paper into fourths along the long axis.

Fold the same sheet of paper into eighths along the short axis, forming four columns and eight rows. Number the columns as illustrated, and use the chart to record the syllables of seven words.

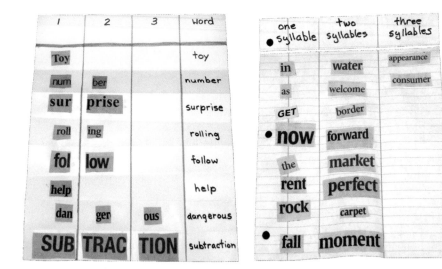

Lined Paper Charts (left):
Fold a sheet of lined paper into thirds. Trace along the fold lines, and use the columns to collect examples of one-, two-, or three-syllable words. See page 308.

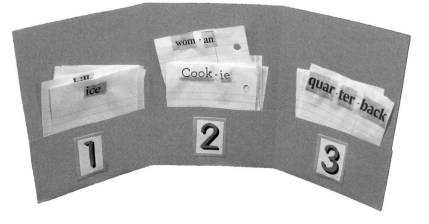

Three-Pocket Foldable® (right):
Make a three-pocket Foldable and use it to collect example word cards of one-, two-, and three-syllable words.

Trifold Foldable® (left): Make and use a trifold to collect examples of one-, two-, and three- syllable words. Have students select a given number of words and use them to write a short story on the back of the Foldable, or use the words to tell a story orally to the class. See page 293.

Really Big One-Syllable Words: The longest one-syllable words are nine letters long. Examples include screeched, scratched, and stretched. Encourage students to find, record, and learn to read "really big" one syllable words.

Words have one or more parts that we can hear as we say them. We can tap our finger, clap our hands, or beat a rhythm stick to the single or multiple sounds of a word.

Numbers

one syllable
one
two
three
four
five
six
eight
nine
ten
twelve

two syllables
seven
thirteen
fourteen
fifteen
sixteen
eighteen
nineteen
twenty

three syllables
eleven
seventeen

Colors:

one syllable
red
blue
green
black
brown
pink
gray

2 syllables
orange
purple
yellow

three syllables
burgundy
magenta

Shapes:

one syllable
ball
box
cube
egg
heart
square

2 syllables
circle
ellipse
oval

3 syllables
octagon
rectangle
triangle

Cube Project: Use two sheets of 11" x 17" or 12" x 18" paper to make this free-standing, collapsible display. Write or glue examples of one-, two-, three-, and four-syllable words. See page 296.

3-D Variation Pictured: Fold the handwritten words or words from RWP into syllables. Glue the last syllable onto the project and leave the other folded syllables extended and dimensional.

Reinforce RWP (right): Clear tape can be used to reinforce words from RWP that have been folded to indicate syllables.

First, glue the word to the project. Second, place tape on the back of the extended syllable and then onto the display cube to make the fold strong and to keep the tab three dimensional.

One-Syllable Words

add	back	cab	dash	ear	game	hail
age	ball	came	date	earth	gas	ham
ail	bed	can	day	east	get	hand
aim	bee	cane	deep	eat	ghost	harp
air	beet	car	den	egg	girl	have
all	bench	care	dig	eight	give	heart
am	bent	case	dish	end	glass	heat
an	best	cast	do	even	go	help
and	bet	cat	dog	ever	goad	hill
ant	big	child	dose	eye	goes	hint
ape	bit	cob	dove	fast	got	hip
as	bite	come	down	fence	gray	hole
at	black	cone	dress	fish	great	home
ate	blue	cost	drink	five	green	hop
aunt	boat		drop	for	grin	hope
	box		dumb	ford	ground	hot
	boy		dust	fort	grow	house
	brain			four	guess	ill
	brown			freeze	gum	in
				frost	gust	is
				fun	gut	it
					guy	jaw
						jazz
						join
						jot
						jug
						jump
						June
						just
						kids
						kin

Accordion Pocket Foldable® (below): Use 11" x 17" index weight paper to make this classroom pocket accordion. Cut sentence strips in half and fold each half into eighths. Write words divided into syllables (or glue words from RWP that have been cut into syllables) on the sections of the sentence strip. Cut off any extra sections and save them for future words. See cards on page 191.

One-Syllable Words

lake	off	rain	sage	skate	tail	up
left	old	ran	sail	skin	take	us
less	on	rat	salt	skit	taste	use
like	one	raw	sand	skull	team	van
look	out	read	sane	sky	teem	vase
lope	own	real	sang	slow	tell	verse
lost	pan	red	sat	sneeze	ten	vest
love	past	rent	scan	snow	tent	view
low	pen	rest	school	so	test	vine
male	pet	rib	sea	some	that	voice
March	pig	rice	send	song	then	vote
May	pin	rich	sense	sow	there	wake
mean	pink	right	serve	spur	thing	want
my	plan	rim	set	square	think	war
near	plant	ring	sew	state	this	warm
need	play	rip	shade	stay	those	well
nest	plum	ripe	shall	still	three	west
next	plus	road	shark	stone	to	when
nice	port	roam	sheep	stop	toast	where
niece	post	roast	ship	stout	toe	which
nine	pot	rock	show	sun	toll	white
no	pull	row	side		too	who
nose	push	run	sign		town	why
not	put	rust	silk		toy	will
note	quail	rye	since		trait	win
	quake		sing		tray	wind
	queen		sir		treat	wipe
	quick		sit		tribe	wire
			six		trunk	wish
					trust	won
					turn	yell
					twelve	yes
					twin	your
					twist	zoo
					two	

Syllable Coverup Card:
Students begin with all tabs open. As a word is called, students cover the number that tells how many syllables they hear. The first student to cover all numbers "wins." See page 140.

The words on this page have two- or three-syllables. As you make flashcards for these words or say them aloud, note that every syllable has a vowel sound.

2	2	3	3
absent	July	animal	national
action	mammoth	another	newspaper
always	marker	apartment	November
answer	mother	banana	octagon
apple	mountain	battery	October
April	nation	beautiful	officer
aqua	nineteen	beginning	pentagon
army	ocean	bicycle	photograph
around	orange	cabinet	pineapple
August	oval	celery	primary
baby	over	chocolate	prisoner
balloon	paper	computer	rectangle
because	pencil	cucumber	remember
before	planet	December	scientists
between	plastic	different	seasonal
butter	pretzel	eleven	September
candy	purple	example	seventeen
carpet	quickly	exercise	surrounded
carry	river	fantastic	syllables
center	science	following	symmetry
children	seven	government	telephone
circle	sixteen	handwriting	together
contest	solid	hemisphere	triangle
country	summer	hospital	tricycle
crayon	thirteen	janitor	vacation
cricket	thunder	lavender	understand
danger	under	magenta	wilderness
dirty	very		
eighteen	water		
fifteen	winter		
flower	woman		
fourteen	yellow		
hamster			
insect			
island			

Folded Syllables: See page 193. Notice the use of ½" clear tape to reinforce this flimsy word to keep it dimensional.

The words on this page have four-, five-, and six-syllables. These are not words that would be commonly used with PreK-2 students, but young children love big words, and they like to tap or clap the syllables as the teacher reads them.

4

adventurous
American
amphibian
automobile
available
carnivorous
circumference
dictionary
discovery
experience
experiment
geography
horizontal
information
photocopy
supervisor
symmetrical
television
temperature
transportation
vaccination

5

abbreviation
administration
auditorium
communication
electricity
elementary
evaporation
hippopotamus
investigation
mathematical
metamorphosis
multiplication
nonrenewable
oceanography
photosynthesis
precipitation

6

autobiography
encyclopedia
extraterrestrial
overpopulation
paleontology
veterinarian

Gigantic Words (below): When making this set of folded syllable flashcards, we glued small sections of colored paper to the first and last tabs to make them look like miniature books. These "really big word books" are pictured in a small plastic storage container used as a bookcase.

Teacher Instructions:
Say the word slowly, but normally several times. Ask students to listen to the "big" word and say the word as you say the word again. Ask students to tap the sounds of the word with you. Say the word slowly emphasizing the syllables as students tap each syllable.

Make VKV syllable Flashcards (left) for "big" words encountered in literature, RWP, textbooks, videos, and daily life to increase auditory vocabulary and relate auditory vocabulary to written words. Students hear and use large words frequently -- *television*, *impossible*, *refrigerator*, *automobile*, *hippopotamus*, *cafeteria*, *Tyrannosaurus*, *gymnasium*, and others.

Syllables Double Letters Word List

Words with double consonants are usually divided between the consonants unless the letters are part of the base word, such as *teller*, *mooing*, or *grassy*.

ad-dress	fid-dle	nan-ny
ar-row	fol-low	nar-row
bal-let	gig-gle	par-rot
bal-loon	goril-la	peb-ble
ber-ry	ham-mer	pep-per
big-gest	hap-pen	pret-ty
blos-som	hap-py	pup-py
bun-ny	jel-ly	puz-zle
but-ton	ket-tle	rab-bit
can-non	kit-ten	rac-coon
car-rot	let-ter	rat-tle
cat-tle	let-tuce	scis-sors
cof-fee	lit-ter	spar-row
col-lege	lit-tle	sum-mer
com-ma	lob-by	sup-per
cot-ton	mam-mal	swim-mer
dad-dy	mam-moth	traf-fic
des-sert	mat-ter	up-per
din-ner	mid-dle	val-ley
dol-lar	mil-lion	waf-fle
drib-ble	mis-sile	wed-ding
driz-zle	mit-ten	whit-tle
	muf-fin	wig-gle
		win-ner
		zuc-chi-ni

Half Book Foldable® (below):
Write, or find a word in print, that has double consonants in the medial position. Glue the word across the fold of a half book. Position the word so that the double consonants are on opposite sides of the fold. See page 289.

Have students illustrate the word, or find an appropriate illustration or photograph and glue it onto the half book.

You can also take pictures with a digital camera and place them on your Foldables. Students love to see things from their world. For example: Take a photograph of a student giggling, student scissors, a classroom puzzle, a muffin, or a dessert served at lunch.

VKV® Rings: Cut a quarter sheet of paper into long fourths to make single flashcards (approximately 1" x 5½") and use them to make mini-double consonant cards. Punch holes and store cards on small rings.

Extension: These Foldable half books can be glued side by side to make one booklet with four pages. Add more side-by-side pages throughout the school term.

Make several VKV flashcards and use them to teach synonyms. It is not necessary to make flashcards for all the synonyms listed in this section; however, do make VKV flashcards for synonyms encountered in reading and writing throughout the year. Store synonyms flashcards in the *Synonyms* section of your VKV Flashcard Box, page 16.

Synonyms are words that have the same or almost the same meaning:

gift	*present*
fix	*repair*
sound	*noise*

Tabbed Project Foldable® (right): Use narrow strips of paper to make small matchbooks, glue them onto a sheet of paper, write synonyms under the tabs, and play synonym concentration. See page 305.

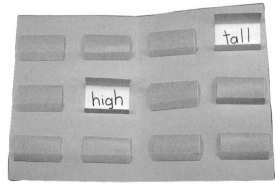

(VKV) Flashcard: Synonyms in Sentences

1. Write a sentence under the tab of a double flashcard as seen in the photographs below.
2. Select a word that could have a synonym tab. On the top tab, mark the location of the word that will have a synonym. (See first photograph below.)
3. Cut away the top tab leaving the small, marked tab to cover the word that will have a synonym.
4. Close the tab and write a synonym for the word on the top of the tab.
5. Read the sentence with one word and then the other. Explain how they are alike. List other synonyms on the back of the flashcard.

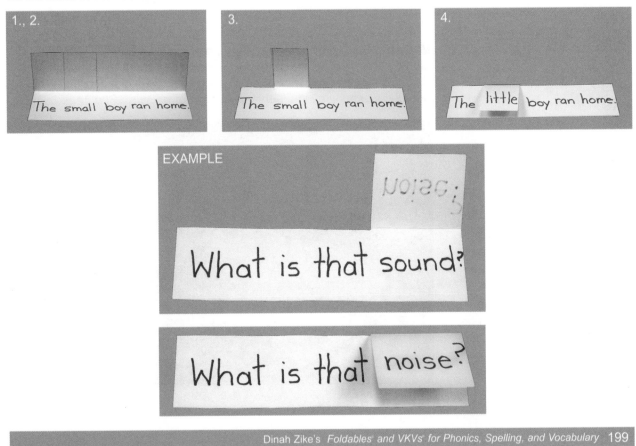

Synonyms Word List

Synonyms have the same meaning, or nearly the same meaning, as another word.

add	increase	make	build
after	following	name	title
all	every	near	close
angry	upset	part	piece
ask	question	place	put
begin	start	present	gift
below	under	rear	back
car	automobile	right	correct
close	near	salary	pay
divide	separate	sound	noise
eat	dine	start	begin
end	finish	stop	halt
find	discover	tale	story
fix	repair	tall	high
give	donate	turn	twist
go	leave	walk	stroll
happy	glad	world	earth
hard	difficult	wrong	incorrect
help	aid		
huge	giant		
hurry	rush		
large	big		
late	tardy		
like	enjoy		
line	mark		
little	small		
look	see		

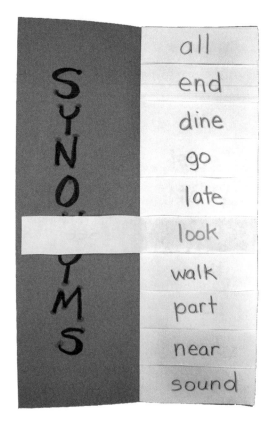

Multi-Tab Foldable® (above): Write words on the front tabs of a multi-tab Foldable, and write synonyms for the words under the tabs. Students might write synonyms on one side of the inside tab and use one of the synonyms in a sentence on the other side. See page 308.

Sentence Strip Synonyms:
Sentence strip holders can be used to sort, match, and display synonym flashcards.
See page 306.

VKV Foldable® Flashcard: **Name a Synonym**

1. Close a double flashcard, then fold it in half.
2. Cut along the top middle fold line. Do NOT cut the back tab.
3. Cut away the top left rectangle.
4. Write a word on the remaining single tab to the left.
5. Write a synonym or multiple synonyms of the word under the right tab.
6. Students look at the left word, independently try to determine a synonym for the word, and then look under the right tab to read a synonym and see if the word they guessed is listed. Explain that the word or words under the tab might not be the only synonyms for the given word.   For younger students, use only the most common synonym. For older or more advanced students, write several synonyms.

VKV Flashcard: **Synonym Rings**

1. Fold a single flashcard in half.
2. Write a word on one side and it's synonym (or multiple synonyms) on the other.
3. For younger students or ELL students, include pictures when appropriate.
4. Punch holes and store cards on a ring. Students read the cards of one color and try to determine their synonyms. Then students read the cards from the opposite direction, reading the cards of the second color, and try to determine their synonyms.

For younger students, use only the most common synonym. For older or more advanced students, write several synonyms on the back of the word cards.

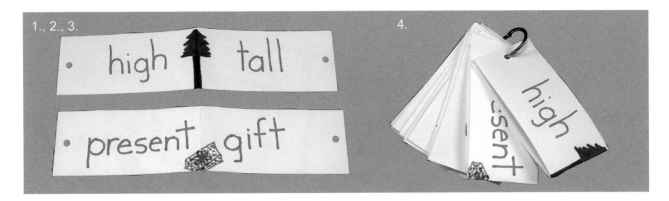

In Pre-Kindergarten, Kindergarten and first grade classrooms, color, shape, and number words are spoken, written, and read frequently. Students will also be exposed to numerous terms that denote time -- seasons, months, weeks, days, hours. Make some of the following Foldable activities, and use them to collect and record frequently used terms and to immerse students in relevant print.

Foldable® Pockets: Colors, Numbers, Shapes, Vowels

1. Make numerous two-pocket Foldables and glue them side by side to make a multi-pocket activity to introduce and reinforce color vocabulary terms. (See instructions on page 291.)
2. Label the pockets with the names of colors to be observed.
3. Collect magazine pictures, student-colored pictures, and fabric samples that illustrate each color, and sort the examples into the appropriate pockets.

Variation: Use the above Foldable activity for numbers 1-10, shapes, vowel sounds and example words.

Four-Door Display (right):
Use to collect physical objects and/or the quarter sheet study cards above. See page 303.

Alternate: Display is labeled "Two", and two objects are displayed within.

Pictured (right): Display is labeled "Blue," and blue objects are displayed within.

Vocabulary

Foldable® Pyramid:
1. Use a sheet of poster board to make the pyramid in the photo to the right. See instructions on page 294 of this book.
2. Write the primary color words and/or glue examples of the primary colors on the three sides of the pyramid -- *red, yellow, blue*.
3. Collect and glue pictures and objects that illustrate these color words on the appropriate sides of the pyramid.
Variation Pictured: Glue the secondary colors formed by mixing the primary colors over the folds.

Venn-Diagram Foldable® (right):
Use this three-tab Foldable to illustrate what happens when colors are mixed.

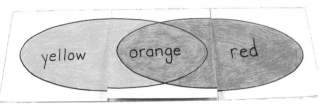

       yellow + red = orange
       yellow + blue = green
       red + blue = purple
       black + white = gray
       red + white = pink

Gross Motor Variation: Use butcher paper to make a giant Venn diagram. Guide students as they use fingerpaints to illustrate what happens when colors are mixed.

Four-Door Foldables® (below): Use 11" x 17" or 12" x 18" paper to make a four-door Foldable and use it to collect examples of letters, numbers, colors, shapes, food, body parts, seasons, and other vocabulary enhancing activities. See page 299.

Daddy got three tomato plants.

They are very small.

When they are big, they will grow red tomatoes.

We will eat the red tomatoes.

red
big
tomato
tomatoes
plants

Large Top-Tab Foldables® (above and below): Make top-tab Foldables to focus on common vocabulary terms. Students help determine vocabulary words they want to know. These words are typed in a large font by the teacher (above right). Have students dictate sentences using the words. These can also be typed by the teacher. Print the words and sentences, and glue them on the appropriate page of the Top-Tab Book. Students read the books and add words from RWP to the pages. See pages 141 and 298.

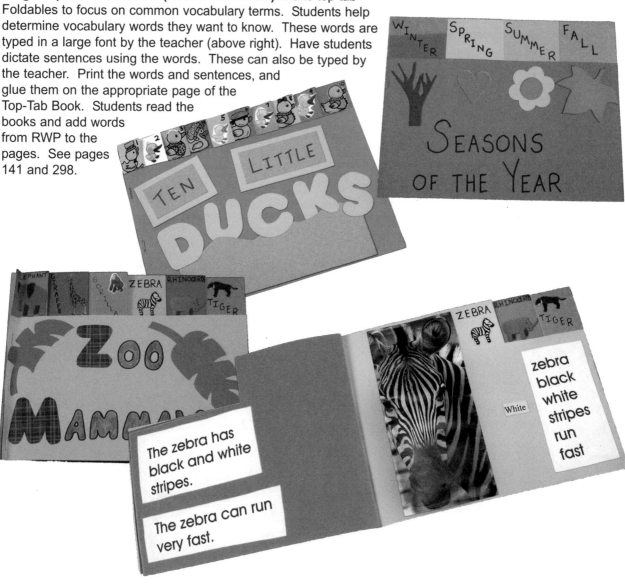

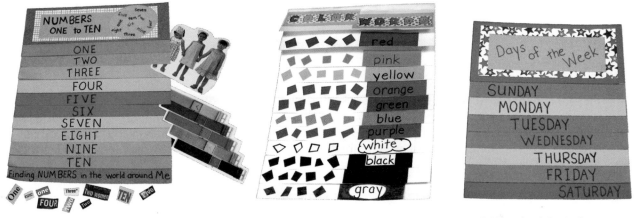

Foldable using 6 sheets of paper.

Foldable using 6 sheets of paper.

Folding using 4 sheets of paper.

Layered Foldables® (above and below): These versatile Foldables can be made student-size or bulletin board-size depending on the paper used. They are perfect for presenting main ideas and supporting facts, sequencing activities, collecting information for review or immersion, illustrating before and after, and presenting new vocabulary terms. Use pictures from worksheets, magazine pictures, original student art, student dictation, teacher-generated print, and words from RWP under the tabs. See page 295.

Foldable using 3 sheets of paper.

Foldable using 3 sheets of paper.

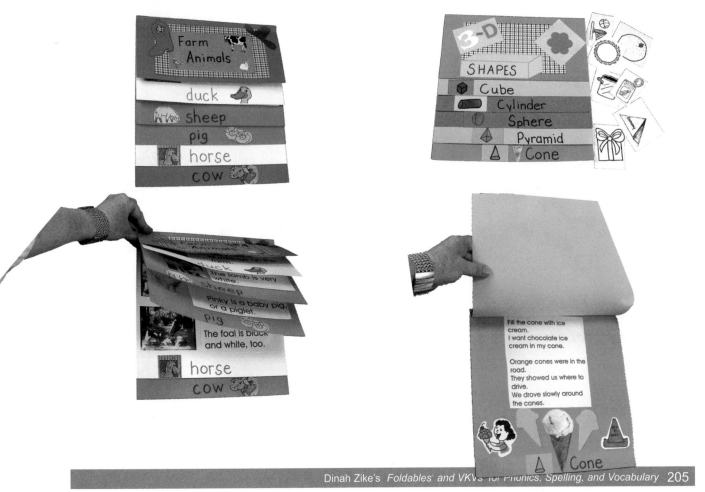

Pop-Up Books (below):

Use 8½" x 11" copy paper or 9" x 12" art paper to make the books photographed on these two pages. Make as many pages as needed for the pop-up booklet and glue them side by side. Use clothespins to help hold the pages together until dry. See instructions on page 299.

Notes From Dinah: I have saying for pop-up books that students hear so often during the school year that they repeat it with me as they make their own pop-ups. It goes like this: "Always cut on a fold, never glue on a fold." To make a tab pop-up, students have to cut the tab on a fold line. When gluing closed pop-up pages side by side, students never put glue on the folded/cut edge or it might glue the tab and prevent it from popping up.

Students love commercially published pop-up books and they are surprised at how easy they are to make. I make pop-up books while students are gathered around my chair. They observe the process numerous times and enjoy watching me make the class pop-up book before they try to make their own books.

This is also one of the first books I teach parents to make with their children. Parents can make pop-up books to commemorate a family vacation, a child's first years, a special occasion, and other important family events. Parents can help students learn concepts they are having difficulty with by making things "pop." For example, a student who is having difficulty identifying colors might benefit from the pop-up book pictured below. This book was made by a parent, and it is a beautiful example of how a parent might make a fun teaching aid for their child.

Vocabulary Cover-Up: Use 12" x 12" scrapbook paper or cut a sheet of 12" x 17" paper to form a 12" square. See photographs and instructions on page 140. Write 12 vocabulary words under the tabs. Begin the activity by opening all tabs. When students hear a word that they have on their card, they cover the word by closing the tab over the word. The students try to cover all words on their vocabulary card.

Pop-Up Pets: See information on the preceding page.

Foldable® Bound Book Journals: In the primary grades, some words are spoken, written, and read more frequently than others. Make some of the following Foldable journals to help collect and record these words when they are encountered in reading and writing. Depending on the age and gross-motor abilities of students, the following Foldables can be made either small (using 8½" x 11" paper) by/for each individual student, or they can be made large (using chart paper or art paper) and used by the class as a classroom vocabulary study aid.

Student- and Parent-Made Journals: Use 11" x 17" or 12" x 18" paper to make the journals pictured below. These are journals that parents can make with their children during summer months, helping to prepare them for a new school year. See page 290 for instructions.

Technology and Print: Technology can be highly motivational! Students love to send and receive e-mail. Students learn letters to form words and type messages to friends and family. They enjoy reading messages they receive from others. In the parent-made book below, relatives were encouraged to send e-mails to the children in the family, and the e-mails were placed in a journal for the children to read.

Teachers, take advantage of this love of technology by frequently incorporating teacher- and student-computer generated print into primary classrooms.

Establish an e-mail "pen pal" link with another classroom. Make a large journal using at least 10 sheets of construction paper. Place a copy of a "sent" e-mail to the left and a copy of the e-mail "received" to the right. Encourage students to read the e-mails and think about ways to respond.

Foldable® Bound Book Journals:

Use four sheets of 11" x 17" or 12" x 18" paper to make this journal. Young children love to see pictures of themselves and they love to "read" about their life. This beautiful Foldable scrapbook was made by a parent. See page 290.

Foldable® Cube:
Use Foldable Cubes for seasons, numbers, shapes, colors, vowels, consonants, and more. Also see pages 43 and 193 for other examples of display cubes in use, and page 296 for instructions.

Fold and Store: Remember, this display cube folds flat and can be "read" like a book. This also allows it to be stored in a file drawer or unit box.

A Year-Long Project: Use two sheets of 11" x 17" or 12" x 18" paper and make a Foldable cube display that can be used throughout the school year to collect words, review concepts, sequence steps, and stimulate discussion and writing about the four seasons. When not in use the cube can be stored in a file or in a large cereal box storage container labeled *Seasons*. Other Foldables and VKVs that relate to seasons could also be stored in the box. See page 32.

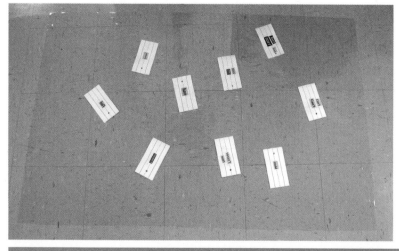

Clear Vinyl Vocabulary Twister:
Place VKV or quarter-sheet flashcards under a two-yard length of clear vinyl and play Twister. For example, a student might be told to place left hand on the contraction "didn't" and right foot on the contraction "haven't." Students take turns "calling" and "twisting." See photographs on page 144.

In the primary grades, some words are spoken, written, and read more frequently than others. Make some of the following VKV activities to help collect and record these words when they are encountered in reading and writing activities.

VKV Flashcards: Word Steps

1. Fold a triple flashcard into fourths.
2. Cut off two of the top fourths, one of the middle fourths, and none of the last section of fourths.
3. Write a two-letter word on the top step.
Write a three-letter word on the middle step. Write a four-letter word on the bottom step.
4. Fold and refold the three sections forward and backward, vertically and horizontally, to alternately view the words or the letters that form the words. See photos below.

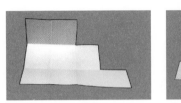
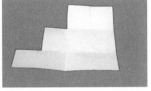

Example Word Steps: Initial consonants (onsets, left) or words in which *y* sounds like a long vowel (right).

do	my
did	buy
door	many

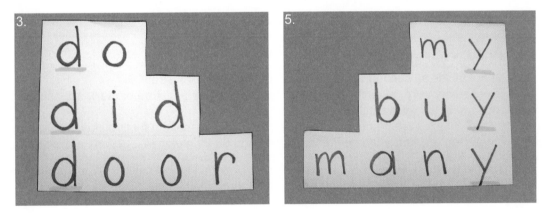

Number Word Steps:

- Fold a sheet of chart paper into tenths along both the long and short axis.
- Cut off 9 of the first row tabs, 8 of the second row, tabs, seven of the third row tabs, etc.
  Do not cut the bottom row, leaving 10 squares.
- Show one object in the single section.
- Show two objects on the second section.
- Continue until there are ten objects on the last tab.

Color Word Steps:

- Write color words on the steps and color the steps to match the featured words -- red (three letters), blue (four letters), green (five letters), yellow (six letters).

Two-Pocket Foldable® for Collecting Vocabulary Cards:

1. Make a two-pocket Foldable. See page 291 of this book for instructions.
2. Label one pocket Vocabulary Terms I Know and label the other pocket, Vocabulary Terms I Need to Know.
3. Students move vocabulary cards from the "Need to Know" pocket to the "Know" pocket as the words are mastered.

Variations: Label the pockets Easy Words and Hard Words.
Make a three-pocket Foldable and use it to collect words that are the following:
  -Too Easy
  -Just Right
  -Too Hard

Two-Tab Foldable® Vocabulary "Books":

1. Make two-tab Foldables as needed. See page 291 of this book for instructions.
2. Write a new vocabulary word on each tab. Define the word, place a picture of the word, and/or use the word in a sentence under the word's tab.
3. As more two-tab Foldables are made, glue them (side by side) to make a multi-tabbed vocabulary booklet that contains new and previously learned terms. See page 68 for gluing instructions and photographs.

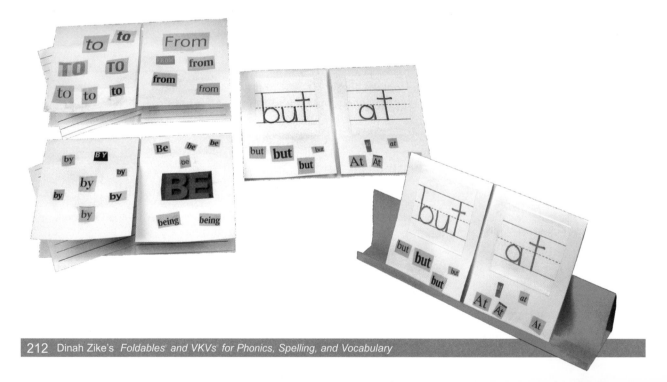

Vocabulary Foldables®

Multi-Tab Foldables® for Vocabulary:

1. Make a Foldable with tabs. See pages 294, 295, 308.
2. On the front tabs do any of the following:
    - Write a vocabulary term.
    - Glue terms cut from RWP.
    - Glue a picture representation of the term.
    - Glue a photograph of something representing the term.

3. Depending on what was placed on the front tabs, place any of the following under the word tabs:
    - Glue or draw a picture of the word.
    - Write the definition of the word.
    - Use a dictionary to determine and write the part of speech, the proper pronunciation, multiple definitions.
    - Use the word in a simple sentence.
    - Write a synonym or an antonym for the term.
    - Write the singular or plural form of a noun, or past or present form of a verb.

Note From Dinah: I can not stress enough how important I think it is to use photographs of signs and print from the student's world. I find using real world print (RWP) in in the classroom turns students, the teacher, and parents into word detectives in and out of class. I now find it difficult to read a newspaper or magazine without a pair of scissors in hand.

Mini-Book Library of Colors, Numbers, Shapes (right): To make the miniature books pictured, fold and cut a sheet of 8½" x 11" photocopy paper into eighths. Fold the eight sections in half like hamburgers. Staple twice along the inside fold line. (This will place the sharp, claw ends of the staples along the outside fold and they will be covered by the book cover glued around the book.) This results in a 32-page mini-book with 30 pages that can be filled with print (a cover will be glued to the outside first and last pages). See page 307.

Cut a sheet of 9" x 12" art paper into eighths. Fold one of the eight pieces of art paper in half and glue it around the mini-book. Since the art paper is glued to the copy paper it makes the book cover extra thick.

Concentration with Matchbook Foldables® (below): Use a sheet of 11" x 17" or 12" x 18" paper to make the base of this concentration game. (Index weight paper or card stock makes a sturdier game board.) Use narrow strips of paper to make eighteen small matchbooks. Glue them on the base as seen in the photographs below. Select nine words. Each word will be used twice. Randomly write or glue each word pair under two tabs until all nine word pairs are hidden under the tabs. Students play concentration by opening and closing tabs trying to match the word pairs. See page 292.

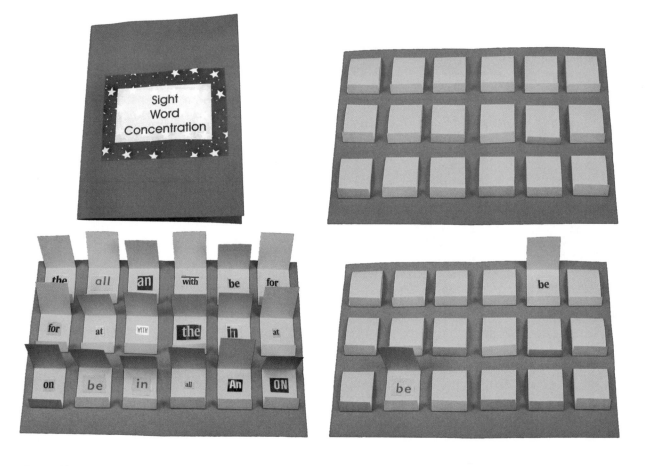

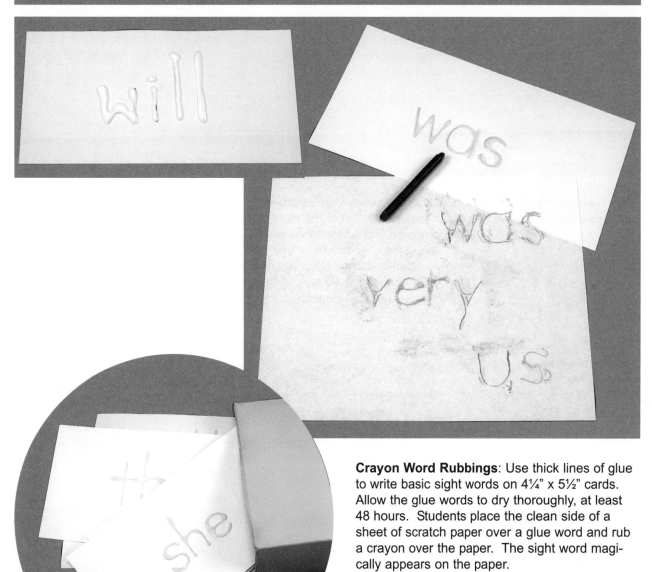

Crayon Word Rubbings: Use thick lines of glue to write basic sight words on 4¼" x 5½" cards. Allow the glue words to dry thoroughly, at least 48 hours. Students place the clean side of a sheet of scratch paper over a glue word and rub a crayon over the paper. The sight word magically appears on the paper.

Store glue sight word cards in cereal box storage containers. Label the box so students can find and use the cards in free time.

Other Vocabulary Enhancing Activities for Young Children:
  -Write vocabulary words in cornmeal or grits tubs. See photograph and recipe on page 85 and 129.
  -Write vocabulary words in colored glue, allow it to dry, and have students trace the word with a finger while saying it. See page 129.
  -Play Twist and Turn with sight words -- left hand on "with," right hand on "come," etc. See page 144 for photographs.

The following word list is a compilation of words based upon research by Fry and Sakiey (1979); Fry (1998, 2000); and Dolch (1948). These word lists are invaluable to the primary teacher and the teacher of ESL/ELL students. During my years of teaching, I meshed these lists, and taught Fry and Dolch words at the same time.

Key: F-D/100 = the word is one of the top 100 most frequently used words (1-100) in both Fry and Dolch lists.

F/200 = the word is one of the top 200 (101-200) most commonly used words in Fry's *Instant Words*, but is not found in the Dolch 220 Word List.

F/300; D/200 = the word is one of the top 300 (201-300) most commonly used Fry Instant Words, and in the top 200 (101-200) Dolch words.

100+ Matchbook Flashcards: Look for the yellow cards pictured on this page and along the bottom of the next three pages. These flashcards feature the 100 of the most common words outlined in the following list. The words on these flashcards were found in RWP, and glued on the front of the cards. Sentences or short paragraphs using the featured words were written under the tabs. Notice a hole was punched along the bottom tab of each matchbook so the flashcards could be stored on a ring. See these matchbooks used on a sentence strip bulletin board on page 31.

Index Flashcards of common words.

The following word list is a compilation of words based upon research by Fry and Sakiey (1979); Fry, Kress, and Fountoukidis (2000); and Dolch (1948).

100 = 1-100 common words
200 = 101-200 common words
300 = 201-300 common words

F = Word is found in the first 300 words of Fry's *Instant Words*..
D = Word is found in the Dolch 220 Word List.

a F-D/100	began F/300	could F-D/100	father F/300	hard F/300
about F-D/100	begin F/300	country F/300	feet F/300	has F-100; D/200
above F/300	being F/300	cut F/300; D/200	few F/300	have F-D/100
add F/300	below F/300	day F/100	find F-100; D/200	he F-D/100
after F-D/200	best D/220	did F-D/100	first F-100; D/200	head F/300
again F-D/200	better D/200	different F/200	five D/200	hear F/300
air F/200	between F/300	do F-D/100	fly F/300; D/200	help F-D/200
all F-D/100	big F/200; D/100	does F-D/200	food F/300	her F-D/100
almost F/300	black D/200	done D/200	follow F/200	here F-D/200
along F/300	blue D/100	don't F/300; D/100	for F-D/100	high F/300
also F/200	book F/300	down F-D/100	found F-D/200	him F-D/100
always F/300; D/200	both F/300; D/200	draw D/220	four F/300; D/100	his F-D/100
am D/200	boy F/200	drink D/200	from F-D/100	hold D/220
an F-D/100	bring D/200	each F/100	full 300 D/200	home F/200
and F-D/100	brown D/200	earth F/300	funny 300 D/200	hot D/220
animal F/200	but F-D/100	eat F/300; D/200	gave 300 D/200	house F/200
another F/200	buy D/200	eight 300 D/200	get F-D/100	how F-D/100
answer F/200	by F/100; D/200	end F/200	girl F/300	hurt D/100
any F/200; D/100	call F-D/100	enough F/300	give F-D/200	I F-D/100
are F-D/100	came F/200; D/100	even F/200	go F-D/100	idea F/300
around F/200; D/100	can F-D/100	every F/300; D/100	going D/200	if F-D/100
as F-D/100	car F/300	example F/300	goes F/300; D/200	important F/300
ask F/200; D/100	carry F/300; D/200	eye F/300	good F/200; D/100	in F-D/100
at F-D/100	change F/200	face F/300	got F/300; D/100	into F-D/100
ate 300 D/200	children F/300	fall D/200	great F/200	is F-D/100
away F-D/200	city F/300	family F/300	green D/100	it F-D/100
back F/200	clean D/220	far F/300; D/220	group F/300	its F-D/100
be F-D/100	close F/300	farm F/200	grow F/300; D/220	it's F/300
because F-D/200	cold D/200		had D/100	
been F-100; D/200	color F/300		hand F/200	
before F-D/200	come F-D/100			

The following word list is a compilation of words based upon research by Fry and Sakiey (1979); Fry, Kress, and Fountoukidis (2000); and Dr. E. W. Dolch.

100 = 1-100 most common words
200 = 101-200 most common words
300 = 201-300 most common words

F = Word is found in the first 300 words of Fry's *Instant Words*..
D = Word is found in the Dolch 220 Word List.

jump D/100	made F/100; D/100	never F/300; D/200	over F-200; D/100	ride D/100
just F/200; D/100	make F/100; D/200	new F-D/200	own F/300; D/200	right F/200; D/100
keep F/300; D/200	man F/200	next F/300	page F/200	river F/300
kind F-D/200	many F/100; D/220	no F-D/100	paper F/300	round D/200
know F/200; D/100	may F-D/100	not F-D/100	part F-100	run F/300; D/200
land F/200	me F/200; D/100	now F-D/100	people F/100	said F-D/100
large F/200	mean F/200	number F/100	pick D/100	same F/200
last F/300	men F-D/200	of F-D/100	picture F/200	saw F/300; D/200
late F/300	might F/300	off F-D/200	place F/200	say F-D/200
laugh D/220	miss F/300	often F/300	plant F/300	school F/300
learn F/200	more F/100	oil F/100	play F-D/200	sea F/300
leave F/300	most F/200	old F-D/200	please D/220	second F/300
let F/300; D/200	mother F/200	on F-D/100	point F/200	see F-D/100
letter F/200	mountain F/300	once F/300; D/200	present 200	seem F/300
life F/300	move F/200	one F-D/100	pretty 200 D/100	
light F/300; D/100	much F-D/200	only F-D/200	pull D/100	
like F-D/100	must F-D/200	open F/300; D/200	put F/200; D/100	
line F/200	my F-D/100	or F/100; D/200	ran D/200	
list F/300	myself 300 D/100	other F/100	read D/200	
little F/200; D/100	name F-D/200	our F-D/200	really F/300	
live F/200; D/220	near F/300	out F-D/100	red D/100	
long F-D/100	need F/200			
look F-D/100				

The following word list is a compilation of words based upon research by Fry and Sakiey (1979); Fry, Kress, and Fountoukidis (2000); and Dr. E. W. Dolch.

100 = 1-100 most common words
200 = 101-200 most common words
300 = 201-300 most common words

F = Word is found in the first 300 words of Fry's *Instant Words..*
D = Word is found in the Dolch 220 Word List.

sentence F/200	spell F/200	think F-D/200	very F/200; D/100	why F-D/200
set F/200	start F/300; D/200	this F-D/100	walk F/300; D/200	will F-D/100
seven 300 D/200	state F/300	those F/300; D/200	want F/200; D/100	wish 200 D/220
shall 200 D/220	still F/200	thought F/300	warm D/200	with F-D/100
she F-D/100	stop F/300; D/200	three F-D/200	was F-D/100	without F/300
should F/200	story F/300	through F/200	wash D/220	word F/100
show F/200; D/220	study F/200	time F/100	watch F/300	world F/200
side F/300	such F-D/200	to F-D/100	water F-100	work F-D/200
sing D/200	take F-200; D100	today D/200	way F-100	would F-D/100
sit D/200	talk F/300	together F/300; D/220	we F-D/100	write F-100; D/200
six D/200	tell F-D/200	too F/200; D/100	well F-D/200	year F/200
sleep D/200	ten D/200	took F/300	went F/200; D/100	yellow D/200
small F-D/200	than F-D/100	tree F/300	were F-D/100	yes D/100
so F-D/100	thank D/220	try F-D/200	what F-D/100	you F-D/100
some F-D/100	that F-D/100	turn F/200	when F-D/100	young F/300
something F/300	the F-D/100	two F/100; D/200	where F/200; D/100	your F-D/100
sometimes F/300	their F/100; D/200	under F/300; D/200	which F/100; D/200	
song F/300	them F-D/100	until F/300	while F/300	
soon F/300; D/200	then F-D/100	up F-D/100	white F/300; D/200	
sound F/200	there F-D/100	upon 200 D/220	why F/200; D/100	
	these F/200; D/220	us F-D/200	with D/100	
	they F-D/100	use F/100; D/200	who F-100; D/200	
	thing F/200			

The five *vowels* are *a*, *e*, *i*, *o*, and *u*.
Usually vowels make two sounds -- *long* and *short*.

The letter *y* sometimes acts as a long or short vowel as found in the following words: *cry*, *by*, *myth*, *symbol*.
Some clusters of vowels and vowels combined with consonants can make vowel sounds.

The following clusters make long vowel sounds:

a =	*-ai-* in *maid*, *-ay* in *may*
e =	*-ea-* in *meat*
i =	*-igh* in *light*, *-ie* in *pie*
o =	*-oa-* in *boat*
u =	*-ue* in *blue*

The following clusters make short vowel sounds:

e =	*-ea-* in *bread*
i =	*-y-* in *myth*
o =	*-au-* in *caught*, *-ou-* in *thought*
u =	*-ou-* in *rough*, *tough*, *trouble*

Every syllable of a word has a vowel sound.

There are many vowel rules and exceptions to these rules, but two of the most common rules are listed below.

When a four-letter word (CVC*e*) ends in *e*, the *e* is silent and the vowel says its
name -- *cake*, *kite*, *late*, *note*.
When two vowels "go walking" the first "does the talking." This means the first vowel says its name, or is long -- *mean*, *loan*, *pain*. See page 262 for exceptions.

Vowel diphthongs, written as two vowels or one vowel and a consonant, make a unique sound. Common diphthongs include the following: *-oi*, *-oy*, *-ow*, *-ou*, *-aw*.

When vowels are grouped with an *r* the vowel sound is changed and the new sound is said to be *r controlled* -- *star*, *her*, *hire*, *horse*, *turn*.

Look for the following complex vowel patterns and note how they relate to the other letters surrounding them:

-ai- in *aid*, *hair*, *wait*
-ay in *day*, *may*, *spray*
-ea- in *read* and *read*, or *meat* and *bread*
-ee- in *feel*, *green*, *sweet*, *week*
-ei- in *eight* and *receive*, or *neighbor* and *ceiling*
-ie in *pie* and *piece*, or *lie* and *thief*
-oa- in *coat*, *goat*, *float*
-oo- in *book* and *soon*, or *cook* and *balloon*
-ow in *slow* and *cow*, or *know* and *now*

Young writers and readers and ESL/ELL students need lots of experiences with words that contain complex vowel patterns to teach them to think about letter-sound relationships while looking at each word as a whole.

Make several VKV flashcards and use them to teach vowel sounds. With practice, most students will be able to transfer what they learn about vowels from using these VKV flashcards to other situations in which they encounter vowels. It is not necessary to make flashcards for all the vowel example words listed in this section; however, do make VKV flashcards for words that illustrate vowel sounds encountered in reading and writing throughout the year. Store the vowel flashcards in the *Vowel* section of the VKV Flashcard Box, page 16.

Research shows it is beneficial to teach vowel combinations as parts of words rather than teaching them in isolation. The VKV flashcards in this book do this.

VKV Flashcard: CVC Words

1. Fold a double flashcard into thirds.
2. Cut along the fold lines of the top section. Do NOT cut the back section.
3. Write a CVC word under the three tabs.
4. Students can view and analyze the initial consonant, medial vowel, and final consonant separately. When all tabs are raised, students view the word as a whole.

Instructor: What sound does the initial consonant make? What sound does the final consonant make?
View the vowel only and predict what sound it will make.
What is the word?

Variation:

5. Cut away the top middle tab to bring attention to the medial vowel.
6. Students sound the vowel on the tab-less center section of the flashcard before lifting any of the tabs.
7. Students lift the first tab and sound the consonant with the medial vowel.
8. Students lift the last tab and sound all three letters to form the CVC word.

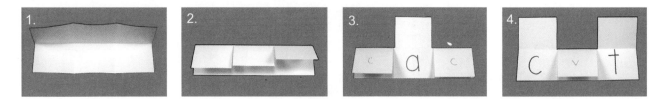

9. Add consonants to the front of the first and last tabs and the VKV will form four words.
Example below right: *hat, had, pat, pad.*

Four-Word CVC Flashcards: Sort numerous VKV flashcards by medial vowel sounds. What conclusions can students draw about the vowels in a CVC word?

Foldable® VKV® Flashcard: Nine-Word CVC and CVCC

1. Close a triple flashcard, then fold it into thirds.
2. Cut along the fold lines of the top and bottom sections. Do NOT cut the middle section. Cut away the top and bottom middle tabs.
3. Write a vowel in the middle of the "tab-less" center section of the flashcard.
4. Write three different consonants, blends, or digraphs on and under the left tabs, and three different consonants, blends, or digraphs on and under the right tabs.
5. Open and close the tabs to form nine different CVC/CVCC words that focus on the medial vowel.

Examples: Medial vowel	*a*	*a*	*e*
Initial C:	*m, p, r*	*t, l, r*	*t, d, b*
Final C or CC:	*t, n, w*	*g, n, p*	*nt, ll, n*
	mat, man, maw	*tag, tan, tap*	*tent, tell, ten*
	pat, pan, paw	*lag, lan, lap*	*dent, dell, den*
	rat, ran, raw	*rag, ran, rap*	*bent, bell, ben*

Note: Since this flashcard uses seven letters to form nine three-letter or four-letter words, there are a limited number of letter combinations that will form "real" words. Some phonics teachers use nonsense words and syllables to teach letter sounds and word formation. This fold is perfect for this use.

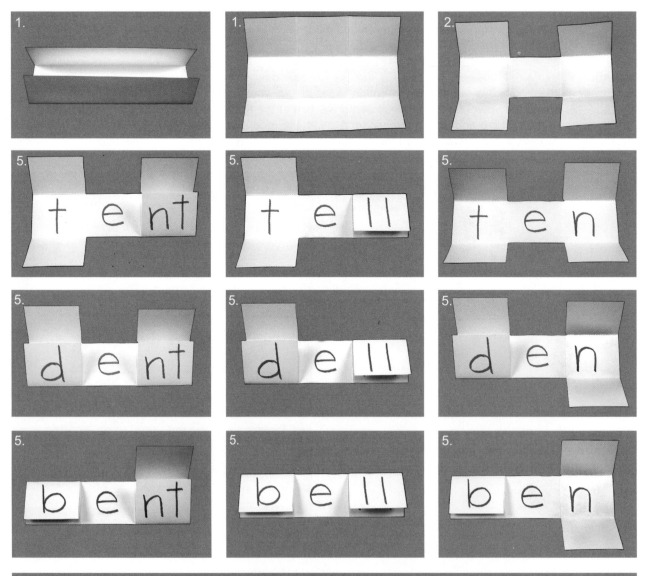

(VKV) Flashcard: CVCe Hidden Letters

1. Fold a double flashcard into fourths.
2. Cut along the fold lines of the top section. Do NOT cut the back section.
3. Write a consonant under the first tab.
4. Write a vowel under the second tab and a consonant under the third.
5. Write an *e* under the last tab.
6. If students need extra help, you can write clues on the front tabs:
   Front of the second tab: *Says its name.*
   Front of last tab: *Shhh.* or *Silent letter.*
7. Students raise the first tab and sound the consonant, raise the second tab and say the long name of the vowel, raise the third tab and sound the consonant, and raise the fourth tab without saying anything.

Note: Select words from the CVCe word list on the next page to make these flashcards, and/or use words encountered in reading, writing, and spelling.

Variation Pictured Below: Cut off the far right tab so the silent *e* is visible, giving students a clue as to the vowel sound.

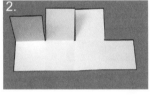

Six-Word Variation (right and below): Fold a triple flashcard into fifths. Cut off the right top and bottom four sections. Write three initial consonants on and under the three left tabs. Write a -VCe phonogram on the sections after the consonants. The far right tab will be blank.

With the far right tab is folded over to cover the *e*, three CVC words are formed with short medial vowel sounds.

With the far right tab is open, three CVCe words are formed. Students experience how the silent *e* changes the medial vowel to a long sound.

(VKV®) Flashcard: CVVC Words

1. Fold a double flashcard into fourths.
2. Cut away the top left rectangle. Do NOT cut the back section. Cut away the top right rectangle. Only the two center top rectangles will remain. Unlike other VKV cards, **do not cut these medial tabs apart**.
3. Write initial and ending consonants to the left and right of the medial tab.
4. Write two vowels under the medial tab.
5. Cover the vowels with the medial tab, then raise it to observe the two vowels ("two vowels walking").
6. Read the word by sounding the initial consonant, the single vowel sound, and the final consonant.
7. What usually happens when two vowels "go walking?"

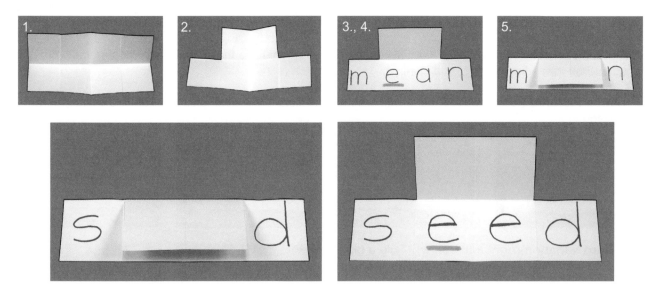

Variation: Cut the medial tabs apart so they can be raised and lowered separately to form three words with each VKV flashcard: one CVVC word and two CVC words.

Examples: Write *m* as the initial consonant and *d* as the final consonant. Write *a* under the first medial tab, and *i* under the second. Alternate raising the tabs and read *mad* and *mid*.
Raise both medial tabs and read *maid*.

Word List:
bead, bed, bad
bean, Ben, ban
beat, bet, bat
coat, cot, cat
laid, lad, lid
lead, led, lad
mean, men, man
meat, met, mat
pain, pan, pin
peat, pet, pat
maid, mad, mid
seat, set, sat
soap, sop, sap

VKV Flashcards: Change Medial Vowels

1. Fold a triple flashcard into thirds.
2. Cut along the fold lines of the top and bottom sections. Do NOT cut the middle section.
3. Cut off the top left and the bottom left sections.
4. Cut off the top right and bottom right sections.
5. Write an initial consonant on the left tab close to the middle section and write a final consonant on the right tab, close to the middle section.
6. Write a vowel on the inside center section of the flashcard. Close one tab and write another vowel. You can leave one tab blank, as illustrated below, or write another vowel on this tab to form three different words.

Initial and Final Consonant Focus with Two Medial Vowels (row a, below): With the blank medial tab in position, observe and sound the initial and final consonants. Raise the tab and read the CVC word formed. Change the medial tab so the second word is formed and repeat the process. After all tabs are opened, close the tabs and read the words again. **Three Different Medial Vowels (row b, below):** Make three CVC words by writing a short vowel on each of the three medial sections as illustrated below in row b.

Examples:

b_t, bet, bat, bit, but	h_m, ham, hem, him, hum	p_g, peg, pig, pug
c_b, cab, cob, cub	j_t, jet, jot, jut	r_g, rag, rig, rug
d_d, dad, did, dud	l_t, let, lit, lot	s_n, sin, son, sun
f_n, fan, fin, fun	m_p, map, mop	t_n, tan, ten, tin, ton
g_t, get, got, gut	n_t, net, not, nut	w_g, wag, wig

Variation: Write two vowels under each of the center tabs to form two words with the same initial and final consonants but different medial vowels.

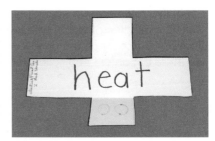

Six Examples: m _ _ t, meet, meat   f _ _ t, foot, feat, feet   r _ _ d, road, read, reed
          f _ _ l, foal, feel   b _ _ t, bait, beet, boat   s _ _ d, said, seed

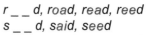

VKV® Flashcards: Medial Vowel Awareness

1. Cut a sentence strip into fourths, or use a single flashcard.
2. Write or glue a CVC word or a CVVC word from RWP in the middle of the card.
3. Fold the left and right edges of the flashcard around so that only the medial vowel or vowels can be seen.
4. Students can observe the medial vowel/vowels before adding the initial and final consonants.

See the RWP examples to the right and below.

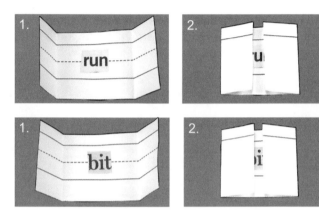

Foldable® Vowel Chart (right): The chart to the right was made using a sheet of 12" x 12" scrapbook paper. It was folded to form five columns. A 2" tab was folded to form a section for labeling the columns.

Label the columns with either long or short vowels. Collect examples of words with long or short vowels from RWP. Record examples of words encountered in literature or content subjects. See page 308.

When a one-syllable word ends in e, the e is silent and the vowel says its own name.

VKV® Flashcards: Short Vowels Become Long

1. Use a single flashcard or half of a sentence strip.
2. Select a word pair from the list on this page.
3. Write a CVC word to the left side of the flashcard. Illustrate the word to the far right if possible.
4. Bend the right edge of the flashcard over to cover the e and form a CVC word. Fold it in place.
5. Write an e on the top of this right tab. Write the e close to the edge of the tab.
6. Open and close the tab, alternately adding and removing the e, and read the short CVC word and the long vowel word which has a silent e.
7. **Variation**: write a CVCC word fold to cover the letter e.

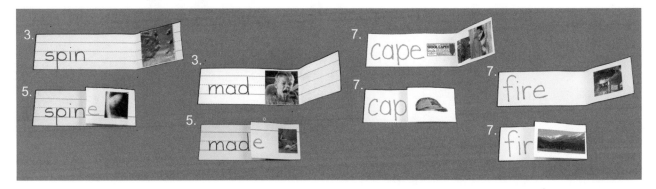

CVC/CVCe and CCVC/CCVCe Examples:

bad	bade	glob	globe	past	paste	sit	site
bar	bare	grim	grime	pin	pine	slid	slide
bit	bite	hat	hate	plan	plane	slop	slope
can	cane	hid	hide	pop	pope	spin	spine
cap	cape	hop	hope	rag	rage	stag	stage
cub	cube	hug	huge	rat	rate	star	stare
cut	cute	kit	kite	rid	ride	strip	stripe
dim	dime	mad	made	rip	ripe	tap	tape
din	dine	man	mane	rob	robe	tot	tote
fad	fade	mat	mate	rot	rote	tub	tube
fat	fate	mop	mope	sham	shame	twin	twine
fin	fine	nap	nape	shin	shine	win	wine
fir	fire	not	note				
gap	gape						

VKV Flashcards: Short Vowel to Long

1. Close a double flashcard, then fold it into fourths.
2. Cut off the top three (left) rectangles leaving the last (right) rectangle to act as a tab.
3. Write an *e* under the right tab, cover the *e* with the tab.
4. Write a CVC word to the left of the tab.
5. Read the CVC word and listen to the short vowel sound.
6. Open the tab to expose *e* and read the CVCe word formed. Note the long vowel sound.

Example: *cub, cube*
pin, pine

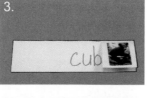

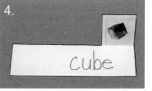

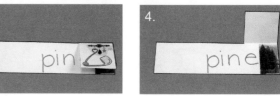

VKV Flashcards: Medial Phonograms

1. Write a word in the middle of a single flashcard.
2. Bend the right edge of the card around to cover the "silent e" and fold in place.
3. Open the right side. Fold the right edge around to cover the initial consonant.
4. When both tabs are folded the medial phonogram will show.
5. Open the left tab and read the CVC word.
6. Open the right tab and read the CVCe word.

Example: *id = rid, ride*   *in = pin, pine*

(VKV) Flashcards: Add a Medial Vowel

1. Fold a single flashcard in half.
2. With the card folded, make another fold about ½" from the center fold.
3. Open the card and write the two vowels of a CVVC word, centering each vowel over the fold lines to the left and right of the center fold. Do not write on the center fold.
4. Write initial and final consonants to the left and right of the vowels.
5. Pinch or paper clip the center folded section and fold it to the left and right to make two CVC words.
6. Stretch and flatten the flashcard completely and read the CVVC word.

(It will take practice to make this card work properly, but when it does it is very demonstrative and effective.)

Example: Write *e* and *a* on the left and right folds.
Write an *s* before the *e*.
Write a *t* after the *a*.
Open and close tabs to read *set* and *sat*.

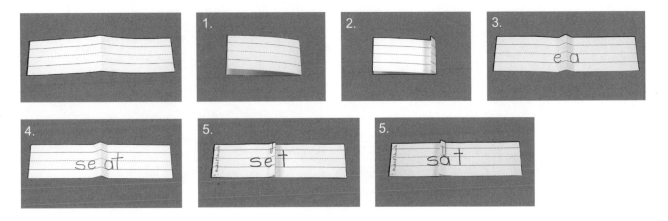

Other Examples:

beat, bet, bat
beet, bet
coat, cot, cat
feed, fed
lead, led, lad
laid, lad, lid
maid, mad, mid
meat, met, mat
road, rod, rad
raid, rad, rid
said, sad, sid
seat, set, sat

The following is a list of the 37 most frequently used *phonograms* (Wylie and Durrell, 1970). Note the most and least frequently used vowels in these 37 rimes. Observe how many of the vowels are long and how many are short.

a = *-ack, -ail, -ain, -ake, -ale, -ame, -an, -ank, -ap, -ash, -at, -ate, -aw, -ay*
e = *-eat, -ell, -est, -ice*
i = *-ick, -ide, -ight, -ill, -in, -ine, -ing, -ink, -ip, -it*
o = *-ock, -oke, -op, -ore, -ot*
u = *-uck, -ug, -ump, -unk*

The phonogram, or *rime*, is the part of a word that follows the initial sound (onset).

Note From Dinah: I was taught to make and use the flashcards pictured above in a college methods class in the early 1970's. I assume these cards had been used for many years before. Stapled flashcards were the inspiration for my VKVs. I wanted to make all phonics and grammar skills kinesthetic, and have every flashcard form two or more words that could be used to teach new skills or to review and apply previously learned skills.

Two-Pocket Foldable® for Collecting Vowels:

1. Make a two-pocket Foldable. See page 291 for instructions.
2. Label one pocket short *a* and label the other short *e*.
   - Make two more pockets and label them--short *i*, *o*, *u*, *y*.
3. Glue the pockets together (side by side) to make a six-pocket Foldable.
4. Use the pockets to collect and/or sort short vowel words. Teacher- or student-generated flashcards, RWP flashcards, and computer written word cards can be stored in the pockets.

Long Vowel Variation: Make this Foldable and use it to collect long vowel words.

Long and Short Vowel Pockets (pictured below): Make this Foldable with ten pockets. Each set of two pockets will be used to collect words with both the short and long vowel sound. When assembled, the book will alternately have short and long vowel pockets for the vowels -- *a*, *e*, *i*, *o*, *u*.

Two-Tab Foldable® Vocabulary Books:

1. Make a two-tab Foldable. See page 291 of this book for instructions.
2. Label one tab short *a* and label the other short *e*.
   - Make two more two-tab Foldables and label them--short *i*, *o*, *u*, *y*.
3. Glue the two-tab Foldables together (side-by-side) to make a six-tab Foldable.
4. Under the tabs, collect and/or list short vowel words.
   - Make this Foldable and use it to collect long vowel words.
   - Make this Foldable with ten tabs (five two-tab Foldables glued side by side) and use it for long and short vowel sounds.

Variation: Each set of two tabs can be used to collect words with both the short and long vowel sound. When assembled, the tabs will alternately be labeled with short and long vowels -- *a*, *e*, *i*, *o*, *u*.

Vowels Foldables®

Billboard Foldable®: Use five sheets of 8½" x 11" paper to make the five vowel cards used on this billboard Foldable. Glue the half sheets edge to edge on a sheet of butcher paper or poster board. When closed, vowel pictures are viewed. When opened sequentially, the letters *a*, *e*, *i*, *o*, and *u* can be seen. Collect examples of words that contain the different vowel sounds and glue them under the appropriate tabs. See page 305 for instructions on making a billboard Foldable, and see page 132 for a photo example of an A,B,C billboard. Use this Foldable for sequencing number words, story lines, events, and steps.

Vowel Pictures

Short *a*

Short *a*
Short *e*

Short *a*
Short *e*
Short *i*

Short *a*
Short *e*
Short *i*
Short *o*

Short *a*
Short *e*
Short *i*
Short *o*
Short *u*

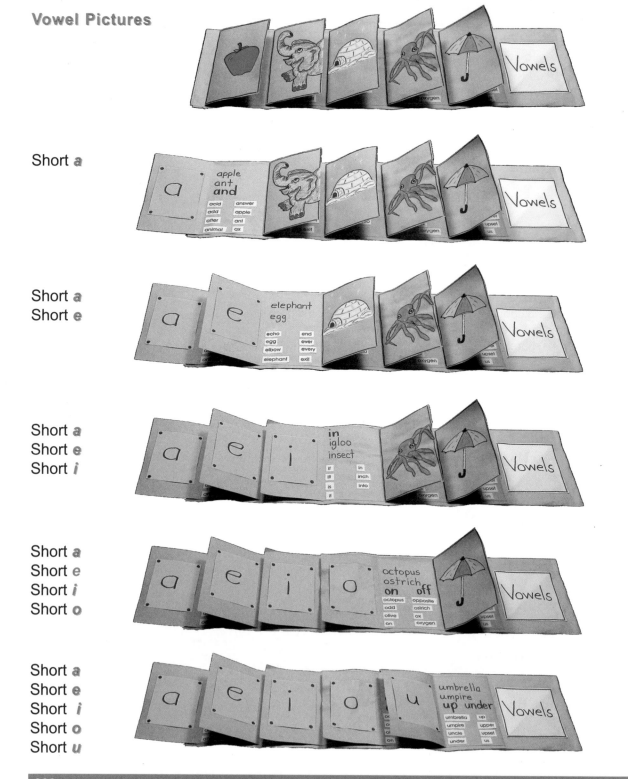

Sentence-Strip Holders and Flashcards (right): Use sturdy 11" x 17" paper or 12" x 18" paper to make these long sentence-strip holders. Cut sentence strips in half or use single-strip flashcards on the holders. You might choose to color code the flashcards and sentence-strip holders to correspond with specific vowel sounds. See page 306 for instructions.

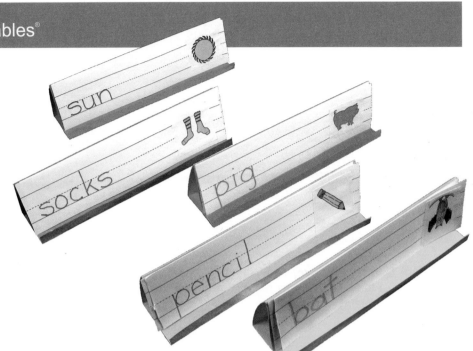

Mini-Book Library (left): Make miniature books for phonograms studied. Use them to collect words formed using the phonograms. The books pictured to the left are stored in a "bookscase" made from the bottom of a large cereal box. The covers of the booklets have been color coded to indicate the vowel sound within the phonogram. (See sentence strips above.) Yellow is used for long and short *a* sounds, blue for *e*, pink for *i*, green for *o*, and orange for *u*. See page 307.

Pop-Up Book (below): The book pictured below can grow as a class or an individual student activity. Add pages as vowels are studied. Collect and add words from RWP as students become familiar with vowel sounds. See page 299.

Four Door Displays (above) and Display Boxes (below): Use 12" x 12" scrapbook paper or 12" x 18" art paper to make the display cases pictured above and 12" x 12" paper to make the display boxes pictured below. These displays are great for collecting and sorting word cards and/or small VKV flashcards.

Top-Tab Foldable® (right): Use five sheets of 11" x 17" paper to make the Top-tab Foldable pictured to the right. Inside the tabbed book, collect and glue words from RWP; feature teacher-written, student-generated print. Glue quarter sheets of lined paper with student-written words and/or sentences, or write short stories on half sheets of lined paper and staple them into the book. See page 298 for top-tab instructions, and see page 141 for another Foldable example.

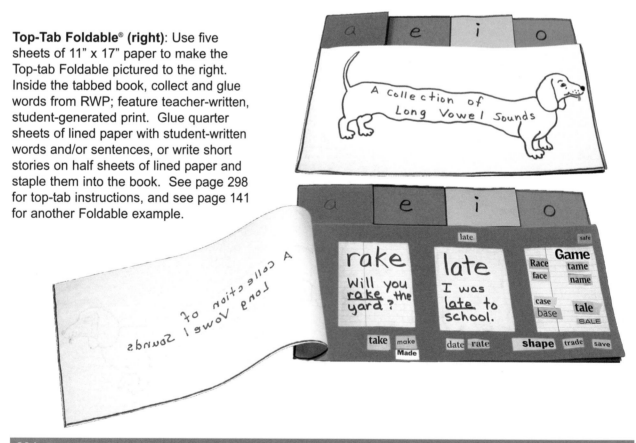

Five-Tab Foldable® (right): Use one sheet of 11" x 17" photocopy paper or 12" x 18" art paper to make the large five-tab vowel Foldable pictured. Use worksheet pictures, RWP, computer-generated words and/or sentences under the tabs. See page 301.

Variation: Make another five-tab Foldable and use it to collect long vowel words.

Foldable® Display Cube (below): Use two sheets of 11" x 17" or 12" x 18" paper to make the cube display case pictured below. Use it to collect examples of long *a*, *e*, *i*, and *o* words. See page 296. (Long *u* words had not been taught at the time this Foldable was made.)

Note: Foldable display cubes can be folded flat so students can easily write on or glue RWP to the sides. When folded, the display case can be used as a four-page booklet, and easily stored in a file cabinet. See page 296.

Initial

<u>a</u>balone
<u>a</u>cid
<u>a</u>dd
<u>a</u>djective
<u>a</u>dverb
<u>a</u>fter
<u>a</u>llergy
<u>a</u>nimal
<u>a</u>nswer
<u>a</u>ntelope
<u>a</u>pple
<u>a</u>steroid
<u>a</u>stronaut
<u>a</u>thlete
<u>a</u>x

a-e

ch<u>a</u>nce
d<u>a</u>nce
enh<u>a</u>nce
gl<u>a</u>nce
h<u>a</u>ve
l<u>a</u>nce
pr<u>a</u>nce

Bound Journal (above left) Picture Frame Foldable® (above): Make and use these Foldables to feature vowels. See page 303.

Top-Pocket Foldable®: Use 11" x 17" paper to make the top pocket pictured (right and below). Collect examples of long and short vowel sounds. VKV flashcards and/or quarter sheets of lined paper can be collected and stored in the top pocket. See page 310.

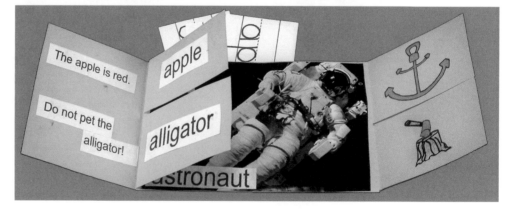

Note that all of these short *a* words are one syllable. Help students realize that words with only one vowel sound will be one syllable.

Miniature Book (above): The copy in the book above was dictated by students, written on a computer (using 7-point type) by the teacher, printed, cut, and glued into the booklet. Students use a magnifying glass to read the text. See page 307.

**Two-Pocket Foldable® (above) or Two-Tab Foldable®
(below)**: Make and use to collect examples of words that are formed using long and short vowel sounds, or phonograms with a featured vowel sound. See page 291.

Medial

back	gab	rack
bad	gag	raft
bag	gram	rag
ban	grand	ramp
band	had	ran
bat	hag	rap
black	ham	sack
blank	hand	sad
brand	has	sag
cab	hat	sand
camp	jab	sap
can	lack	scab
cash	lad	slab
cast	lamp	slam
cat	land	spat
crab	lap	stab
craft	last	stag
crash	mad	strap
dad	man	stamp
damp	mask	strand
draft	mast	tab
drag	mat	tact
drank	nag	tag
fact	nap	tan
fad	pact	tap
fan	pad	task
fast	pan	than
fat	past	that
flag	pat	track
flap	plan	tram
flat		tramp
		wrap
		zap

Phonograms: *-ace, -ade, -age, -ake, -ale, -ame, -ane, -ape, -are, -ase, -ate, -ave, -aze.*

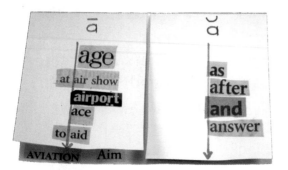

Two-Tab Foldable® (above), see page 291.

Envelope Foldables® (below): Make and use envelope Foldables with (top example) or without (bottom example) a window to view a title or main idea featured in the center of the manipulative. See page 297.

Initial a-	a-e	a-e
able	bake	(continued)
ace	bare	make
age	base	name
agent	blame	page
aid	brace	pale
ail	brake	paste
aim	brave	place
angel	cage	plane
ape	cake	quake
April	came	rage
apron	cane	rate
ate	cape	sale
aviary	care	same
	case	shade
	cave	shake
	chase	shame
	craze	snake
	date	stage
	daze	take
	fade	tale
	fate	tape
	frame	trade
	gate	vase
	grace	wage
	grade	wake
	grate	
	hate	
	lace	
	late	

Sometimes two vowels are combined to form one long vowel sound: b*ai*t, m*ay*, *ei*ght.

-ai-	-ai-	-ay	-ei-
	(continued)		
aid	paid	away	beige
air	pail	bay	eight
bail	pain	bray	freight
braid	paint	clay	geisha
brain	quail	crayon	lei (flowers)
chain	raid	day	neigh (sound)
detail	rain	gay	neighbor
fail	raise	gray	reign
fair	raisin	hay	rein
faith	sail	jay	reindeer
frail	snail	lay	sei whale
gain	stain	May	seine (net)
hail	straight	may	sleigh
hair	tail	pay	veil
jail	tailor	play	veiled
laid	trail	pray	vein
maid	train	ray	weigh
mail	wail	relay	weight
main	waist	say	
nail	wait	spray	
		stay	
		stray	
		tray	
		way	

Miniature Book (above): The copy in the book above was written on a computer using 7-point type, printed, cut and glued into the booklet. Students are encouraged to use a magnifying glass to read the text.

Two-Tab Foldable® (bottom left) and Sentence-Strip Foldable® (bottom right): Make and use to collect RWP and to provide opportunities for students to read the print in sentences they have helped generate.

The two-tab Foldable was made using 8½" x 11" photocopy paper, and the sentence strip Foldable was made using half sheets of copy paper, 8½" x 5½" in size.

Note the use of RWP in the form of photographs of highway signs and words collected from magazines and newspapers. Dictated sentences were printed, cut, and glued under the tabs.

Vowels Short *e*

Common short *e* phonograms include the following: -*ed*, -*eg*, -*en*, -*end*, -*ent*, -*ell*, -*ep*, -*ess*, -*est*, -*et*.

Initial e

<u>e</u>cho
<u>e</u>dge
<u>e</u>dit
<u>e</u>ducation
<u>e</u>gg
<u>e</u>lbow
<u>e</u>lephant
<u>e</u>levator
<u>e</u>lf
<u>e</u>lk
<u>e</u>lse
<u>e</u>mpty
<u>e</u>nd
<u>e</u>nemy
<u>e</u>nergy
<u>e</u>ngine
<u>e</u>njoy
<u>e</u>nter
<u>e</u>pic
<u>e</u>tch
<u>e</u>ver
<u>e</u>very
<u>e</u>xit
<u>e</u>xtra

Medial

b<u>e</u>d
b<u>e</u>g
b<u>e</u>ll
B<u>e</u>n
b<u>e</u>nd
b<u>e</u>nt
B<u>e</u>ss
b<u>e</u>st
b<u>e</u>t
bl<u>e</u>nd
bl<u>e</u>ss
bl<u>e</u>st
c<u>e</u>ll
c<u>e</u>nt
ch<u>e</u>ss
cr<u>e</u>st
d<u>e</u>ll
d<u>e</u>n
d<u>e</u>nt
dr<u>e</u>ss
dw<u>e</u>ll
f<u>e</u>ll
g<u>e</u>nt
g<u>e</u>t
gu<u>e</u>ss
gu<u>e</u>st

(continued)

h<u>e</u>n
j<u>e</u>ll
j<u>e</u>t
K<u>e</u>n
k<u>e</u>pt
l<u>e</u>d
l<u>e</u>ft
l<u>e</u>g
l<u>e</u>nd
l<u>e</u>ss
l<u>e</u>t
l<u>e</u>vel
m<u>e</u>n
m<u>e</u>nd
m<u>e</u>ss
m<u>e</u>t
N<u>e</u>d
N<u>e</u>ll
n<u>e</u>st
n<u>e</u>t
p<u>e</u>n
p<u>e</u>st
p<u>e</u>t
r<u>e</u>d
r<u>e</u>nt
r<u>e</u>st
s<u>e</u>ll

(continued)

s<u>e</u>nd
s<u>e</u>nt
s<u>e</u>t
sh<u>e</u>ll
sl<u>e</u>d
sm<u>e</u>ll
sp<u>e</u>ll
sp<u>e</u>nd
sw<u>e</u>ll
T<u>e</u>d
t<u>e</u>ll
t<u>e</u>n
t<u>e</u>nt
t<u>e</u>st
th<u>e</u>n
tr<u>e</u>nd
v<u>e</u>nt
v<u>e</u>st
v<u>e</u>t
w<u>e</u>d
w<u>e</u>ll
w<u>e</u>nt
w<u>e</u>st
w<u>e</u>t
wh<u>e</u>n
y<u>e</u>ll

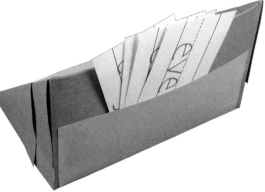

Four-Door Display with a Pocket (above): Make the above display using a sheet of 11" x 17" or 12" x 18" paper. See page 303.

Add a storage pocket for flashcards by gluing a 4" x 8" section of paper (as illustrated) or an envelope to the back of the display.

Two-Tab Bound Book (left): Five sheets of 8½" x 11" paper were used to make this 10-tab book. See page 291.

Sometimes two vowels are combined to form one short vowel sound: *lead*, *thread*, *weather*.

ea

bread
breath
dead
deaf
dread
feather
head
heaven
heavy
lead
leather
meadow
measure
pleasant
ready
spread
steady
swear
sweat
thread
threat
tread
treasure
wealth
weapon
wear
weather

e-e

(Difficult to spell: CVCCe spelling with short e medial sound)

dense
fence
tense

Bound Journal (above left) Picture Frame Foldable® (above right): Make and use these Foldables to collect words with long and short vowel sounds.

Add Word Tabs to any Foldable® (below): Use 2" x 2" sections of lined paper folded in half to make small word tabs. When the tab is closed, students can not see the word represented by the picture. Students say the word they think will be written under the tab, then they check their answer by opening the tab. This simple tab makes any word identification activity more interactive and provides a way in which students can check their own responses.

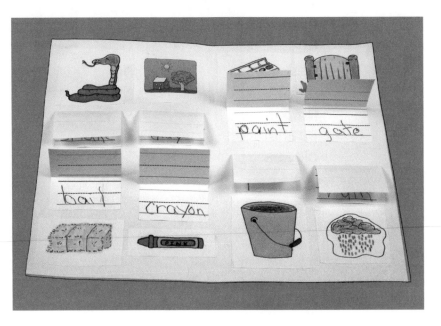

Vowels Long *e*

Sometimes two vowels are combined to form one long vowel sound -- *flea, leaf, key.*

Initial long e

eat
each
eager
eagle
eaglet
earring
ease
easel
east
easy
equal
even
evening
evil

Final long e

(open syllable rule/
end of word)

be
he
me
she

ea

beak
beat
clean
cream
deal
fear
flea
freak
gear
heal
heap
lead
leaf
leak
leap
meal
mean
meat
near
neat
pea
peace
peach
peanut
please

ea (continued)

read
sea
seat
steal
tea
teach
team
tease
veal
weak
weave
year
zeal

-ey

key
monkey
turkey
valley

-i

broccoli
confetti
spaghetti
taxi

Matchbook Foldable® (below top): Use one sheet of 11" x 17" paper for the base of the Foldable pictured below. Glue 18 small matchbooks onto the base. Use to collect long *e* words. Put pictures, definitions, or simple sentences under the tabs. See page 292.

Accordion Foldable® (below bottom): Use three sheets of 8½" x 11" paper to make the accordion Foldable pictured at the bottom of this page. Leave the tab on the last section so more pages can be added in the future. See page 300.

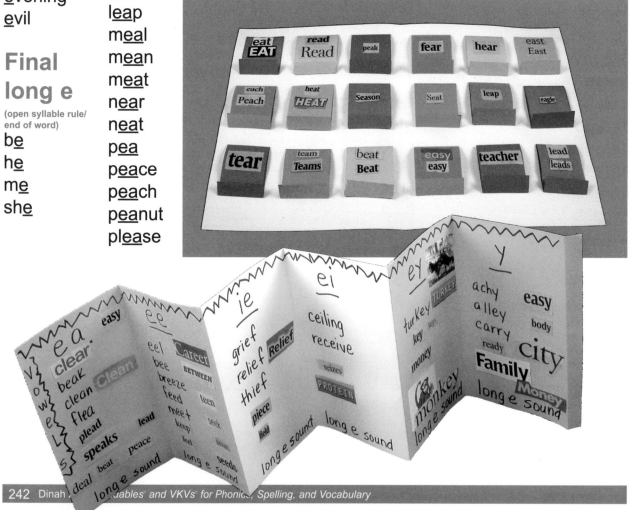

Vowels Long *e*

Sometimes two vowels are combined to form one long vowel sound -- *beef, chief, happy*.

ee	ee (continued)	-ei	-ie	-y	-y
b**ee**	s**ee**	c**ei**ling	bel**ie**ve	an**y**	happ**y**
b**ee**f	s**ee**d	conc**ei**t	br**ie**f	bab**y**	hurr**y**
b**ee**tle	s**ee**k	dec**ei**t*	ch**ie**f	budd**y**	jur**y**
bl**ee**d	s**ee**m	dec**ei**ve	gr**ie**f	bur**y**	Larr**y**
br**ee**ze	sh**ee**t	k**ei**ster	n**ie**ce	carr**y**	marr**y**
ch**ee**k	sl**ee**t	(buttocks)	p**ie**ce	cit**y**	onl**y**
coff**ee**	sn**ee**ze	l**ei**sure	th**ie**f	dair**y**	quickl**y**
cr**ee**k	st**ee**l	rec**ei**ve		dut**y**	read**y**
cr**ee**p	str**ee**t	s**ei**ze		earl**y**	reall**y**
d**ee**p	sw**ee**p	s**ei**zure		empt**y**	scar**y**
degr**ee**	sw**ee**t	w**ei**r (dam)		ever**y**	starr**y**
eel	t**ee**	w**ei**rd		fair**y**	stead**y**
f**ee**d	t**ee**n	z**ei**n		famil**y**	tall**y**
f**ee**l	thr**ee**	(protein powder)		furr**y**	ver**y**
f**ee**t	toff**ee**				worr**y**
fl**ee**	tr**ee**				
fl**ee**t	w**ee**d				
fr**ee**ze	w**ee**k				
gr**ee**n	wh**ee**l				
gr**ee**t					
h**ee**l					
j**ee**r					
k**ee**p					
kn**ee**					
kn**ee**l					
l**ee**ch					
l**ee**k					
m**ee**k					
m**ee**t					
n**ee**d					
n**ee**dle					
p**ee**l					
qu**ee**n					
r**ee**f					
r**ee**l					

Bound Four-Tab Foldable® Book (below): Use 11" x 17" paper to make four-tab Foldables. Fold them in half. Glue them side by side, and bind them as a book. See page 68 for photographic instructions.

Front

Back

Common short *i* phonograms include the following: *-ib, -ick, -id, -ift, -ig, -ill, -im, -in, -ing, -ip, -ist, -it.*

Four-Door Display (above): Make and use to collect word cards and/or VKVs. See page 303.

Two-Pocket Foldable® (below): see page 291.

Initial

if
igloo
ill
import
in
inch
inchworm
income
inner
insect
inside
into
invite
is
it

Medial

bib	gift	pick	spill
bid	gig	pig	stick
big	gill	pin	still
bill	gin	pill	stiff
bin	grill	pit	strip
bit	grim	pitch	swift
bliss	grin	prince	swim
brim	grip	quick	switch
brisk	hid	quill	thrift
chill	him	quilt	thrill
cliff	hip	quiz	thin
crib	hiss	rib	this
did	hit	rid	tick
dig	jig	rig	till
dill	kick	rim	tilt
dim	kid	rip	tin
din	kin	risk	tip
dip	kill	shift	trick
dish	kiss	shin	trim
disk	kit	ship	trip
ditch	lick	silk	twin
drift	lid	sill	twist
drill	lift	since	until
drip	lip	sip	whim
fib	list	sis	whip
fig	mid	sit	whisk
fill	milk	six	wick
film	mill	skid	wig
fin	miss	skill	will
fish	mist	skin	wilt
fit	mit	skim	win
fix	mix	skip	wish
frill	nick	slid	wit
	nip	slip	with
		sniff	zig
			zip

Students will find fewer **y** words that make a short *i* sound than a long *i* sound. More difficult words are included in this list as examples. See **y** as a long *i* sound on the next pages.

-y-
cymbal
crypt
crystal
cystic
dyslexic
gryphones
(part eagle, part lion)
hymn
mystic
myth
platypus
rhythm
symbol
tryst

i-e
give
live

a-e
pillage
village

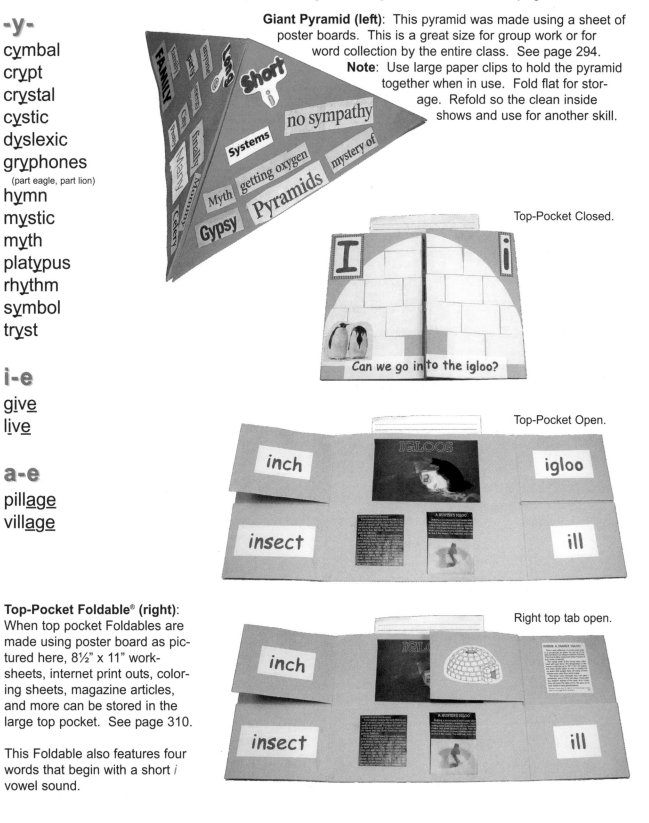

Giant Pyramid (left): This pyramid was made using a sheet of poster boards. This is a great size for group work or for word collection by the entire class. See page 294.
Note: Use large paper clips to hold the pyramid together when in use. Fold flat for storage. Refold so the clean inside shows and use for another skill.

Top-Pocket Closed.

Top-Pocket Open.

Right top tab open.

Top-Pocket Foldable® (right): When top pocket Foldables are made using poster board as pictured here, 8½" x 11" worksheets, internet print outs, coloring sheets, magazine articles, and more can be stored in the large top pocket. See page 310.

This Foldable also features four words that begin with a short *i* vowel sound.

Initial	Medial	Ending
I	b<u>i</u>cycle	h<u>i</u>
<u>i</u>ce	d<u>i</u>nosaur	
<u>i</u>cing	f<u>i</u>nd	
<u>i</u>cicle	gr<u>i</u>nd	
<u>i</u>dea	l<u>i</u>on	
I'm	p<u>i</u>lot	
<u>i</u>sland	rh<u>i</u>no	
<u>i</u>tem	sp<u>i</u>der	
<u>i</u>vy	t<u>i</u>tle	
	tr<u>i</u>angle	

Two-Tab Foldable® (below): The example below was made using one sheet of 8½" x 11" paper folded to leave one side longer than the other. See page 291.

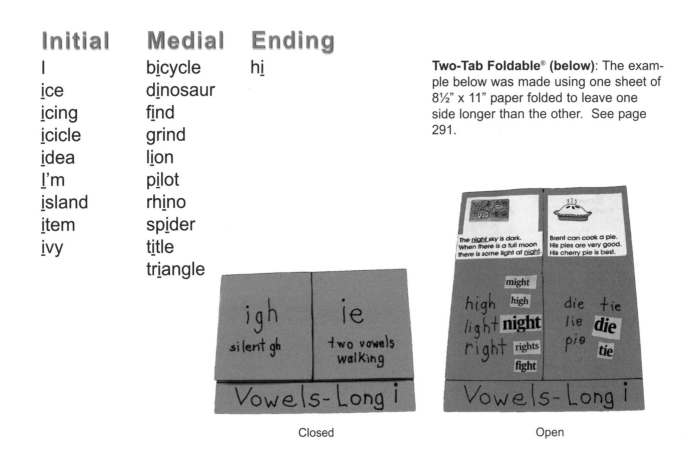

Closed   Open

Four-Door Foldable® (below): Use a sheet of 11" x 17" or 12" x 18" paper to make a classroom four-door Foldable. When an important vocabulary word is spelled in a manner that is not predictable, it is fun to turn it into a special Foldable. Look at the science example that focused on the words "eye" and "eyes". See page 299.

Rimes: *-ibe, -ice, -ide, -ife, -ike, -ile, -ime, -ine, -ipe, -ire, -ise, -ite, -ive, -ize*.

i-e
(silent e)

bide
bike
bile
bite
file
fine
fire
five
gripe
hide
hike
hire
hive
kite
knife
lice (pl)
life
like
lime
line
live
mice
mile
mine
mire
nice
nine
pile
pine
pipe
price
pride
prize

i-e
(silent e)

ride
rile
ripe
rise
side
site
size
slide
smile
strike
stripe
tide
tile
time
tire
while
wide
wife
wipe
wire
wise

-ind
(long i phonogram)

bind v
find v
hind adj/n
kind adj/n
mind n
rind n
wind v

-y
(y as a vowel)

buy
by
cry
cycle
dry
dye
fly
fry
hype
my
ply
pry
python
rely
reply
rhyme
shy
sky
sly
spy
sty
style
try
type
why
wry

-igh
(silent -gh)

bright
fight
flight
high
light
night
might
night
right
sigh
sight
slight
tight

-ie

die
lie
pie
tie

-ei
(two vowels walking/exceptions)

feisty
Geiger
    counter
height
heist
neither
seismic

Two-Column Folded Chart (above):
Use a sheet of 8½" x 11" paper to make the chart pictured below. Use the same sized paper to cut the letter *y* and glue it on the chart. Use the chart to collect RWP words where *y* has the long *i* and long *e* sounds.

Note: Guide students to recognize that the long *i* sound is seldom formed by two vowels combined -- *die, lie, pie, tie*.

Initial

<u>o</u>bject
<u>o</u>ctagon
<u>o</u>ctopus
<u>o</u>dd
<u>o</u>live
<u>o</u>n
<u>o</u>pera
<u>o</u>pposite
<u>o</u>ption
<u>o</u>strich
<u>o</u>x
<u>o</u>xygen

Two-Pocket Foldable® (above): Use one sheet of 8½" x 11" paper to make the two-pocket Foldable pictured closed (left) and open (right). Use it to collect VKVs and/or quarter sheet word cards. See page 291.

Picture Frame Foldables® (below): These picture frame books are made using two sheets of 8½" x 11" paper. One sheet of colored paper is used to make the frame and cover, and one white sheet is glued inside resulting in a quickly bound book. See page 303 for instructions.

Rimes: *-ob*, *-ock*, *-od*, *-og*, *-om*, *-ond*, *-ong*, *-op*, *-ot*.

Medial

blob	dot	knob	shop
blot	drop	knock	slot
Bob	flock	lock	smog
body	flog	log	snob
bog	flop	long	sock
bomb	fob	lot	sob
bop	fog	mom	song
box	fond	mop	sop
broccoli	fox	nod	spot
chop	frog	not	stock
clock	gob	pod	stop
clog	God	pop	strong
cob	gong	pot	tock
cod	got	plot	top
cop	hog	rock	tot
copy	hop	rob	trod
cot	hot	rock	trot
crop	job	rod	wrong
dock	jog	rot	
dog	jot	shock	

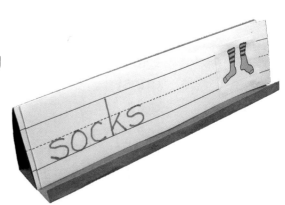

Sentence-Strip Holder (above), Four-Door Display Case (bottom left), and Display Box (bottom right): Use 11" x 17" or 12" x 18" paper to make these Foldables. Use the Foldables pictured to sort, collect, display, and store word cards and VKVs.

Sentence Strip, see page 306.
Four-Door Display, see page 303.
Display Box, see page 304.

Initial

oak
oar
oat
obey
ocean
o'clock
odor
okay
okra
old
oleo
omit
opal
open
oval
over

Medial

bold
cold
fold
ghost
gold
hold
mold
molt
most
poll
post
roll
scold
scroll
sold
stroll
told
toll
troll

Ending

-o

(open syllable rule)

ago
also
alto
auto
bingo
bongo
bronco
buffalo
burro
cello
domino
ego
Eskimo
gecko
go
hello
hero
hobo
hydro
jumbo
lasso
mango
memo

(continued)

mosquito
motto
no
patio
photo
piano
potato
so
tango
tomato
tornado
trio
typo
volcano
zero

Eight-Tab Foldable® (above): make a four-tab Foldable, see page 295. Cut each of the four tabs in half to form eight tabs.

Mini-Book Foldable (above), see page 307.

**Sentence-Strip Foldable®
(below)**: See page 306.

Back

Front

Rimes: *-obe, -ode, -oke, -ole, -ome, -one, -ope, -ore, -ose, -ote, -ove, -oze*.
Sometimes two vowels are combined to form one vowel sound: d**oe**, b**oa**t.

-oa	o-e	(continued)	-ow	-oe
boast	bone	slope	blow	doe
boat	broke	smoke	bow	foe
coal	choke	sole	bowl	hoe
coast	clone	spoke	crow	Joe
coat	close	stole	flow	toe
foal	code	stone	follow	woe
foam	cone	stove	glow	
float	dome	stroke	grow	**-ough**
gloat	dove	tone	grown	dough
goal	drove	tote	know	thorough
goat	froze	tote	low	
groan	globe	vote	mow	
load	gnome	whole	mower	
loaf	hole	woke	owe	
loam	home	zone	own	
loan	hope		owner	
moan	hose		row	
moat	joke		show	
oak	lone		shown	
oar	lope		slow	
oat	mole		snow	
road	mope		sow	
roam	nose		stow	
roar	note		tow	
roast	phone		throw	
soap	poke		thrown	
soak	robe		yellow	
soar	rode			
shoal	role			
toad	rope			
toast	rose			
throat	rote			

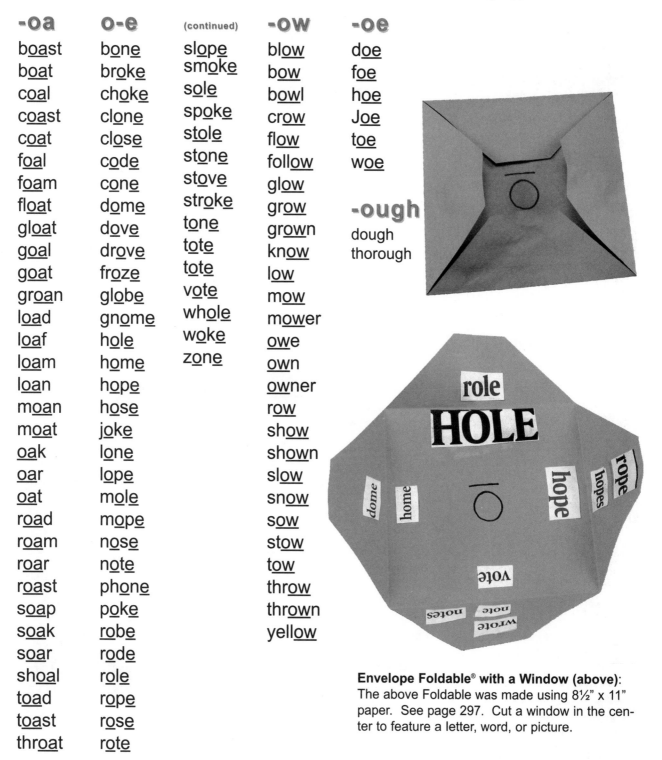

Envelope Foldable® with a Window (above):
The above Foldable was made using 8½" x 11" paper. See page 297. Cut a window in the center to feature a letter, word, or picture.

Initial

udder
ugly
umbrella
umpire
uncle
under ᴰ
until
up ᴰ ꜰ
upon ᴰ
upper
upset
us ᴰ ꜰ
usher

a-

above
about
ago
appalled
away
award

-o-

none
son
ton
violet
won

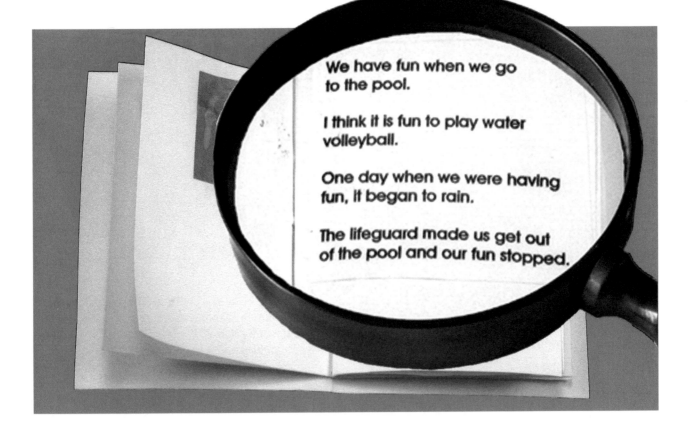

Two-Tab Foldable® (above): The letter *a* can sound like a short *u* as seen on the right tab of this Foldable. Students collected the words from RWP -- newspapers, magazines, advertisements, and other forms of print. See page 291.

Miniature Book (below): The copy in the book below was written on a computer using 7-point type, printed, cut, and glued into the booklet. Have students read the text with a magnifying glass. See page 307.

We have fun when we go to the pool.

I think it is fun to play water volleyball.

One day when we were having fun, it began to rain.

The lifeguard made us get out of the pool and our fun stopped.

Rimes: *-ub, -ud, -ug, -um, -un, -up, -ut*.
Note that each of the medial *u* words has one vowel sound and one syllable.

Medial u

	(continued)	(continued)	(continued)	-ou
bluff	fluff	puff	stuff	country
blunt	flung	pump	stump	couple
brush	flunk	punch	stun	double
buck	flush	punt	stung	enough
bud	fun	pup	stunt	rough
buff	glum	rub	sum	tough
bug	grub	rug	sun	trouble
bum	gruff	run	sung	
bump	grunt	rung	thud	
bun	gull	runt	thug	
bunch	gum	rush	thumb	
bunk	gun	rust	thus	
bus	huff	scrub	truck	
but	hug	scuff	trunk	
chuck	hum	scum	trust	
chum	hung	shrub	tub	
chunk	hush	shrug	tuck	
club	jug	shrunk	tug	
cluck	jump	shut	yuck	
crunch	just	skunk	yum	
crush	luck	slug		
cub	lump	slum		
cuff	lunch	slump		
cut	lung	snub		
drug	muck	snuff		
drum	mud	snug		
dub	mug	spud		
duck	mum	struck		
dug	nun	strum		
dull	plug	stub		
dumb	plum	stuck		
dump	plumb			
dust	plump			
	plus			

RWP Immersion: Find examples of short vowel words in commercial print, and use them to make quarter-sheet flashcards as pictured above. Students might be asked to underline the onset in one color and the rime in another.

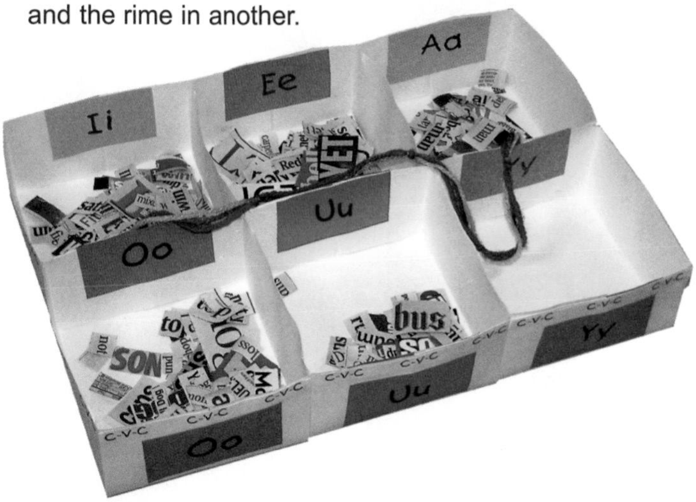

Compare and contrast how many primary words have long *u* sounds compared to other long vowel sounds. See *long oo* words on page 257.

Initial u
(open syllable)

unicorn
uniform
union
unit
united
universe
use
useful
usual

Medial u

butane
cucumber
cute
cuticle
duke
fluke
flute
fume
lube
mute
plume
rule

Final u
(open syllable)

emu
flu
menu

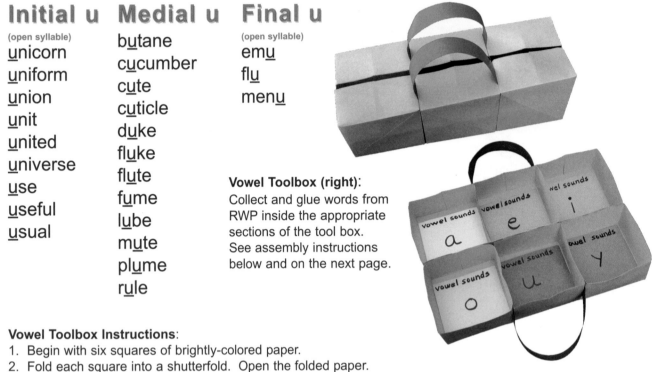

Vowel Toolbox (right):
Collect and glue words from RWP inside the appropriate sections of the tool box. See assembly instructions below and on the next page.

Vowel Toolbox Instructions:
1. Begin with six squares of brightly-colored paper.
2. Fold each square into a shutterfold. Open the folded paper.
3. Refold the paper into another shutterfold on the opposite axis. Open the folded paper.
4. Cut along the top and bottom fold lines to form tabs on the left and right sides. Fold these tabs over the large left and right tabs and cover them with glue.
5. Glue the sections to the inside of the top and bottom tabs to form a box (e). Use clothespins to hold the tabs in place until the glue dries.

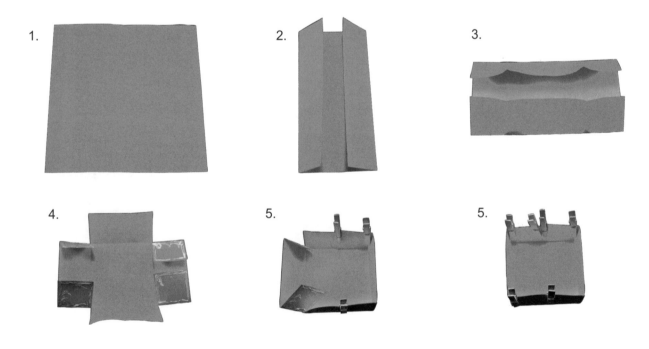

1.

2.

3.

4.

5.

5.

Vowel Toolbox Instructions (continued):

6. Glue three boxes together side by side. If a handle is desired, cut a 1" x 12" strip of paper and glue the ends between the boxes. Use clothespins to hold the boxes and handle together until the glue dries.
7. Make a hinge using 2" clear tape along the bottom of the vowel tool box.
8. Use three small sections of 2" clear tape inside the box to reinforce the hinge.
9. The hinge allows the box to open flat, or to close to form a tool box.
10. Cut and glue a section of paper to form a pocket (or glue envelopes cut to fit) inside the sections to collect and hold quarter sheets and/or small flashcards.
11. Pockets hold and keep word cards organized when the toolbox is closed for storage.

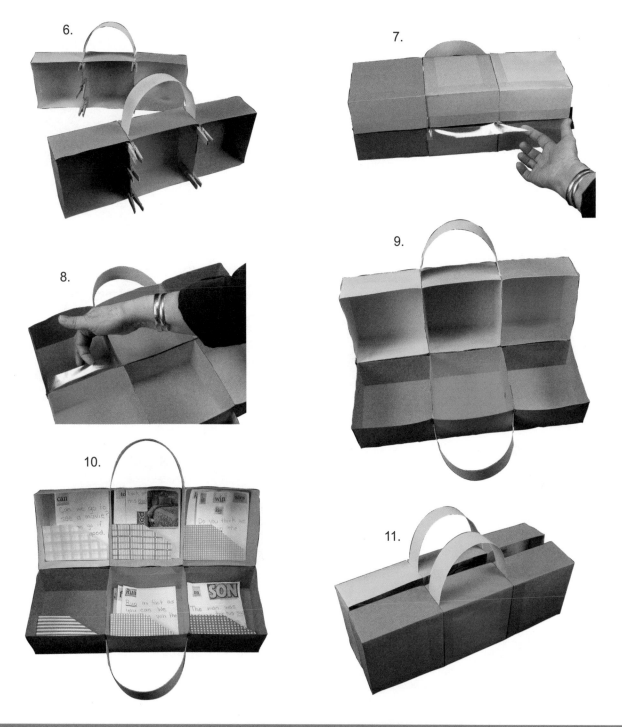

/*u*/ vowel sound: *bull*   1 dot *oo*, or short *oo*

-oo	-ou, -oul	-o	-u
book	could	wolf	bull
brook	should		bullet
cook	would		bush
cookie			full
crook			pull
foot			push
good			put
hood			sugar
hoof			
hook			
nook			
rook			
rookie			
shook			
soot			
stood			
took			
wood			
wool			

Bound Four-Tab Foldables® (right):
Fold multiple four-tab Foldables in half and glue them side by side to make a bound book. Use to collect short *oo* words, pictures, and sentences using the words. See page 68.

Three-Tab Foldable® (left): On the front tabs, collect examples of words with the short *oo* sound -- *-oo-*, *-ou-*, and *-u-*. Write sentences using several of the words collected under the tabs. See page 293.

/**u**/ vowel sound: ruler   *2 dot* **oo***, or long* **oo** *sound*

-o (ending)

do
to
two
who

-oo (ending)

bamboo
boo
cockatoo
coo
goo
igloo
kangaroo
moo
shoo
tattoo
too
voodoo
woo
yahoo
zoo

-oo (medial)

balloon
baboon
boom
boost
boot
cartoon
cool
cocoon
food
fool
goof
goose
harpoon
kook
loop
loose
mood
moon
noodle
noon
poodle
pool
proof
roof
room
root
school
shoot
smooth
spook
tool
tooth
troop
zoom

-ue

avenue
blue
barbecue
clue
continue
cruel
cue
due
duel
fuel
glue
hue
sue
tissue
true
value

-ui

bruise
cruise
fruit
juice
recruit
suit
suitcase
tuition

-ew

blew
cashew
chew
crew
dew
drew
few
flew
grew
hew
jewel
knew
mildew
nephew
new
newbie
newt
pew
review
screw
slew
spew
stew
threw
view
yew

o-e

approve
lose
move
prove
remove

-oe

canoe
shoe

**-ou,
-ough**

coup
group
grouper
groupie
route
soup
through
troupe

u-e

abuse
accuse
cube
crude
cute
excuse
fume
fuse
huge
June
plume
produce
rude
rule
tube
tune
use

**Bound Two-Tab Foldables®
(above):** See page 68.

Vowels *r* Controlled-/*ar*/ and /*or*/ sounds

When a vowel is combined with an *r*, the vowel sound changes. Sometimes these vowels are referred to as being *r controlled vowels*, or *vowel plus r sounds*.

-ar

arm
army
art
bar
barn
car
cart
charge
charm
dark
dart
far
farm
hard
harm
harsh
jar
large
market
mart
polar
quart
quarter
scar
shark
sharp
star
start
tar
tardy
tarp
war
warm
wart
yard

Shutterfold (below):
Use a shutterfold to collect examples of words containing *r-controlled* vowels. Note the use of RWP. See page 292.

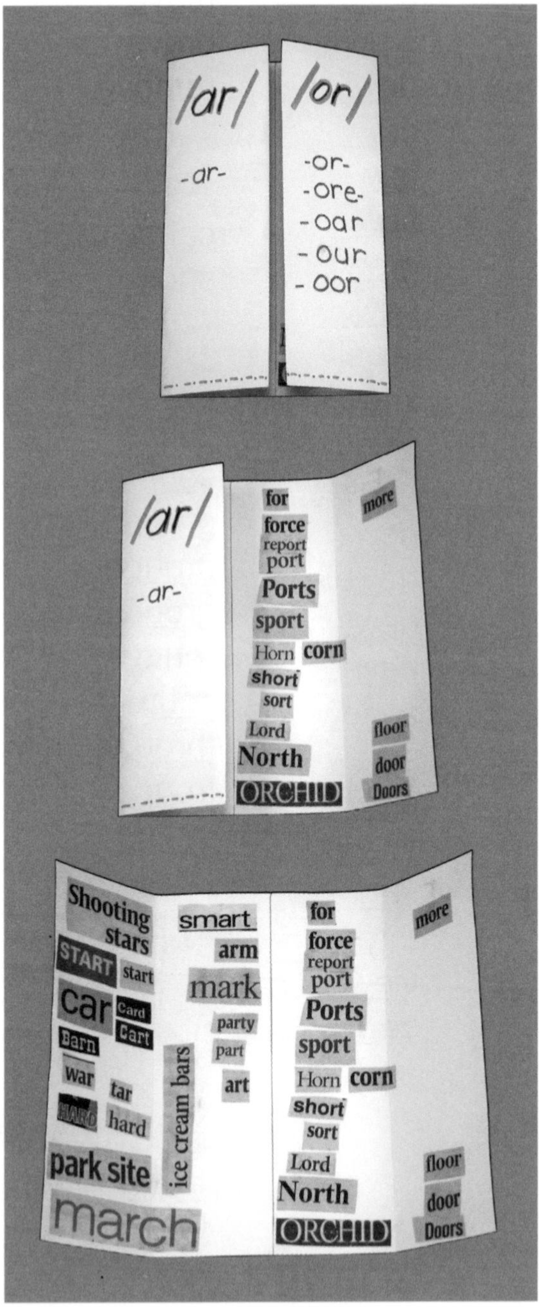

-ore

bore
chore
gore
more
ore
pore
shore
store
tore

-oo

door
floor

-our

court
four
pour
your

-oar

boar
board
hoard
hoarse
oar
roar
soar

-or

born
color
cord
corn
dorm
floor
for
fork
form
fort
honor
horn
horse
labor
mirror
more
morning
north
or
order
ore
organ
port
short
storm
story
sword
terror
thorn

Vowels *r* Controlled-/ur/ sound

When a vowel is combined with an, the vowel sound changes. Sometimes these vowels are referred to as being *r controlled,* or *vowel plus r sounds.*

-er

allergy
baker
battery
berm
camera
certain
dessert
expert
father
fern
fever
germ
her
herd
lever
liver
mother
nerd
nerve
never
over
perm
person
river
serpent
serve
shower
supper
term
verse
water
winter

-ere

were

ear

(spelled *ear*, sounds like *ur*)

early
earn
earth
heard
learn
pearl
search

(spelled *ar*, sounds like *ur*)

collar
dollar
lunar
solar

(spelled *or*, sounds like *ur*)

word
work
world
worm
worse
worth

(spelled *our*, sounds like *ur*)

journal
courtesy

Picture Frame Foldable® (above): Feature a skill or a special word and/or picture inside the front frame. Collect RWP, dictation, student writing inside the book. The example above is examining words ending in -*er*. See page 303.

Accordion Pocket Chart (right): Use a sheet of poster board to make a large six-column chart, and use it to collect examples of *r-controlled* vowels. This example was folded to include a pocket and a sentence-strip holder along the bottom. See page 309.

-ir

bird
birth
chirp
circle
circus
dirt
fir
firm
first
flirt
girl
shirt
sir
skirt
stir
third
thirsty
thirteen
thirty
whirl

-ur

blur
burden
burn
burp
burr
burro
burst
church
curb
curl
curtain
curve
fur
hurry
hurt
nurse
purple
purse
spur
surf
surface
turkey
turn
turtle
urn
urban
yurt

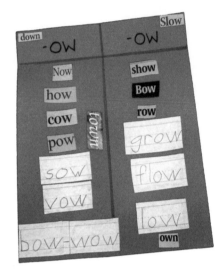

Two-Column and Three-Column Foldable® Charts (above): Use 11" x 17" paper or poster board to make charts for students to record diphthongs they encounter in reading or for students to glue diphthongs found in RWP. See page 308.

Two-Pocket Foldable® (left): Collect and store diphthong word cards in the pockets. See page 291.

Multi-Tabbed Foldable® Variation (below): After making a multi-tabbed Foldable, write or glue words with diphthongs under the tabs as illustrated and cut small notches in the top tabs to expose the diphthongs within the words below. This focuses the students' attention onto the featured diphthong.

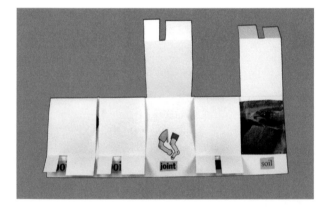

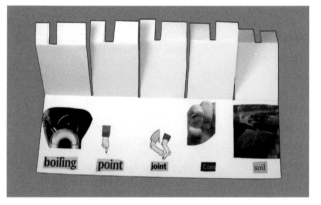

Vowels Diphthongs

Diphthongs are two vowels with two sounds glided together and pronounced as one.
Examples: *ou-* in out, *-oi-* in soil

-ow-	-ow	ou-	-oy	oi	aw
brown	allow	about	annoy	boil	awkward
clown	bow	around	boy	coil	awl
cow	brow	cloud	boysenberry	coin	crawl
crowd	cow	count	convoy	doily	dawn
crown	how	counter	cowboy	foible	drawn
down	now	county	coy	foil	fawn
drown	row n	doubt	coypu (nutria)	foist	hawk
flower	sow	drought	destroy	hoist	jaw
frown	vow	flounder	employ	join	law
glower	wow	flour	enjoy	joint	lawn
gown		found	foyer	joist	maw
growl		ground	joy	koi (fish)	paw
how		hound	loyal	loin	pawn
howl		hour	oyster	loiter	saw
now		house	ploy	moist	shawl
owl		loud	royal	moisture	straw
plow		mountain	soy	noise	trawl
power		mouth	toy	oil	yawn
powder		ouch	voyage	oily	
prowl		our	zoysia (grass)	poi	**au**
shower		out		poignant	auburn
sow		pound		poinsettia	auction
towel		proud		point	audience
tower		pout		poise	audio
town		round		poison	auditorium
vowel		scout		soil	autumn
wow		sound		toil	cause
		shout		toilet	daughter
				voice	haul
				void	haunt
					maul
					sauce
					taught
					vault

slow   bow   narrow

Three-Tab Foldable®, see page 293.

There are many words that follow the "*i* before *e* except after *c*, or when sounded like *a* as in n*ei*ghbor or w*ei*gh" rule, but there are just as many exceptions.

ie-

(follow the rule)

bel*ie*f
bel*ie*ve
br*ie*f
ch*ie*f
d*ie*
d*ie*sel
d*ie*t
f*ie*ld
f*ie*sta
fr*ie*nd
gr*ie*f
l*ie*
n*ie*ce
p*ie*ce
pr*ie*st
rel*ie*f
sh*ie*ld
s*ie*sta
th*ie*f
th*ie*ves
y*ie*ld

ei- after c

(follow the rule)

c*ei*ling
conc*ei*t
conc*ei*ve
dec*ei*t
rec*ei*pt
rec*ei*ve
perc*ei*ve

ei-

(exceptions to rule)

caff*ei*ne
cod*ei*ne
*ei*ther
f*ei*sty
h*ei*fer
h*ei*ght
h*ei*st
l*ei*sure
n*ei*ther
prot*ei*n
s*ei*smic
s*ei*ze
s*ei*zure
st*ei*n
w*ei*rd

ei-

(-*ei*- can also make the long /a/ sound)

b*ei*ge
*ei*ght
fr*ei*ght
h*ei*r
n*ei*ghbor
r*ei*gn
r*ei*n
r*ei*ndeer
sl*ei*gh
v*ei*l
v*ei*led
v*ei*n
w*ei*gh
w*ei*ght

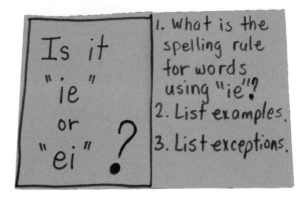

Three-Fourths Book (above): The main idea, or in this example, a question is written to the left of a three-fourths book, and related questions are on the front of the right tab. Answers to the questions on the right are under the tabs and numbered to correspond to the questions on the front. This is a great Foldable to teach students how to write test-like questions that can be shared with and answered by classmates. Students might include an answer key on the back of their Foldable. See page 290.

Students will encounter silent vowels in CVVC words, in CVCe words, and in some final digraphs.

Silent a
(two vowels walking: long o sound)

boat
boast
coach
coal
coast
coat
foal
foam
foamy
goad
goal
goat
goatee
hoax
load
loaf
loam
loan
loathe
moan
moat
poach
roach
road
roam
roar
roast
soak
soap
soar
toad
toast

Silent e
(final -e rule, see pages____ and ____)

entire
fire
close
home
nose
robe
side
snake
state
time

Silent e
(final -le digraph)

able
apple
battle
cattle
circle
double
pickle
rattle
sample
tickle
title
trouble
twinkle
whittle
wiggle

Silent e
(two vowels walking: long o sound)

roe
toe
woe

(two vowels walking: long i sound)

die
lie
pie

(two vowels walking: long u sound)

cue

Silent e
(final -e in other words)

above
come
fence
lettuce
massive
silence
some

Silent i
(i before e rule, but the i is silent in these words)

chief
field
grief
lien
niece
piece
priest
thief
yield

Peacekeepers aid board
deals YEAR
year weak hear

Sometimes...when two vowels go "walking" the first says its name, and the second vowel is silent.

COAST

beat jail Teen
raise road **Rain**
beat

base **RATE**
LIFE jeans
side
same CVCe fire
name mute

When a word ends in an "e" it might be silent.

game
lead fine hope
slide role home
face

ai
ea
ie
oa

SILENT VOWELS

_ate
_ite
_ote
_ute

Top-Pocket Foldable® (right): See page 310 for instructions, and see page 121 for photographs of another top-pocket activity.

ai
ea
ie

SILENT VOWELS

1. gate 4. late
2. fate 5. date
3. hate 6. rate

_ite
_ote
_ute

1. boat 4. float
2. coat 5. load
3. goat 6. road

7. roam 10. goal
8. foam 11. loaf
9. foal 12. oak

Word-Friendly Classroom:
The activities in this book make classrooms word-friendly places. Students learn to read, write, and collect words at their level, below their level for review, and slightly above their level for extension, application of word analysis skills, and oral vocabulary enhancement.

Expand Speaking and Reading Vocabulary:
Expose students to a rich vocabulary environment through the collection of real world print (RWP), observation of print; listening to print being read; and the use of Foldables, VKVs, and other immersion activities. This will reinforce and enrich student vocabulary and illustrate relationships between words.

Flabbergasted or Flustered:
A first-grade class might not be expected to know the words *flabbergasted* or *flustered,* yet if they are asked to clap when they hear an initial *fl* sound, and they can successfully do this with words like *fly* and *flow*, it would not be inappropriate to include more complicated words that include the same sound for auditory identification. This book is filled with words at, below, and above the ability levels of primary students.

Form Words Using Letters of Different Fonts, Sizes, and Colors:
- Wooden or plastic letter sets
- Magnetic letters
- Tactile letters -- sandpaper, colored glue dots, page 129.
- Teacher- or student-printed letter cards
- Letter cards made by using stickers or stamps
- Computer-generated letter cards using different fonts and font sizes
- Real world print (RWP) cut from commercially printed materials and products

Categories of words to be Written, Read, or Found in RWP:
- Naming words: persons -- first names only, last names only, or both
- Naming words: places -- common nouns, proper nouns, or a mixture of both
- Naming words: things -- common nouns, proper nouns, or a mixture of both
- Initial consonants or consonant clusters -- black, blue, blot, blow
    Words that begin or end with a given consonant or consonant cluster -- bat, cab
    Nouns that begin with the same consonant or consonant cluster -- cloud, clam, class, clown
    Verbs that end with the same consonant or consonant cluster -- wish, wash, splash
- Words that contain the same vowel sound -- eat, beet, seat
- Words with a given vowel -- bat, ban, dad, cat, fan, grand
- Words with silent letters -- lamb, comb, bomb, crumb, thumb
- Special groups of words -- color words, animal words, number words, holiday words
- Rhyming words, words with the same rime -- bail, fail, mail, pail, sail, tail
- Words formed from a given set of letters -- c,a,o,r, t -- cat, car, cot, coat, cart, rot, rat, tar, art, oar, oat
- Words with a given number of syllables -- one-, two-, three-syllable words
- Words with the same ending: ring, sing, thing, or cats, dogs, cows, hogs
- Contractions -- do not, don't
- Compound words -- open, closed, and hyphenated
- Compound words that are always capitalized and compound words that are not -- New Year, Mother's Day, White House, Pacific Ocean, New Jersey, North Dakota, blue jeans, ice cream
- Words with prefixes and/or suffixes (unfasten, recalling, disliking)
- Homographs: dove_n, dove_v
- Homophones: aisle, I'll, isle

Definition Review:

Sight word A word encountered during reading that contains parts students might not be familiar with; but students can probably predict the word's
meaning from the context.

Loan word A word that originates in another language but has become common in its foreign-language setting. Loan words are usually pronounced using the phonics of the original language -- tortilla, amigo, burro, beret, faux, bouquet, safari, koala, yen, prima donna, spaghetti, origami, hula, klutz, polka, totem, wigwam.

Syntax The way words are organized in a language to form phrases, clauses, or sentences.

Decode Refers to a method or methods of word identification.

Word attack skills and *decoding skills* are one and the same. Word attack skills allow readers to recognize graphic symbols and relate them to language.

Word attack skills include the following:
1. recognizing the parts of words and analyzing them phoneme by phoneme
2. blending onsets and rimes and other word parts into new words
3. recognizing symbols for consonant and vowel sounds
4. recognizing syllable patterns

Word map or *word web* Maps and webs organize words to show how the words are perceived to relate to a topic or idea.

Word Sorts Students collect and sort words by a given characteristic -- onset, rime, prefixes, suffixes, plurals. Word sorts are often described as *closed* or *open*.

Closed Word Sorts: deductive thinking
Students are asked to find something specific -- CVCe words, words
that begin with the consonant blend *bl*-, plural nouns, rhyming words.
Open Word Sorts: inductive thinking
Students find plural nouns in RWP, and discover that some nouns add -*s* to form the plural, some nouns add -*es* to form the plural, and some nouns that end in *y*
change the *y* to *i* before adding -*es*.

Word wall A space dedicated to the collection and display of words students need to be able to read, spell, and use in writing and oral presentations. To facilitate use, word walls are usually organized so the words are displayed alphabetically.

Word Wall: The word wall in this second-grade classroom is ready for the first day of school. It has been placed at the front of the classroom, and the squares were measured and designed to surround the front board. The squares were laminated, and words will be written using an erasable marker.

This word wall will be used to display words used frequently in second-grade writing: through, which, ever, because, after, other, another. Students will be taught to refer to the words on the word wall when writing and editing their writing.

1. Students might enter a classroom for the first time to find a word wall with a few high-frequency, grade-level-appropriate terms listed. These teacher-selected words are usually review words that the teacher feels might be challenging for students returning from a break.

2. High-frequency words will be added as they are studied by the class.

3. Teacher and students note words that are frequently misspelled in student work, and discuss whether they should be added to the word wall. Allow students to help make decisions about which words are or are not added, as there is limited space.

4. The teacher and the students determine when words should be deleted from the wall, or the teacher gives notice that certain words will be omitted in a given amount of time. For example, a green dot next to a word might be an indicator that the word is "going away" within a two-week period.

RWP Word Bank or File:
Use envelopes or file folders to collect words from RWP. Parents who are actively collecting letters or words for your class would benefit from having their own RWP word files.
- a-z letter banks
- a-z word banks, CVC and CVCe words
- initial, medial, final consonant word banks
- long vowel and/or short vowel word banks
- rime word banks
- number banks
- color word banks
- antonym word banks

Classroom Word Journals and Dictionaries (right): Use eight sheets of poster board to make a giant bound book journal, as pictured, for social studies. Sequentially label 26 of the inside pages with the letters of the alphabet. Within the classroom dictionary, write social studies terms, definitions, and pronunciation guides when needed. Include examples of the terms used in RWP. Also, collect and include pictures that help define terms and concepts. See page 290.

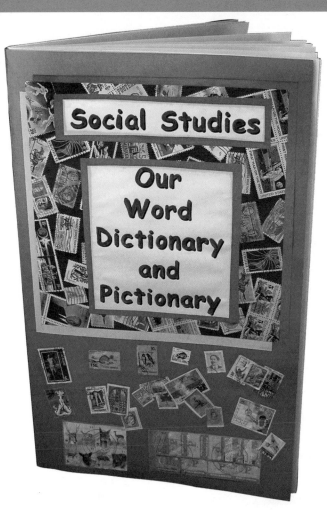

Spelling Word Dictionary (left): Word journals can be made by or for individual students to collect words that they need to learn to spell. Teachers might mark developmentally important misspelled words within student writing with a pink highlighter, and write the corrections next to the misspelled words. When work is returned to students, they look for "pink" words, enter these highlighted words (spelled correctly) into their pink spelling journals, and use their journals during future writing activities to check the spelling of words they frequently misspell. Students might be asked to select words from their dictionaries to individualize and supplement their spelling word lists. Use eight pieces of photocopy paper to make 32-page spelling word dictionaries. Make spelling dictionaries for the class and be ready to present them to students the first or second week of school. Recruit parent volunteers to help mass-produce these books for student use. See page 290.

Word Mittens:

1. Make a 1½" pocket along one long edge of a piece of 8½" x 11" paper.
2. Fold the paper in half like a hamburger, with the pocket to the outside.
3. Glue three sides together, leaving the pocket side open. This will form a square mitten like the red and white example, top left.
4. Use quarter-sheet flashcards or 3" x 5" index cards to make answer cards to be displayed in the pockets.

Variation: Trim the edges of the square pocket to form a rounded or mitten-shaped word pocket before gluing.

Example Using *first* and *last* Word Cards: Teacher instructs students to listen for the *p* sound. The teacher says the word *pat* and students raise their cards and indicate if they hear the sound at the *first* or *last* of the word.

Example Using *living* and *nonliving* Word Cards: Teacher says the word *wood* and students raise their cards to indicate that it is living matter.

CVV

bee
boy
day
may
sea
see
tea
too
way
you

VVC

ear
eat
oar
oat
oil
out
our

VVCC

each

CCVV

blue
clue
flea
flee
free
glee
glue
knee
play
they
tree
true

CVVC

bean
been
book
feet
food
four
good
head
hear
hook
keep
look
mean
near
read
seam
seem
seen
soon
took
year
your

CCVVC
CCCVVC

cream
crook
dream
gleam
great
greet
sheaf
shear
sheer
sheet
shook
shoot
snail
sneer
snoop
stream
street
their
treat

CVVCC

could
found
learn
point
sound
teeth
tooth
world
would
young

CCVVCC

should
smooth

days

DAY

Day

CVV

CVVC

good

Read

week

teen

need

Long a Rimes: -ace, -ade, -age, -ake, -ale, -ame, -ane, -ape, -are, -ase, -ate, -ave, -aze
Long i Rimes: -ice, ide, -ife, -ike, -ile, -ime, -ine, -ipe, -ire, -ise, -ite, -ive
Long o Rimes: -obe, -ode, -oke, -ole, -ome, -one, -ope, -ose, -ote, -ove
Long u Rimes: -ube, -ude, -uge, -uke, -ule, -ume, -une, -upe, -ure, -use, -ute

bake	cube	fake	hale	lace	pace	site	
bale	cute	fame	hate	lake	page	size	
base	date	fate	haze	lame	pale	take	
bike	dice	file	here	lane	pane	tale	
bite	dime	fine	hide	late	pile	tame	
bone	dine	fire	hike	lice	pine	tape	
cage	dive	five	hire	life	pipe	tide	
cake	dome	gale	hive	like	poke	tile	
came	dose	game	hole	lime	pole	time	
cane	dove	gape	home	line	pose	tire	
cape	duke	gate	hope	live	puke	tone	
care	face	gave	hose	lobe	race	tote	
case	fade	gaze	jade	lode	rage	tube	
cave			joke	lope	rake	vane	
			kite	made	rate	vase	
				make	rave	vine	
				male	raze	vise	
				mane	rice	vote	
				mate	ride	wade	
				maze	ripe	wage	
				mice	rode	wake	
				mike	role	wane	
				mile	rope	wave	
				mine	rose	wide	
				mole	sage	wife	
				more	sale	wipe	
				name	same	wire	
				nice	sane	wise	
				nine	save	woke	
				note	side		
				nose			

(No long vowel sound: difficult to spell because they don't follow the pattern.)
come
give
have
here
move
some
were

(Proper Nouns: CVCe)
Dale
Gale
Jane
Lane
Luke
Nile
Pope
Rome

[Foldable illustration labeled "CVCe Words" with tabs a, e, i, o, u and small images labeled fire, game, bite]

Poster Board Bound Journal: Use three sheets of poster board to make this twelve-page big book. Use two inside pages for each vowel. Make paper labels for the vowels and attach them with 2" tape so they extend past the right edge of the book. Extended tabs make it easy for small children to find pages in large floor books. See page 290.

Word Patterns CCVCe

Add a consonant blend or digraph (onset) to a -VCe word family to get this word pattern.

blade	crane	glade	knife	skate	these	(No long vowel sound: difficult to spell because they don't follow the pattern.)
blame	crate	glaze	phone	slave	those	
blaze	craze	glide	place	slice	trace	
brace	crime	globe	plane	smile	trade	there
brave	drive	glove	plate	snake	trove	where
bribe	drone	grace	price	space	twice	
bride	drove	grade	quake	spade	twine	
brine	flake	grape	scale	spine	whale	(Proper Nouns: CVCe)
chase	flame	grate	shade	stage	while	Blake
chide	fluke	grave	shake	stake	white	Brice
chime	flute	graze	shale	stale	whole	Drake
chive	froze		shame	state	whose	Grace
chore			shape	stole	write	Shane
chose			shave	store	wrote	Steve
clone				strife		
close						
clove						

Space (CCVCe Word) and Relationships: The four-door Foldable below features words that describe space -- inside, outside, above, below, top, bottom. See page 299.

bled	drip	knit	show	snap	thin	(Difficult to spell.)
blew	drop	knob	shut	snob	this	knew
blob	drug	know	skid	snow	thud	they
blog	drum	play	skin	snug	thug	what
blot	flap	plod	skip	spat	trap	
blow	flat	plot	skit	sped	tray	
brad	flaw	plug	slap	spot	trim	
brat	fled	plum	slat	spud	trip	
brim	flew	plus	sled	spun	trod	
chap	flip	pray	slew	stem	twig	
chat	flog	prim	slid	stew	twin	
chew	flop	prop	slim	stir	when	
chin	flow	shed	slip	stop	whim	
chip	flub	shin	slot	stow	whip	
chop	fret	ship	slug	stub	wrap	
chug	frog	shod	slum	swim	wren	
chum	from	shop	smog	than		
clad	glib	shot		that		
clap	glum			them		
clay	gnat			then		
clip	gray					
clog	grew					
clop	grey					
clot	grow					
club	grid					
crab	grim					
craw	grin					
crew	grit					
crop						
drab						
draw						
drew						

CCVC

stay
shop
drug
draw
than

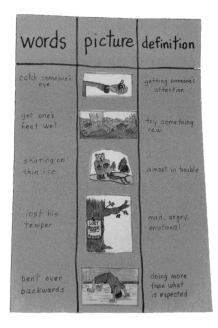

words	picture	definition
catch someone's eye		getting someone's attention
get one's feet wet		try something new
skating on thin ice		almost in trouble
lost his temper		mad, angry, emotional
bent over backwards		doing more than what is expected

back	fact	lack	part	tack
ball	fang	lamb	pass	talk
band	farm	land	past	tall
bang	fast	lass	pill	task
bank	fell	last	pink	tell
bask	felt	left	pond	tent
bass	fill	lend	pony	test
bell	find	less	rack	tint
belt	fist	lest	raft	told
bend	fold	lick	rang	tout
bent	fond	lift	rank	turn
best	form	limb	rent	vend
bilk	full	lint	rest	vent
bill	gift	list	rift	verb
bold	girl	lock	rind	vest
boss	gold	loft	ring	walk
both	hand	long	rock	wall
buck	hard	loss	rust	want
bull	held	luck	sack	well
call	help	lung	sand	went
card	herd	mask	sank	west
cell	high	mass	sell	will
cent	hill	melt	send	wilt
cold	hint	mess	sent	wind
curb	hold	miss	sick	wing
dent	hunt	mold	sing	wind
dirt	jest	molt	sink	with
disk	jump	moss	silt	word
dock	junk	most	sock	work
down	just	much	sold	yank
duck	kept	must	song	yell
dust	kick	nest	such	zest
	kind	next		zing
	king			
	kiss			

CCVCC and CCCVCC

black	draft	knell	skiff	stuck	track
bland	drank	knock	skull	stuff	trend
blank	drawl	knoll	slang	stunt	trick
blast	dress	krill	slick	swift	troll
blend	drift	plank	slump	swing	truck
bless	drill	plant	smack	thank	trunk
blest	droll	pluck	small	thick	trust
block	drunk	plush	smash	thing	which
blunt	dwell	prank	smell	think	whiff
brand	flank	press	smirk	thrift	wrong
brass	flash	print	smock	thrill	
brick	flask	scent	snack	throng	
bring	flick	scold	sniff	thumb	
brink	fling	shack	spank		
brush	flint	shaft	spell		
chess	flock	shall	spend		
chest	floss	shank	spill		
chill	flunk	shard	sprang		
chunk	frank	shark	spring		
clack	frill	sharp	sprint		
clang	gland	shawl	stack		
clank	glass	shelf	stand		
clash	glint	shell	stank		
class	glitch	shift	start		
cliff	glory	shirt	stick		
clock	gloss	shock	still		
cluck	graft	short	stock		
crack	grand	shrank	storm		
craft	grant	shunt	story		
crank	grass		strand		
crash	grill		stress		
crest	grunt		strict		
crumb			string		
crush			strong		

CVCCC

bunch
catch
ditch
first
hatch
latch
light
lunch
match
munch
night
patch
right
watch

CCVCCC

branch
brunch
chinch bug
crunch
drench
flinch
glitch
scratch
stench
thatch
trench
wrench

CVCVC

biker
cabin
colon
color
hiker
humid
humor
rider
safer
timid
tumor
water

VKV® Phonogram Syllables (above): instruction on page 156.

Note From Dinah: As a teacher, during the summer I would outline the reading, phonics, spelling, grammar, and writing skills I would be teaching and reviewing during the upcoming school year. I would then go through my grade-level text books and curriculum guides and list all content vocabulary I had to teach. I sorted the content vocabulary by the reading, phonics, spelling, grammar, and writing skills on my skills outline. This resulted in a master word list organized by language skills that included content words and high-frequency reading and writing words from my reading program. For example, this merger yielded a list of content terms spelled with a silent letter as well as reading and spelling terms with a silent letter.

Content vocabulary words are usually not high-frequency words, and I found that the more I exposed students to them orally, in writing, and by including them on Foldables and VKV flashcards, the easier they were for students to comprehend and retain when studied in the content subject. And, if any of these terms were studied in the content subject before they were studied and analyzed using language skills, it was great reinforcement and review for the students to see them again, associated with their reading terms.

Geography Terms From the List (right) Sorted By Example Skills:

Initial Consonant Blends/Digraph:
crust
drought
glacier
globe
grass
ground
plain
plateau
prairie
precipitation
smog

Double Final Consonants:
atoll
compass
grass
hill
krill
landfill

Double Medial Consonants:
hurricane, irrigation
summer

Onsets and Rimes:
bog, smog
gulf
hill, krill
hot
land
map
west

CVCe words:
lake
pole

Long and Short oo Words:
typhoon

Two Vowels:
beach
coast
east
geography
green
rain
reef
refugee
year

r Controlled Vowels:
arctic
coral
desert
earth
marine
prairie
rural
tornado
winter

y = Vowel:
city
cycle
cyclone
geography
industry
recycle

oi and oy Words:
oil
soil

ou and ow Words:
drought
mountain
town

Final o words:
tornado
volcano

Compound Words
Closed:
  coastline
  earthquake
  evergreen
  farmland
  grassland
  greenhouse
  groundwater
  landfill
Open:
  compass rose
  coral reef
  evergreen forest

  map key
  rain forest
  water cycle
  water vapor

-ph- = /f/:
geography
hemisphere
pictograph
typhoon

Silent Letters:
drought
tsunami

Suffixes:
-ment
environment

Singular and Plural Nouns:
valley, valleys
tornado, tornadoes

Drop e and Add -ing:
precipitating
recycling

Homographs and Homophones:
bay, bay
coast, coast
desert, desert
desert, dessert
ground, ground
land, land
plain, plane
pole, pole
rain, reign
soil, soil

Geography Terms

arctic
atlas
atoll
axis

basin
bay
beach
bog

cave
city
coast
coastline
cold
compass
compass rose
continent
coral reef
country
crust
culture
cyclone

desert
distance
drought

earth
earthquake
east
elevation
environment

equator
erosion
evaporation
evergreen
    forest
export

farmland
forest

geography
geyser
glacier
globe
grass
grassland
greenhouse
ground
groundwater
gulf

habitat
hemisphere
highway map
hill
hot
humid climate
hurricane
iceberg
ice sheet
import
industry
irrigation
island

krill

lake
land
landfill

magma
map
map key
marine
migrate
mountain

nature
north

ocean
oil

pictograph
plain
plateau
pole
poles
pond
population
port
prairie
precipitation

rain
rain forest
recycle
refugee
river
rural

sea
smog
soil
south
state
suburb
summer

tornado
town
tsunami
tundra
typhoon

urban

valley
volcano

water
water cycle
water vapor
weather
weathering
west
winter

year

Health Terms

absent	deaf	gang	organ	values
accident	death	growth	overweight	vegetables
activity	decision	habit	oxygen	vein
aerobic	dentist	hair	parent	vision
age	depression	handicap	peer	vitamin
aging	diet	harmful	physical	warm-up
air	digest	hazardous	physician	water
allergy	digestion	headache	poison	weight
anger	disease	health	pollution	wellness
antibiotic	doctor	health care	pulse	workout
aspirin	drug	hear	relax	wound
asthma	ear	heart	rest	x-ray
attitude	eat	heat	risk	
backache	emergency	hunger	safety	
bacteria	energy	infant	scab	
behavior	exercise	infection	scrape	
birth	eye	injury	shock	
blood	eye exam	intestines	skeleton	
body	fad	itch	sleep	
braces	family	joint	smog	
brain	farsighted	junk food	smoke	
bully	fat	kidney	snack	
burn	fatigue	learn	sports	
caffeine	feelings	liver	sprain	
cancer	fever	lung	stomach	
cavity	fiber	medicine	stress	
cell	filling	mental health	sty	
cartilage	fire	mood	sweat	
choke	first aid	motion	swell	
cold	floss	movement	symptom	
common	flu	muscle	tartar	
cough	food	nail	taste buds	
cut	friend	noise	teeth	
	friendship	nose	throat	
		nurse	tobacco	
		nutrition	toothbrush	

Math Terms

add
addends
addition
additive identify
additive inverse
amount
angle
area
arithmetic
average
axis
bar graph
between
billion
cardinal number
cent
center
centimeter
change
circle
circle graph
circumference
compare
compass
cone
count
counting principle
cube
cubed
cup
customary
  measures
cylinder

decimal
decimal point
decrease
denominator
diagonal
diamond
difference
differences
digit
distance
divide
dollar
double
edges
eight
eighth
endpoints
equal
equation
equivalent
error
estimate
estimation
evaluate
even
even number
fewer
fifth
figure
first
five
four
fourth
fraction

gallon
globe
graph
graphing
greater than
grid
grid paper
group
grouping
half
height
hemispheres
heptagon
hexagon
horizontal
hundred
increase
interior
intersect
least
less
less than
line
line graph
liter

many
mathematics
measure
measurement
meter
metric measure
metric system
midpoint
minus
mixed number
more
most
nine
ninth
number line
number
numeral
numerator
numerical
octagon
odd
odd number
one
one-to-one
opposite
ounce
outline
oval

Math Terms

pair	straight
parallel	straightedge
parallel lines	subset
pattern	substitution
pentagon	subtract
percent	subtraction
perimeter	sum
pictograph	symbols
pint	symmetric
place holder	symmetry
place value	table
plane	temperature
plus	ten
point	tenth
pound	term
problem	thermometers
protractor	third
pyramid	thousand
quart	three-dimensional
rectangle	time
ruler	times
second	total
set	triangle
seven	triangular
seventh	two-dimensional
side	unequal
similar	union
six	unit
sixth	Venn diagram
solid	vertical
solid figure	vertical lines
solution	volume
solve	whole
sphere	whole number
square	width
	zero

Science Terms

absorb	community	expand	habitat
air	compost	extinct	hardness
allergy	condensation	fat	hatch
amphibian	constellation	fertilizer	hazardous waste
animal	control	focus	heat
antibiotic	crater	fog	herbivore
asteroid	crust	food chain	heredity
astronaut	crystal	food web	hibernation
astronomer	day	force	horizon
astronomy	decay	fossil	host
atmosphere	dew	fossil fuel	hot spot
atom	desert	freeze	human being
axis	digestion	freezing point	humid
bacteria	disease	friction	humidity
balance	dissolve	front	humus
beach	diurnal	frost	hurricane
behavior	dune	full moon	hypothesis
blizzard	Earth	fungus	ice
blood	earthquake	galaxy	ice sheet
blood vessel	eclipse	gas	igneous rock
boiling	ecology	gem	inclined plane
brain	ecosystem	geologic time	incubate
calorie	egg	geyser	insect
capillary	electricity	giant	invertebrate
carbohydrates	electromagnet	gill	Jupiter
carbon dioxide	element	glacier	land
carnivore	endangered	global warming	larva
cast	species	grasslands	lava
cave	energy	gravity	lever
cell	environment	greenhouse	life science
classification	erosion	effect	light
climate	evaporate	groundwater	liquid
cold-blooded	evaporation	group	litter
comet			lunar
			lunar eclipse

Science Terms

machine
magma
magnet
magnetism
mammal
mantle
marine life
Mars
marsupial
mass
matter
Mercury
metal
meteor
meteorite
meteorologist
microscope

migration
mildew
mineral
mixture
mold
molecule
moon
moon phases
moss
muscle
natural
Neptune
night
nucleus
nutrients

observation
observatory
orbit
organ
organic
organism
oxygen
pesticide
planet
plant
Pluto
polar
pollen
pollution
population
precipitation
prey
pulley
push, pull
radio
recycle
revolution
rock
rock cycle
rotation
sap
satellite
Saturn
scale
science
screw
season
sediment
skeletal system
smog
soil

solar
solar system
solid
sound
space
speed
star
state of matter
static
symmetry
table
technology
temperate
temperature
tide
tissue
tools
tornado
tsunami
universe
Uranus
vein
Venus
vertebrate
volcano
warm-blooded
water cycle
wave
waxing
weather
weathering
wedge
weight
wetland
wheel
work

Find 5 words that have 2 syllables

Find 5 words that have the long a sound

Find 5 words that have double consonants

Find 5 compound words

Find 5 contractions

Find 5 in Science/Chapter 3

Social Studies Terms

address
adobe
agriculture
America
American
ancestor
ancient
atlas
autobiography
barbed wire
battle
boundary
calendar
canyon
capital
capitol
century
chart
circle graph
city
climate
coast
colonist
community
compass
compass rose
continent
country
court
culture
custom

democracy
desert
direction
drought
earthquake
environmental
equator
erosion
explorer
export
factory
family
famine
farm
festival
flag
freedom
frontier
fuel
geography
geyser
ghost town
glacier
globe
goods
government
governor
graph
harvest
hemisphere
hero
hill
history

holiday
hurricane
import
income
independence
industrial
Internet
interview
invention
irrigation
island
judge
jury
lake
lava
law
leader
legend
manufacture
map
map key
map symbol
market
mayor
merchant
migration
mission
monument
mountain
mural
museum

nation
Native American
natural resource
navigate
needs
neighbor
ocean
peninsula
picture graph
Pilgrim
pioneer
plain
plantation
plateau
polar
pollution
population
port
poverty
precipitation
president
property
Puritan
pyramid
railroad
rain forest
ranch
recycle
reservation
revolution
river
road map
rural

Social Studies Terms

season
service
services
settlement
settlers
shelter
skyscraper
slave
slavery
state
suburb

supply
surplus
surrender
symbol
tax
technology
telegraph
temperature
teepee
timber
time
tornado
tourist
town
trade
tradition
transportation
trust

urban
valley
vegetation
volcano
volunteer
vote
voyage
wagon
wants
war
water cycle
weather
welfare
wetland
wilderness
wildlife
working class

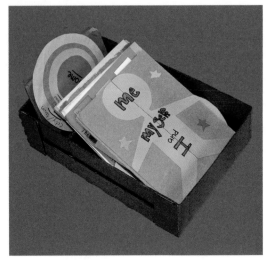

Shutterfold Project (above): Made using 11" x 17" art paper. See page 292.

Three-Tab, Venn Diagram Foldable®: This large classroom Foldable was made using 11" x 17" heavy-weight paper (80# or 110#). Since students will be using these terms frequently during the year, this Foldable will be stored in a cereal box entitled *Communities* which will be retrieved as terms are used and reviewed. Information, examples, and definitions will be collected under the tabs. As illustrated in the photograph, when students find RWP that applies to this concept, they are encouraged to add it to the Foldable and share their addition with the class. This results in continued review and use of content vocabulary terms. See three-tab book page 293.

Social Studies, Science, Health, and Geography: Some content terms apply equally to several subjects.

The water cycle is studied...

   ... in earth science because it applies to weather, seasons, erosion, weathering.
   ... in health and life sciences as it relates to the importance of water to life.
   ... in social studies and geography because it helps to explain climate, the world's ocean, and the organization of geographic regions.

Science, social studies, geography, and health terms that relate to the water cycle include *evaporation*, *condensation*, *precipitation*, *perspiration*, *transpiration*, and *percolation*. Remember, young children can be auditorially, visually, and kinesthetically exposed to large words to extend their vocabulary without expecting mastery. They will hear the above terms during weather reports, in conversations at home, in television and movie dialog, and when studying content subjects.

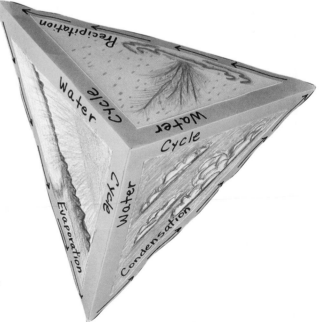

Water Cycle Pyramid Foldable® (below): This pyramid can be made using 8½" x 11" paper for individual student use, or it can be made using poster board for classroom use. When the poster board pyramid below is turned on its side so the precipitation side is down, students can describe and illustrate different types of precipitation. Continue this process until information is recorded on each of the three inside sections. See page 294.

Four-Door Poster Board Project (above left): The water cycle plays an important part in the study of seasons, too. This large project is perfect for small-group or entire-classroom use. See page 299.

Evidence-Based Resources to Support 12 Common Instructional Skills & Tools Used with Foldables® and VKVs®

Cause and Effect

- Williams, J. P.; Nubla-Kung, A.M; Pollini, S.; Stafford, K. B.; Garcia, A.; Snyder, A. E. 2007. Teaching cause-effect text structure through social studies content to at-risk second graders. *Journal of Learning Disabilities*, 40. 111-120.
- "Cause & Effect." www.literacymatters.org/content/text/cause.htm
- "Cause and Effect Reading Lesson Plan." An introduction for science teachers to the concept of cause & effect. Offers a chart, chain of events, problem/solution diagram, and Venn diagram to analyze different aspects of cause and effect. www.everestquest.com/read2.htm

Compare and Contrast

- Hall, K.M.; Sabey, B. L.; and McClessan, M. 2005. Expository text comprehension: helping primary-grade teachers use expository texts to full advantage. *Reading Psychology*, 26. 211-234.
- Marzano, R.J.; Pickering, D.J.; and Pollock., J.E. 2001. Classroom Instruction That Works. Identifying similarities & differences is the #1 way to raise student achievement. Representing similarities & differences in graphic or symbolic form enhances learners' understanding of and ability to use knowledge.
- Chen, 1999; Cole & McLeod, 1999; Glynn & Takahashi, 1998, Lin, 1996. Combining the instructional strategies of asking students to construct their own means for comparing similarities and differences with the use of nonlinguistic representation significantly enhances student achievement.

Concept Maps & Webs

- Horten et al. 1993. Meta-analysis of studies using concept mapping as a learning strategy showed that concept mapping raised student achievement on average 0.46 standard deviations and contributed to strong improvement in student attitude.
- Novak & Gowan. 1984. In addition to a key role as assessment tools (consider differences before, during and after instruction), concept maps offer a useful way to help students learn how to learn.
- Readence, J. E., Moore, D. W., and Rickelman, R. J. 2000. Pre-reading Activities for Content Area Reading and Learning. 62-81. Describes seven graphic representation strategies.
- Constructing concept maps is a demanding cognitive task that requires training. www.flaguide.org/cat/minutepapers/conmap4.php
- Concept maps, used for over 25 years, help students focus on the "big picture," enabling them to devote more time to conceptual understanding versus rote learning. www.flaguide.org/cat/minutepapers/conmap7.php

Graphs and Diagrams

- Disess, Hammer, Sherin & Kopakowski. 1991. One of the difficulties with conventional instruction is that students' meta-knowledge is often not engaged, so they come to know "how to graph" without understanding what graphs are for or why the conventions make sense.
- Friel, S.N., Curcio, F.R, Bright, G. W. 2001. *Journal for Research in Math. Education*, 32, 2, 124-158. Four critical factors influence graph comprehension: purposes for using graphs, task characteristics (visual decoding, judgment, tasks, and the context or semantic content of a graph), discipline characteristics, and reader characteristics . . . Graph sense or comprehension develops gradually as one creates graphs and uses already-designed graphs in a variety of problem-solving contexts that involve the use of data" . . . Consider using a constructivist perspective to enable students to organize and make sense of information before introducing formal work with the traditional types of graphs.
- Pressley et. al, 1988; Woloshy et al., 1990. Non-linguistic representations are important for engaging students in elaborative thinking in two ways. When students elaborate on knowledge, they not only understand it in greater depth, but also recall it much more easily.

Journaling and Bookmaking

- Fordham, N.W., Wellman, D. & Sandman, A. 2002. Taming the text. The Social Studies. 93. 149-158. Writing to learn in all content areas is vital, because considering a topic under study and then writing requires more extensive processing than reading alone entails.
- NWP & Nagin. 2003. Writing to Learn (WTL) advocates encouraging writing to help students discover new knowledge--to sort through previous understandings, draw connections, and uncover new ideas as they write. WTL activities can also encourage reflection on learning strategies and thereby increase students' meta-cognitive skills. (exs: journals, learning logs, exit slips)
- Sprenger, M. 2005. Students reinforce their learning when they communicate and especially write about "their content, be it concepts, facts or procedures."

KWL and Variations

- Eshelman, John W., Ed.D. 2001. Commentary on Behavior and Instruction: Ausubel, Advance Organizers, and Replicable Research. www.members.aol.com;johneshleman/comment12.html
- Frey, N. and Fisher, D.B. 2006. 19-20. *Language Arts Workshop: Purposeful Reading and Writing Instruction.*
- Merkley, D.M. and Jeffries, D. 2001. Guidelines for Implementing a Graphic Organizer. *The Reading Teacher* 54 (4), 538-540.
- Ogle, D. M. *The Reading Teacher*, 39, 564-570. KWL: A teaching model developed by Ogle in 1986 that develops active reading of expository text.
- Readence, J.E., Bean, T.W., & Baldwin, R. S. 1998. Teachers can vary the way to expose students to information before they "learn" it. KWL is a good, logical graphic application.

Main Idea & Supportive Facts

- Barton, J. and Sawyer, D. 2004. Our students are ready for this: Comprehension instruction in the elementary school. *The Reading Teacher*, 57, 334-347.
- Just, M. and Carpenter, P. 1992. A capacity theory of comprehension: Individual differences in working memory. *Psychological Review*, 1992, 122-149. In most reading situations we read for the main points, in part, due to memory constraints. We can't process every line in the text at the same level if our work ing memory is overloaded with too much information. Part of the information then is displaced or 'forgotten.'
- Tomitch. L.M.B. 2000. Teaching main ideas -- Are we really teaching? *Linguagem & Ensino*, 45-53. Main idea identification is one of the most important literacy comprehension skills. Textbooks typically provide tasks or practice involving the main ideas, but do not actually provide explicit procedures and instruction in main idea identification and formulation.

Opposites (Pairing of Antonyms)

- Heidenheimer, P. 1978. Logical relations in the semantic processing of children between six and ten: emergence of antonym and synonym categorization. *Child Development*. 49. 1243-1246.
- Jones, Steven. 2007. "Opposites" in discourse: a comparison on antonym use across four domains. *Journal of Pragmatics*. 39. 1105-1119.
- Jones, S. and Murphy, M. L. Antonymy in childhood: a corpus-based approach to acquisition.
- McKeown,M. G. 1993. Creating effective definitions for young word learners. *Reading Research Quarterly*, 27, 16-31.

Questioning

- Cotton, K. Teaching questioning skills: Franklin Elementary School. *School Improvement Research Series*. http://www.nwrel.org/scpd/sirs/4/snap13.html. Research on questioning reveals among other findings that teaching students how to respond to and how to frame higher-level questions is positively related to their voluntary participation in such higher cognitive processes in classroom discussions.
- McKenzie, Jamie. 2005. Learning to Question to Wonder to Learn.
- Raphael, T. E., 1986. Promotes replacing traditional cognitive hierarchies of questions relative to text and graphics with classifications that identify the kinds of transactions that learners/readers use with the text to answer questions. One way to teach these important QAR strategies is with the help of graphic organizers.

Sequencing Events/Cycles/Ordering

- Cusimano, A., M.Ed. 2006. Auditory Sequential Memory Instructional Workbook. Within the area of the brain controlling the processing of information presented in isolation or sequential order, each aspect (numbers, letters and words) is specific unto itself. Students who have mastered the skill of number memory may not have developed the skill of remembering letters and words, or vice versa. Thus, we must consider the development of all numbers, letters, and words separately.
- Frey, N.and Fisher, D. B. 2006. 337-340. *Language Arts Workshop: Purposeful Reading and Writing Instruction.* Focus on temporal or sequential text structure and signal words in expository text with explicit instruction on structure and styles used in content area texts and informational trade books.

Tables and Charts

- Bruning, Schraw, Norby & Roning. 2003. Research on the effects of students self-generating material that involves recoding, as is built into interactive graphic organizers, shows that students consistently do better.
- Katayama & Robinson, 2000. Evidence suggests that blank or partially completed graphic organizers promote greater text comprehension than those completed in advance for students.
- Graphic displays outside of text, such as pictures, geographic and concept maps, tables and charts, and the like promote recall of text when used in concert with each other. The belief is that such displays are effective because they provide the learner with two avenues to memory: verbal (text) and spatial (the placement of information in relation to other facts), and that the spatial and verbal work in concert with one another (Kulhavy, Lee, & Caterino, 1985 as cited in Fischer et. al., 2007, *50 Content Area Strategies for Adolescent Literacy.* p. 3). "For real learning to occur, students must use the graphic organizer to transform information. The goal . . . is not to fill it out; that's a worksheet." The graphic organizer "is an external storage device for information" and to be useful, it "should be used to transform information into verbal or written form" so that students can make the information their own. Fischer et. al., 2007. *50 Content Area Strategies for Adolescent Literacy.* p. 3.

Vocabulary Development

- Baumann, F.F. and Kame'enui, E.J. 2004. *Vocabulary Instruction: Research to Practice.* Three of four research-based modes for teaching vocabulary: wide reading, explicit teaching of specific words, teaching of word-learning strategies, and development of word consciousness can be well supported by interactive graphic organizers. Marzano's vision for direct vocabulary instruction aims for a top-level linguistic understanding of words accompanied by visual representation of terms that students encounter in their academic reading.
- Beck, I. L, McKeown, M. G, & Kucan, L. 2002. *Bringing Words to Life: Robust Vocabulary Instruction.*
- Dolch, E. W. Problems in Reading, 1948. First publication of the Dolch high frequency list.
- Fry, E. B. 2004. The Vocabulary Teacher's Book of Lists.
- Fry, E. B. and Kress, J. E. 2006. The Reading Teacher's Book of Lists, 5th Edition.
- Moore, D. W. and Readence, J. 1984 . A qualitative and quantitative review of graphic organizer research. Journal of Educational Research. 78. 11-17. Meta-analysis of 24 studies suggests that vocabulary knowledge gains following graphic organizer use may be even greater than comprehension gains.
- Sakiey, E. and Fry, E. B. 1979. 3000 Instant Words. Presents the 3,000 most frequently used words in rank and alphabetical orders. ERIC ID169516
- White T.G., Sowell, V., and Yanagihara, A. 1989. Teaching elementary students to use word-part clues. *The Reading Teacher.* 42. 302-309. Includes list of 20 most common prefixes and suffixes.

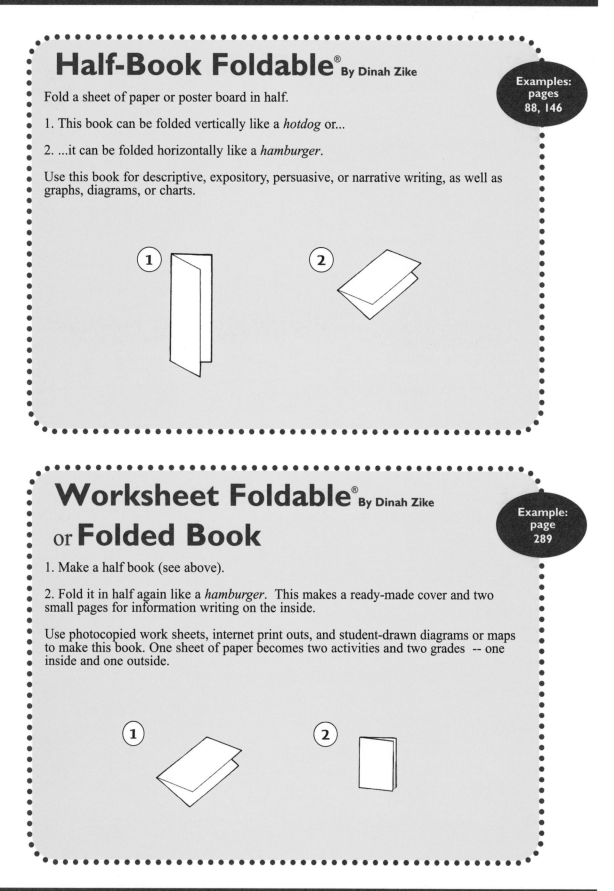

Half-Book Foldable® By Dinah Zike

Examples: pages 88, 146

Fold a sheet of paper or poster board in half.

1. This book can be folded vertically like a *hotdog* or...

2. ...it can be folded horizontally like a *hamburger*.

Use this book for descriptive, expository, persuasive, or narrative writing, as well as graphs, diagrams, or charts.

① ②

Worksheet Foldable® By Dinah Zike
or Folded Book

Example: page 289

1. Make a half book (see above).

2. Fold it in half again like a *hamburger*. This makes a ready-made cover and two small pages for information writing on the inside.

Use photocopied work sheets, internet print outs, and student-drawn diagrams or maps to make this book. One sheet of paper becomes two activities and two grades -- one inside and one outside.

① ②

Three-Fourths Foldable® By Dinah Zike

Example:
page
262

1. Make a two-tab book. Raise the left-hand tab.

2. Cut the tab off at the top fold line.

3. A larger book of information can be made by gluing several three-quarter books side by side.

Sketch or glue a graphic to the left, write one or more questions on the right, and record answers and information under the right tab.

Bound Journal Foldable® By Dinah Zike

Examples:
pages
108, 118, 209

1. Take two sheets of paper or poster board and separately fold them like hamburgers. Place the papers on top of each other, leaving one sixteenth of an inch between the mountain tops.

2. Mark both folds 1" from the outer edges.

3. On one of the folded sheets, cut from the top and bottom edges to the marked spots.

4. On the second folded sheet, start at one of the marked spots and cut the fold (or "shave it of"f by cutting it off) between the two marks.

5. Take the cut sheet from step 3 and fold it like a burrito. Place the burrito through the other sheet and the open the burrito. Fold the bound pages in half to form an eight-page book.

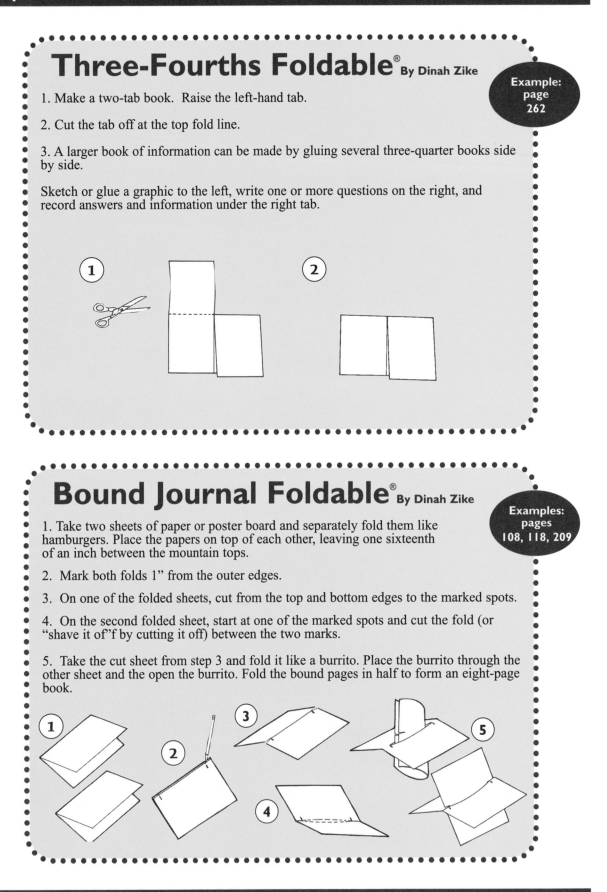

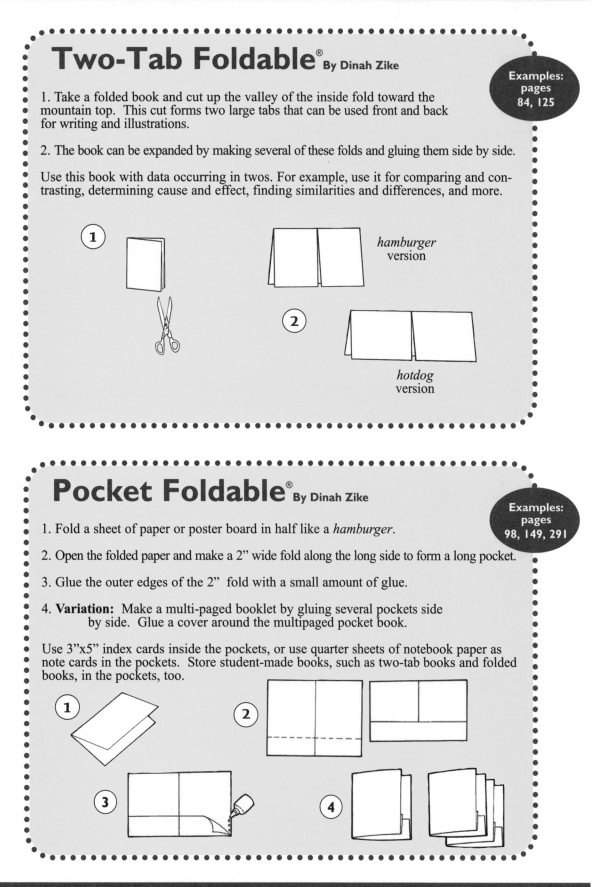

Two-Tab Foldable® By Dinah Zike

Examples: pages 84, 125

1. Take a folded book and cut up the valley of the inside fold toward the mountain top. This cut forms two large tabs that can be used front and back for writing and illustrations.

2. The book can be expanded by making several of these folds and gluing them side by side.

Use this book with data occurring in twos. For example, use it for comparing and contrasting, determining cause and effect, finding similarities and differences, and more.

① ②

hamburger version

hotdog version

Pocket Foldable® By Dinah Zike

Examples: pages 98, 149, 291

1. Fold a sheet of paper or poster board in half like a *hamburger*.

2. Open the folded paper and make a 2" wide fold along the long side to form a long pocket.

3. Glue the outer edges of the 2" fold with a small amount of glue.

4. **Variation:** Make a multi-paged booklet by gluing several pockets side by side. Glue a cover around the multipaged pocket book.

Use 3"x5" index cards inside the pockets, or use quarter sheets of notebook paper as note cards in the pockets. Store student-made books, such as two-tab books and folded books, in the pockets, too.

① ② ③ ④

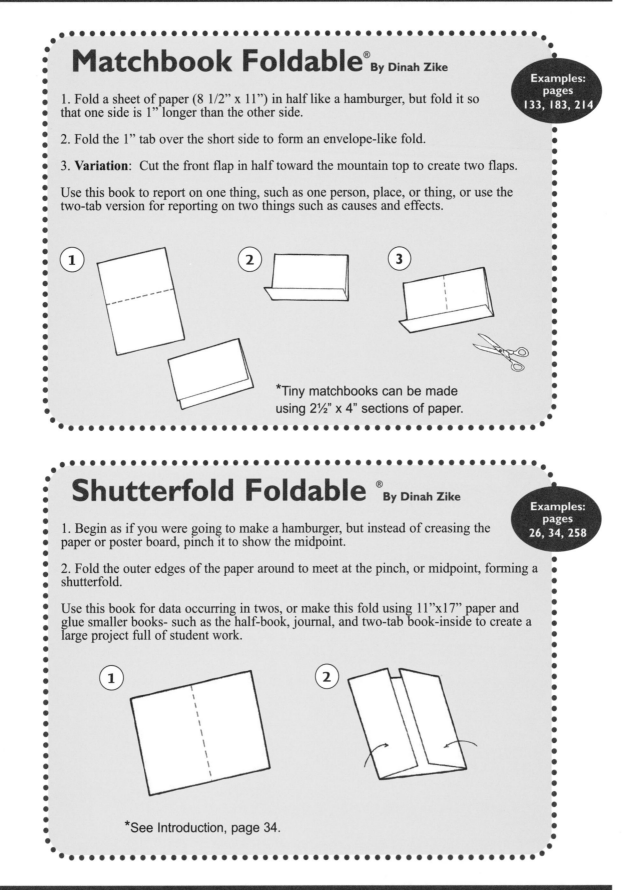

Matchbook Foldable® By Dinah Zike

Examples: pages 133, 183, 214

1. Fold a sheet of paper (8 1/2" x 11") in half like a hamburger, but fold it so that one side is 1" longer than the other side.

2. Fold the 1" tab over the short side to form an envelope-like fold.

3. **Variation**: Cut the front flap in half toward the mountain top to create two flaps.

Use this book to report on one thing, such as one person, place, or thing, or use the two-tab version for reporting on two things such as causes and effects.

*Tiny matchbooks can be made using 2½" x 4" sections of paper.

Shutterfold Foldable® By Dinah Zike

Examples: pages 26, 34, 258

1. Begin as if you were going to make a hamburger, but instead of creasing the paper or poster board, pinch it to show the midpoint.

2. Fold the outer edges of the paper around to meet at the pinch, or midpoint, forming a shutterfold.

Use this book for data occurring in twos, or make this fold using 11"x17" paper and glue smaller books- such as the half-book, journal, and two-tab book-inside to create a large project full of student work.

*See Introduction, page 34.

Trifold Foldable® By Dinah Zike

Examples:
pages
153, 166, 192

1. Fold a sheet of paper or poster board into thirds.

2. Use this book as is, or cut into shapes. If cutting, leave plenty of fold on both sides of the designed shape so the book will still open and close in three sections.

Use this book to make charts with three columns or rows, large Venn diagrams, reports on data occurring in threes, or to show and write about the outside and inside of something.

Three-Tab Foldable® By Dinah Zike

Examples:
pages
19, 77, 114

1. Fold a sheet of paper or poster board like a *hotdog*.

2. With the paper horizontal and the fold of the *hotdog* up, fold the right side toward the center, trying to cover one half of the paper.

Note: If you fold the right edge over first, the final graphic organizer will open and close like a book.

3. Fold the left side over the right side to make a book with three folds.

4. Open the folded book. Place one hand between the two thicknesses of paper and cut up the two *valleys* on one side only. This will create three tabs.

Use this book to record data occurring in threes or to create a two-part Venn diagram, see pages 25 and 114 for examples.

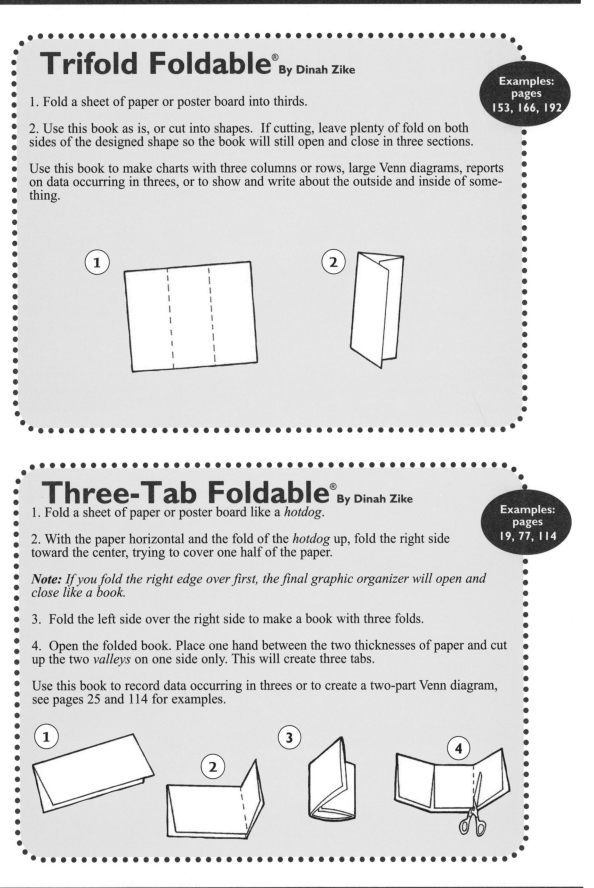

Pyramid Foldable® By Dinah Zike

Examples: pages 147, 203

1. Fold a sheet of paper or a poster board into a *taco*. Cut off the excess rectangular tab formed by the fold.

2. Open the folded taco and refold it like a *taco* the opposite way to create an X-fold pattern.

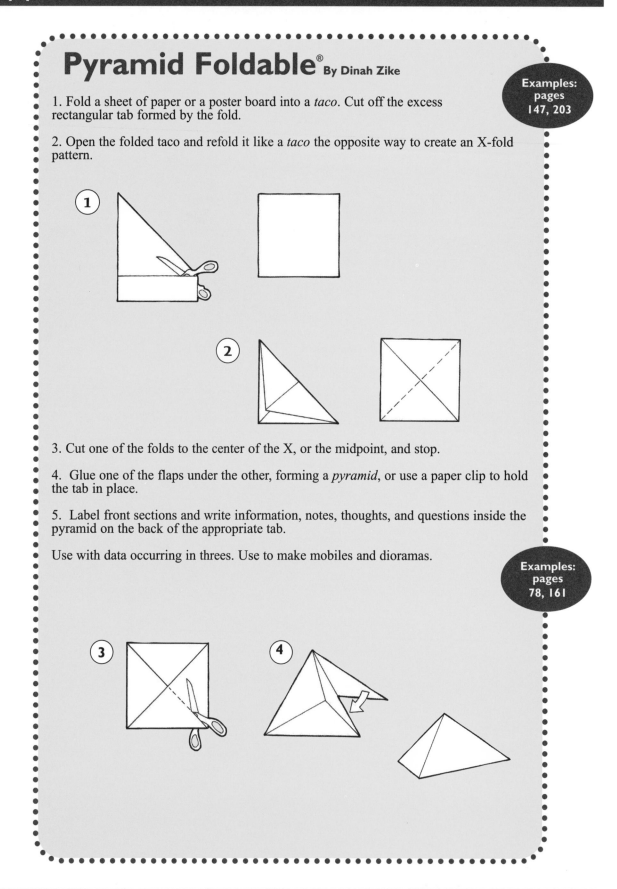

3. Cut one of the folds to the center of the X, or the midpoint, and stop.

4. Glue one of the flaps under the other, forming a *pyramid*, or use a paper clip to hold the tab in place.

5. Label front sections and write information, notes, thoughts, and questions inside the pyramid on the back of the appropriate tab.

Use with data occurring in threes. Use to make mobiles and dioramas.

Examples: pages 78, 161

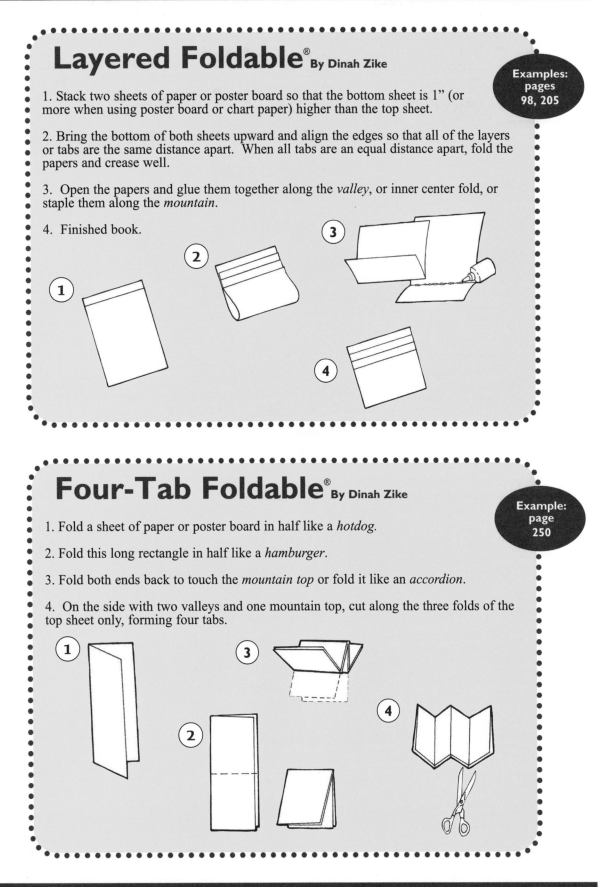

Layered Foldable® By Dinah Zike

Examples: pages 98, 205

1. Stack two sheets of paper or poster board so that the bottom sheet is 1" (or more when using poster board or chart paper) higher than the top sheet.

2. Bring the bottom of both sheets upward and align the edges so that all of the layers or tabs are the same distance apart. When all tabs are an equal distance apart, fold the papers and crease well.

3. Open the papers and glue them together along the *valley*, or inner center fold, or staple them along the *mountain*.

4. Finished book.

Four-Tab Foldable® By Dinah Zike

Example: page 250

1. Fold a sheet of paper or poster board in half like a *hotdog*.

2. Fold this long rectangle in half like a *hamburger*.

3. Fold both ends back to touch the *mountain top* or fold it like an *accordion*.

4. On the side with two valleys and one mountain top, cut along the three folds of the top sheet only, forming four tabs.

Standing Cube Foldable® By Dinah Zike

Examples: pages 43, 134, 193

1. Use two sheets of the same size paper or poster board. Fold each like a *hamburger*; however, fold one side ½" shorter than the other side.

2. Fold the long side over the short side on both sheets of paper, making tabs.

3. On one of the folded papers, place a small amount of glue along the tab, next to the *valley* but not in it.

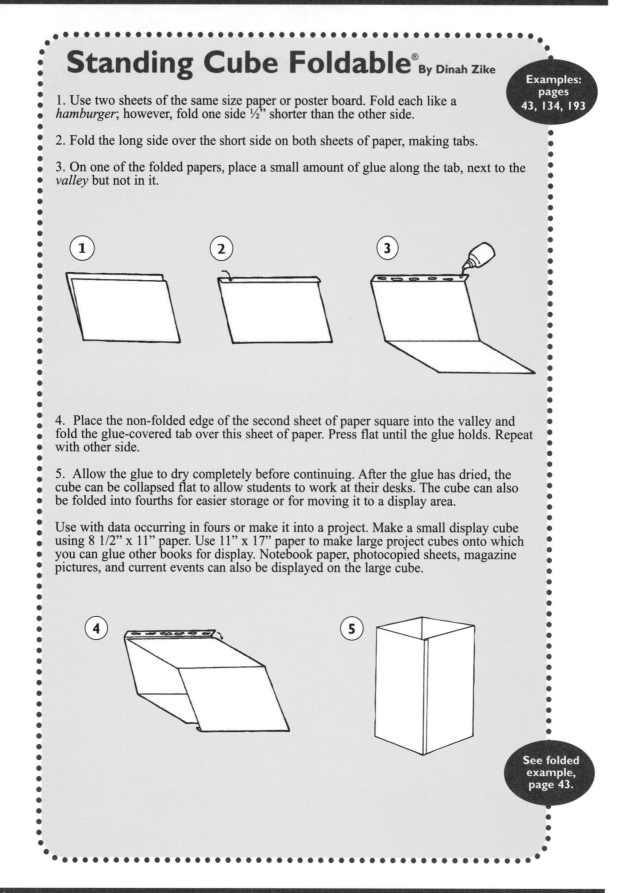

4. Place the non-folded edge of the second sheet of paper square into the valley and fold the glue-covered tab over this sheet of paper. Press flat until the glue holds. Repeat with other side.

5. Allow the glue to dry completely before continuing. After the glue has dried, the cube can be collapsed flat to allow students to work at their desks. The cube can also be folded into fourths for easier storage or for moving it to a display area.

Use with data occurring in fours or make it into a project. Make a small display cube using 8 1/2" x 11" paper. Use 11" x 17" paper to make large project cubes onto which you can glue other books for display. Notebook paper, photocopied sheets, magazine pictures, and current events can also be displayed on the large cube.

See folded example, page 43.

Envelope Foldable® By Dinah Zike

Examples:
pages
100, 136, 238

1. Fold a sheet of paper (8 1/2" x 11") into a *taco*. Cut off the excess paper strip.

2. Open the folded *taco* and refold it the opposite way forming another taco and an X-fold pattern on the sheet of paper.

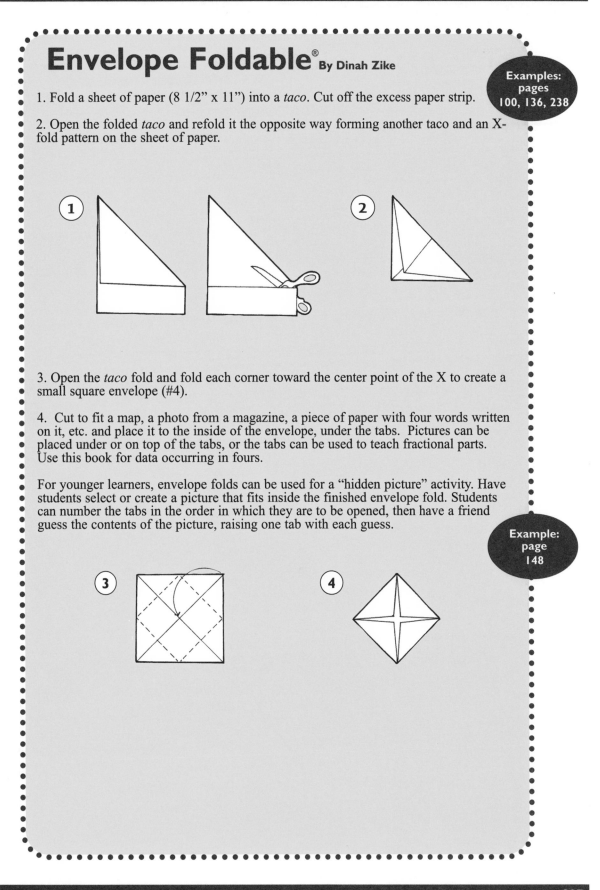

3. Open the *taco* fold and fold each corner toward the center point of the X to create a small square envelope (#4).

4. Cut to fit a map, a photo from a magazine, a piece of paper with four words written on it, etc. and place it to the inside of the envelope, under the tabs. Pictures can be placed under or on top of the tabs, or the tabs can be used to teach fractional parts. Use this book for data occurring in fours.

For younger learners, envelope folds can be used for a "hidden picture" activity. Have students select or create a picture that fits inside the finished envelope fold. Students can number the tabs in the order in which they are to be opened, then have a friend guess the contents of the picture, raising one tab with each guess.

Example:
page
148

Top-Tab Foldable® By Dinah Zike

Example: page 160, 204

1. Fold a sheet of paper or poster board in half like a *hamburger*. Cut the center fold, forming tow half sheets.

2. Fold one of the half sheets four times, each time folding in half like a hamburger. This folding has formed your pattern of four rows and four columns, or 16 small squares.

3. Fold two more sheets of paper or poster board in half like a hamburger. Cut the center folds, forming four half sheets.

4. Hold the pattern vertically and place a half sheet of paper under the pattern. Cut the bottom right-hand square out of both sheets. Set this first page aside.

5. Take a second half sheet of paper and place it under the pattern. Cut the first and second right-hand squares out of both sheets. Place the second page on top of the first page.

6. Take a third half sheet of paper and place it under the pattern. Cut the first, second, and third right-hand squares out of both sheets. Place this third page on top of the second page.

7. Place the fourth, uncut half sheet of paper behind the three cut-out sheets, leaving four aligned tabs across the top of the book. Staple several times on the left side. You can also glue along the left paper edges and stack them together. The glued spine is very strong.

8. Cut a final half sheet of paper with no tabs and staple along the left side to form a cover.

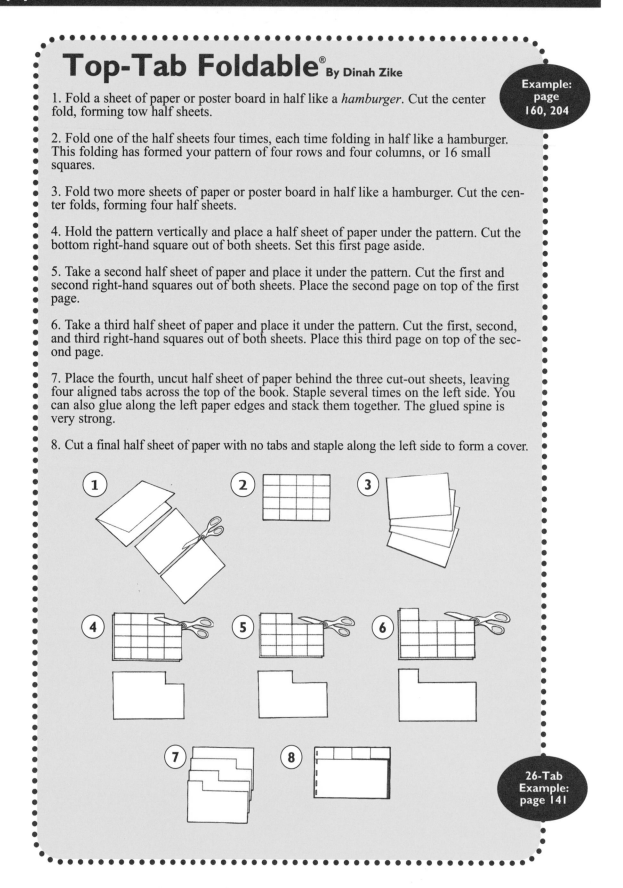

26-Tab Example: page 141

Four-Door Foldable® By Dinah Zike

Examples:
pages
139, 203, 285

1. Make a shutterfold using paper or poster board.

2. Fold the shutterfold in half like a hamburger. Crease well.

3. Open the project and cut along the two inside valley folds.

4. These cuts will form four doors on the inside of the project.

Use this fold for data occurring in fours. When folded in half like a hamburger, a finished four-door book can be glued inside a large (11" x 17") shutterfold as part of a larger project.

Pop-Up Book

Examples:
pages
206-207

1. Fold a sheet of paper (8 1/2" x 11") in half like a *hamburger*.

2. Beginning at the fold, or *mountain top*, cut one or more tabs.

3. Fold the tabs back and forth several times to make good fold lines.

4. Partially open the *hamburger* fold and push the tabs through to the inside.

5. With one small dot of glue, glue figures for the pop-up book to the front of each tab. Allow the glue to dry before going on to the next step.

6. Make a cover for the book by folding another sheet of paper in half like a *hamburger*. Place glue around the outside edges of the *pop-up book* and firmly press inside the *hamburger* cover.

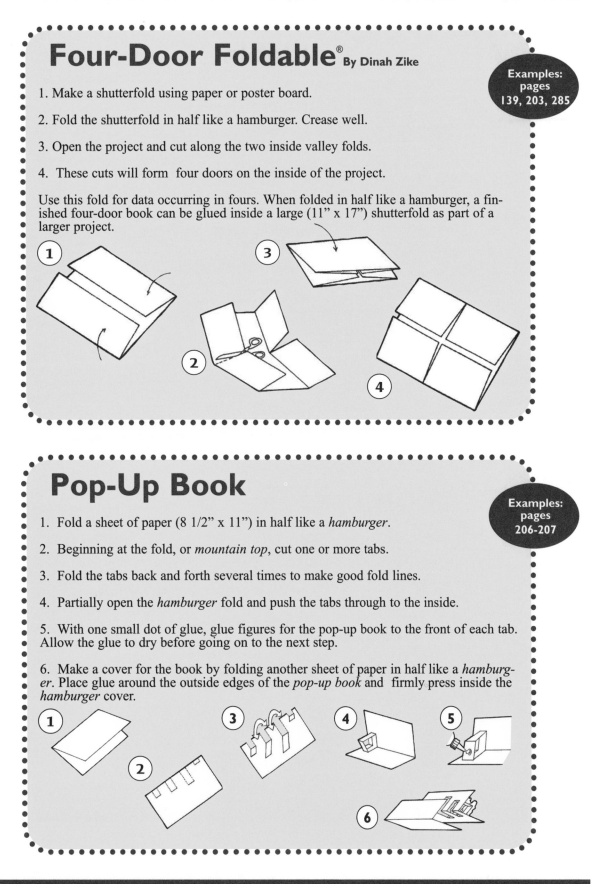

Accordion Foldable® By Dinah Zike

Examples:
pages
131, 147, 149

1. Fold the selected paper into hamburgers.

2. Cut the paper in half along the fold lines. (Omit this step to make a large accordion.)

3. Fold each section of papers into hamburgers; however, fold one side 1" shorter than the other side. This will form a tab that is 1" long.

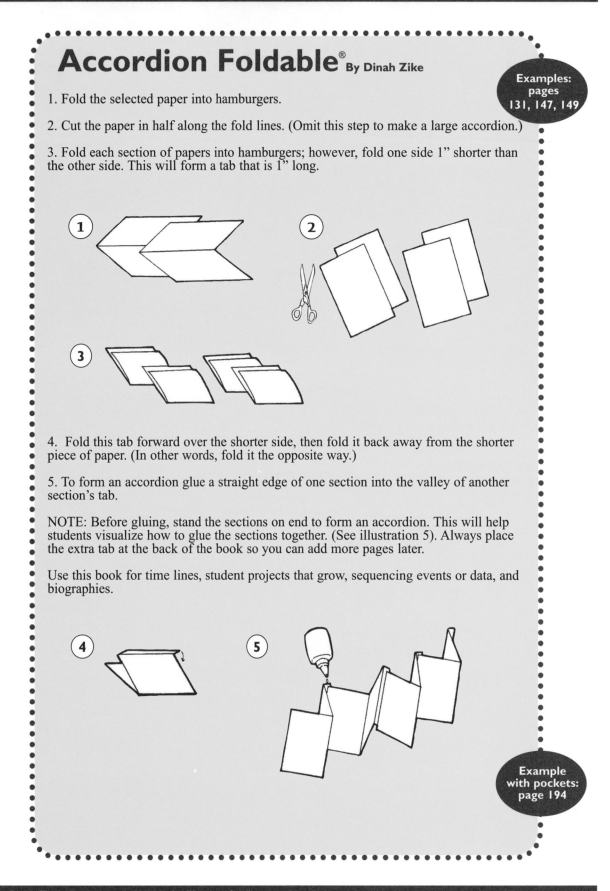

4. Fold this tab forward over the shorter side, then fold it back away from the shorter piece of paper. (In other words, fold it the opposite way.)

5. To form an accordion glue a straight edge of one section into the valley of another section's tab.

NOTE: Before gluing, stand the sections on end to form an accordion. This will help students visualize how to glue the sections together. (See illustration 5). Always place the extra tab at the back of the book so you can add more pages later.

Use this book for time lines, student projects that grow, sequencing events or data, and biographies.

Example
with pockets:
page 194

Folding Fifths

Example of Five-Tabs, page 235

1. Fold a sheet of paper in half like a hotdog or hamburger.

2. Fold the paper so that one-third is exposed and two-thirds are covered.

3. Fold the two-thirds section in half.

4. Fold the one-third section (single thickness) backward to form a fold line.

5. Leave open for a five-part folded table or chart, or cut along each fold to create a five-tab book.

Folding a Circle into Tenths

1. Fold a paper circle in half.

2. Fold the half circle so that one-third is exposed and two-thirds are covered.

NOTE: *Paper squares and rectangles are folded into tenths the same way. Fold them so that one-third is exposed and two-thirds are covered. Continue with steps 3 and 4.*

3. Fold the one-third (single thickness) section backward to form a fold line.

4. Fold the two-thirds section in half.

5. The half circle will be divided into fifths. When opened, the circle will be divided into tenths.

Circle Graph By Dinah Zike

1. Cut out two circles using a pattern.

2. Fold each of the circles in half on each axis, forming fourths. Cut along one of the fold lines (the radius) to the middle of each circle. Flatten the circles.

3. Slip the two circles together along the cuts until they overlap completely.

4. Spin one of the circles while holding the other stationary. Estimate how much of each of the two (or you can add more) circles should be exposed to illustrate given percentages or fractional parts of data. Add circles to represent more than two percentages.

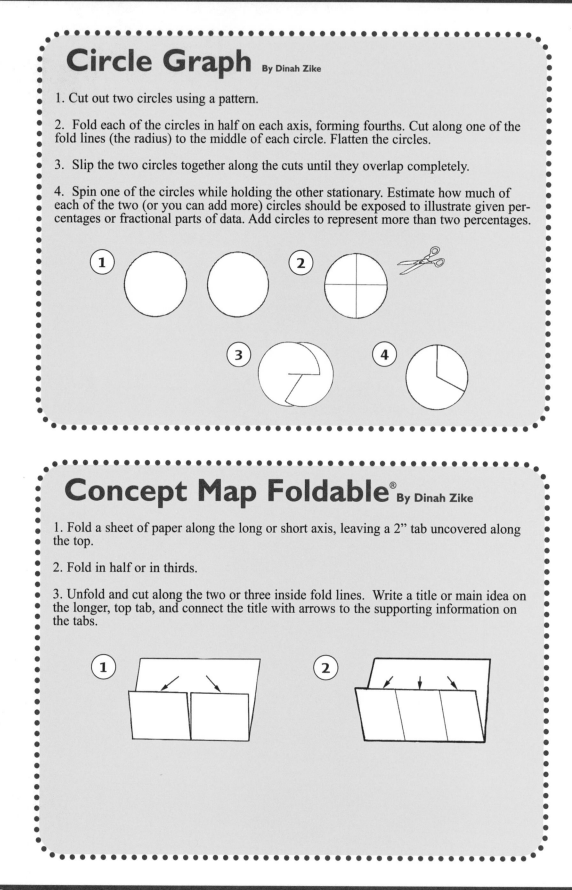

Concept Map Foldable® By Dinah Zike

1. Fold a sheet of paper along the long or short axis, leaving a 2" tab uncovered along the top.

2. Fold in half or in thirds.

3. Unfold and cut along the two or three inside fold lines. Write a title or main idea on the longer, top tab, and connect the title with arrows to the supporting information on the tabs.

Four-Door Foldable® Diorama By Dinah Zike

**Examples:
pages
18, 86, 155**

1. Make a four-door Foldable out of a shutterfold.

2. Fold the two inside top corners back to the outer edges (mountains) of the shutterfold. This will result in two tacos that will make the four-door Foldable look like it has a shirt collar. Do the same thing to the bottom of the four-door Foldable. When finished, four small triangular tacos have been made.

3. Form a 90-degree angle and overlap the folded triangles to make a diorama display that doesn't use staples or glue. (It can be collapsed for storage.)

4. **Variation**: If you prefer, you can cut off all four triangles or tacos. Staple or glue the sides to create the diorama display.

Picture Frame Foldable® By Dinah Zike

**Examples:
pages
164, 248, 259**

1. Fold a sheet of paper or poster board in half like a hamburger.

2. Open the hamburger and gently roll one side of the hamburger toward the valley. Try not to crease the roll.

3. Cut a rectangle out of the middle of the rolled side of the paper to leave a ½" border and form a frame.

4. Fold another sheet of paper (the same size) in half like a hamburger. Apply glue to the inside border of the picture frame and place the folded, uncut sheet of paper inside.

Use this book to feature a person, place, or thing. Inside the picture frames, glue photographs, magazine pictures, computer-generated graphs, or have students sketch pictures. This book has four inside papers for writing and recording notes.

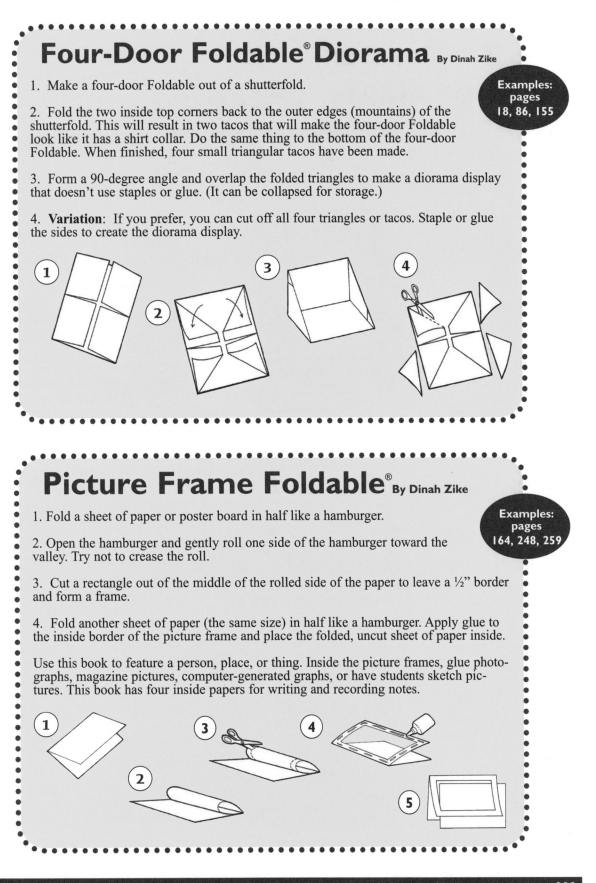

Display Box

Examples: pages 134, 254

1. Make a taco fold and cut off the rectangular tab formed. This will result in a square. (See page 254 for photographs of fold instructions.)

2. Fold the square into a shutterfold.

3. Unfold and fold the square into another shutterfold perpendicular to the direction of the first. This will form a small square at each of the four corners of the sheet of paper.

4. As illustrated, cut along two fold lines on opposite sides of the large square.

5. Collapse in and glue the cut tabs to form an open box.

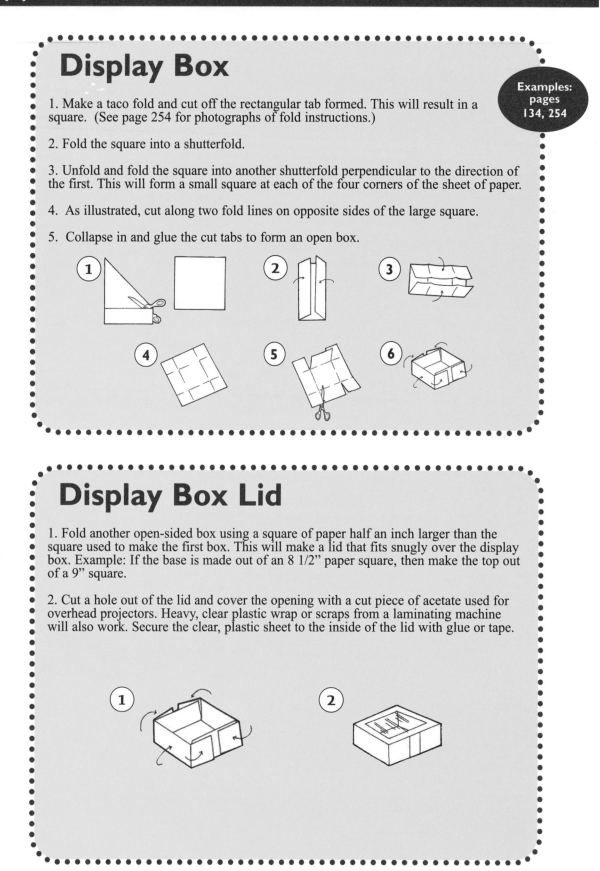

Display Box Lid

1. Fold another open-sided box using a square of paper half an inch larger than the square used to make the first box. This will make a lid that fits snugly over the display box. Example: If the base is made out of an 8 1/2" paper square, then make the top out of a 9" square.

2. Cut a hole out of the lid and cover the opening with a cut piece of acetate used for overhead projectors. Heavy, clear plastic wrap or scraps from a laminating machine will also work. Secure the clear, plastic sheet to the inside of the lid with glue or tape.

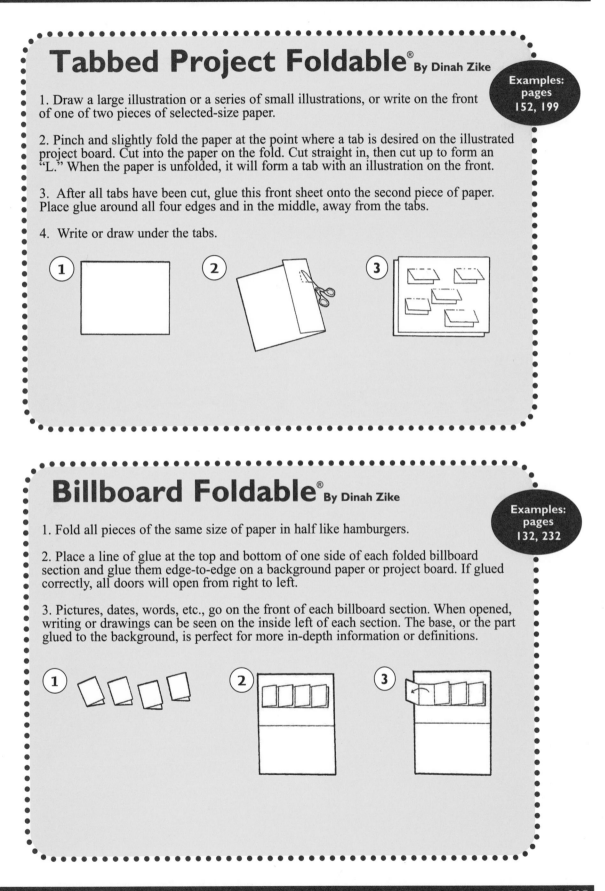

Tabbed Project Foldable® By Dinah Zike

Examples: pages 152, 199

1. Draw a large illustration or a series of small illustrations, or write on the front of one of two pieces of selected-size paper.

2. Pinch and slightly fold the paper at the point where a tab is desired on the illustrated project board. Cut into the paper on the fold. Cut straight in, then cut up to form an "L." When the paper is unfolded, it will form a tab with an illustration on the front.

3. After all tabs have been cut, glue this front sheet onto the second piece of paper. Place glue around all four edges and in the middle, away from the tabs.

4. Write or draw under the tabs.

Billboard Foldable® By Dinah Zike

Examples: pages 132, 232

1. Fold all pieces of the same size of paper in half like hamburgers.

2. Place a line of glue at the top and bottom of one side of each folded billboard section and glue them edge-to-edge on a background paper or project board. If glued correctly, all doors will open from right to left.

3. Pictures, dates, words, etc., go on the front of each billboard section. When opened, writing or drawings can be seen on the inside left of each section. The base, or the part glued to the background, is perfect for more in-depth information or definitions.

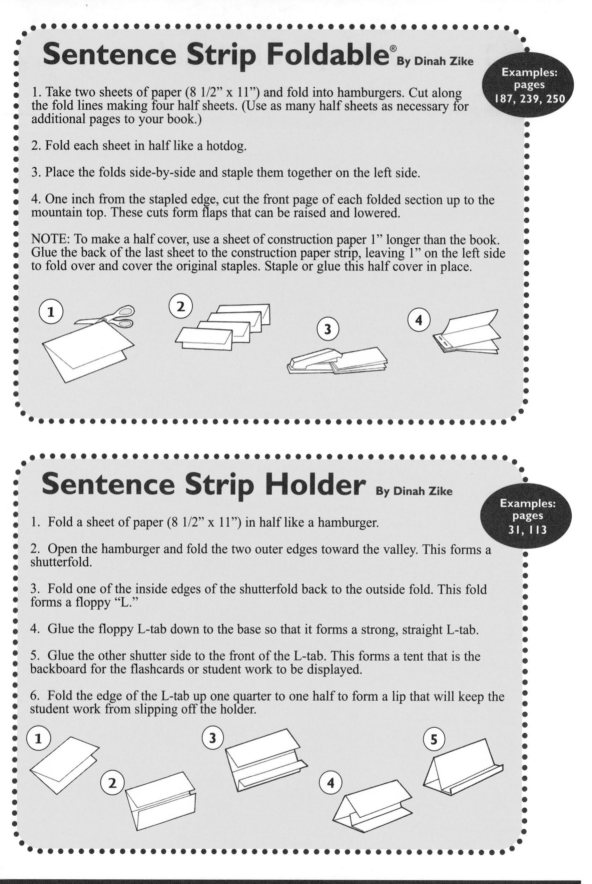

Sentence Strip Foldable® By Dinah Zike

Examples: pages 187, 239, 250

1. Take two sheets of paper (8 1/2" x 11") and fold into hamburgers. Cut along the fold lines making four half sheets. (Use as many half sheets as necessary for additional pages to your book.)

2. Fold each sheet in half like a hotdog.

3. Place the folds side-by-side and staple them together on the left side.

4. One inch from the stapled edge, cut the front page of each folded section up to the mountain top. These cuts form flaps that can be raised and lowered.

NOTE: To make a half cover, use a sheet of construction paper 1" longer than the book. Glue the back of the last sheet to the construction paper strip, leaving 1" on the left side to fold over and cover the original staples. Staple or glue this half cover in place.

Sentence Strip Holder By Dinah Zike

Examples: pages 31, 113

1. Fold a sheet of paper (8 1/2" x 11") in half like a hamburger.

2. Open the hamburger and fold the two outer edges toward the valley. This forms a shutterfold.

3. Fold one of the inside edges of the shutterfold back to the outside fold. This fold forms a floppy "L."

4. Glue the floppy L-tab down to the base so that it forms a strong, straight L-tab.

5. Glue the other shutter side to the front of the L-tab. This forms a tent that is the backboard for the flashcards or student work to be displayed.

6. Fold the edge of the L-tab up one quarter to one half to form a lip that will keep the student work from slipping off the holder.

Book Jacket Foldable® By Dinah Zike

Examples: pages 57, 139

1. Fold a sheet of paper (8 1/2" x 11") in half like a hamburger, leaving one side a quarter inch shorter than the other side, then crease.

2. Move the short side up, making it ½" longer than the long side, and crease. This forms the ½" spine of the book.

3. Fold the outer edges toward the valley, forming two flaps 1½" wide.

4. Fold the book jacket in half like a hotdog and cut along this fold to create two mini book jackets.

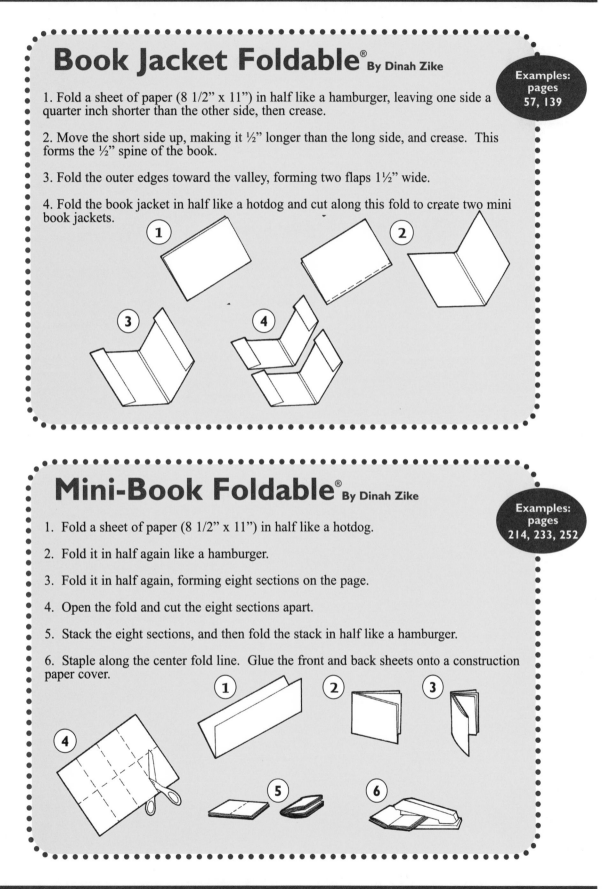

Mini-Book Foldable® By Dinah Zike

Examples: pages 214, 233, 252

1. Fold a sheet of paper (8 1/2" x 11") in half like a hotdog.

2. Fold it in half again like a hamburger.

3. Fold it in half again, forming eight sections on the page.

4. Open the fold and cut the eight sections apart.

5. Stack the eight sections, and then fold the stack in half like a hamburger.

6. Staple along the center fold line. Glue the front and back sheets onto a construction paper cover.

Folded Table or Chart

Examples: pages 95, 70, 113

1. Fold the number of vertical columns needed to make the table or chart.

2. Fold the horizontal rows needed to make the table or chart.

3. Label the rows and columns.

Remember: Tables are organized along vertical axis and horizontal axis, while charts tend to be are organized along one axis, either vertical or horizontal.

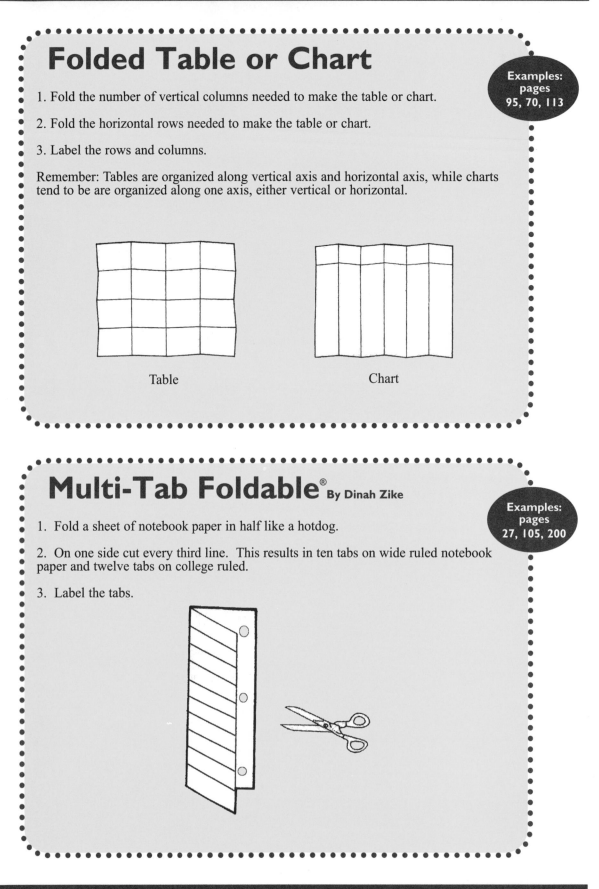

Table   Chart

Multi-Tab Foldable® By Dinah Zike

Examples: pages 27, 105, 200

1. Fold a sheet of notebook paper in half like a hotdog.

2. On one side cut every third line. This results in ten tabs on wide ruled notebook paper and twelve tabs on college ruled.

3. Label the tabs.

Pocket Chart Foldable® By Dinah Zike
Optional Sentence Strip Holder

Examples: pages 55, 71

Help students create this large Pocket Chart Foldable and use it to collect examples of student work, student art and illustrations, digital photographs, current events, and other items that help students visualize things past and present.

1. Fold a sheet of poster board into half or into thirds.

2. Fold a 5" tab along the bottom of the poster to form a pocket.

3. As an option, you can make a sentence strip holder at the bottom of the Pocket Chart. Make a 1" tab along the bottom of the poster pocket to make a sentence strip holder. Staple ¼ inch along the ends of the folded pocket and sentence-strip holder.

4. Label the top of the three columns with titles.

Student work and art can be stored in the three pockets, and sentence strips and vocabulary cards can be displayed along the bottom of the Foldable as illustrated.

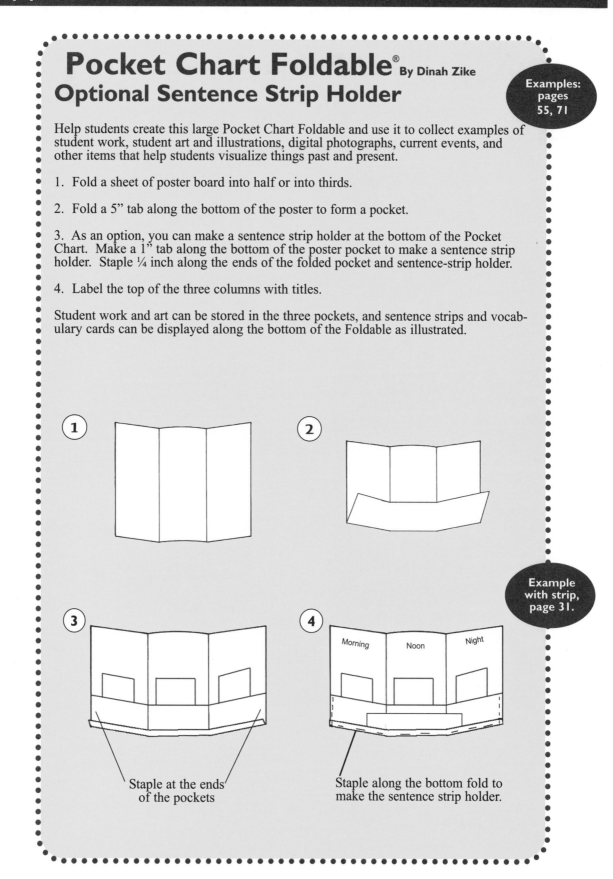

Example with strip, page 31.

Staple at the ends of the pockets

Staple along the bottom fold to make the sentence strip holder.

Top Pocket Foldable® By Dinah Zike

Examples: pages 121, 142, 236

1. Hold a sheet of poster board with the long edge held horizontally and fold in half like a hamburger, but instead of creasing the paper, pinch it to show the midpoint.

2. Fold the outer edges of the paper to meet at the pinch, or midpoint, forming a shutterfold. Write the unit title on the front of the shutterfold.

3. Crease the folds well and then open the shutterfold.

4. Fold the poster board upwards like a hotdog so that the two horizontal edges meet.

5. Use the left and right creases to fold the edges of the hotdog inward, which will create a large central pocket that can hold student work. Glue or staple the left and right creases to reinforce the pocket.

6. Cut off the bottom fold line of the right and left tabs allowing them to open and close.

7. Label the front of the Foldable and the four inside tabs.

Write terms and definitions as well as student dictated information and thoughts under the tabs. Collect pictures, illustrations, student worksheets, photographs, and current events and store them in the top pocket.

Variation: Make small top-pocket Foldables using 8½" x 11" paper and store quarter-sheet flashcards in the top pocket, or make using 11" x 17" paper and store half-sheet flashcards in the top pocket.

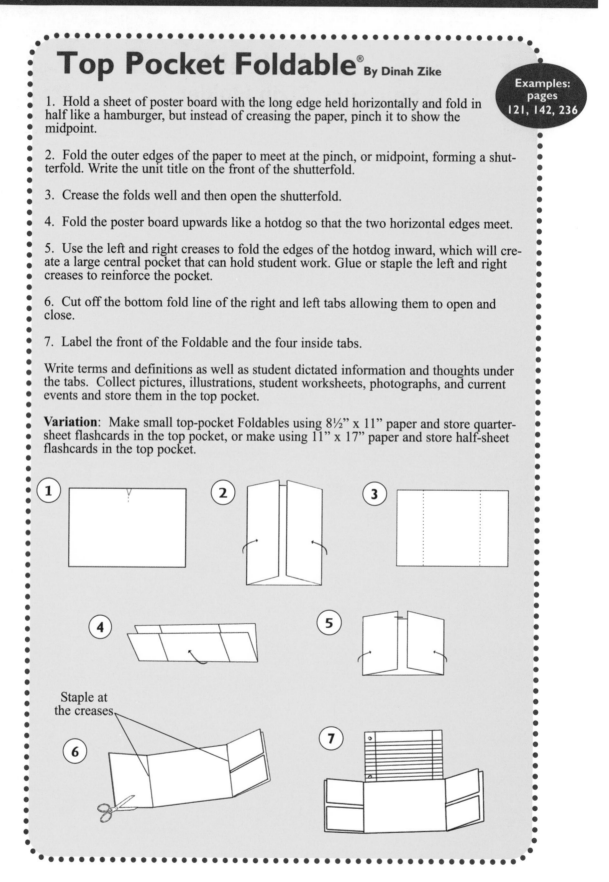

Staple at the creases

Dinah Zike Academy   dzacademy.com

Dinah Zike is proud to introduce the Dinah Zike Academy, a teacher training institute outside of San Antonio in the beautiful and historic Texas Hill Country.

Dinah: *It has always been my dream to have a location for teachers to immerse themselves in a fully developed, hands-on lab setting that will provide strategies to address diverse learners, meet state and national benchmarks, and build student learning skills for life. I also want to provide the opportunity for teachers to become Dinah Zike Certified trainers for their district, state, or nationwide, because I can't physically reach all the teachers who want to learn more about Foldables and my other teaching strategies.*

In three-day, jam-packed sessions at the Academy, Dinah and/or DZA's pro facilitators will engage and immerse you in the power and potential of 3-D interactive graphic organizers, dynamic and efficient classroom organization, and effective teaching strategies across age-grade levels and content areas. Research grounding, implementation for a variety of learners, and practicality are built in. A session maximum of 24 participants allows for hands-on individual and small-group work, technology use, and direct application to participants' teaching practices. Some seminars are cross-curricular and targeted to either elementary or secondary levels. Others are focused on specific content/subject areas, such as science, mathematics, social studies, and reading/language arts.

The expansive Academy is well-equipped with group and individual classrooms, high-speed Internet access, computer work stations, working design areas and tools, easily replicable supply stations, displays and publishing centers plus resources including artifacts, a research and reference library, and the list goes on.

The Academy is located in the heart of the historic and charming village of Comfort, Texas, in the beautiful Texas Hill country, 45 minutes from San Antonio and 1½ hours from Austin. Most convenient airport is San Antonio. Antiquing, shopping, golfing, fishing, bicycling, sightseeing, caving, natural and historic-site adventuring are popular area pursuits. Or just relaxing on the porch of your B&B!

Testimonial: "*I just returned from the Dinah Zike Academy, and I'm overwhelmed with the vast amount of information provided. This is my 37th year in education, and I've never enjoyed a course of study as much as the Academy.*"

For More Information, or to reserve your spot:

WEBSITE: www.dzacademy.com
PHONE: 830-995-3800
FAX: 830-995-5205
MAIL inquiries to:
DZ Academy, P. O. Box 340, Comfort TX 78013

Equivalency Flips®

Dinah's Newest Math Manipulative
One sheet of colored 8½ x 11 paper magically folds to teach multiple equivalencies! For example, the "**Cup and Ounces Equivalency Flip**" (left) folds to form a tabbed activity that illustrates the relationship between cups, ounces, tablespoons, and milliliters. Others illustrate fractions, percentages, time (right), measurement, weight, and more. Quickly and easily make a classroom set: just pop out the diecut sections, fold, and glue. **Each packet contains a classroom set of 12 identical diecut color sheets with full-color instructions, or get a mixed set with one of each.**

New
Product
Line!

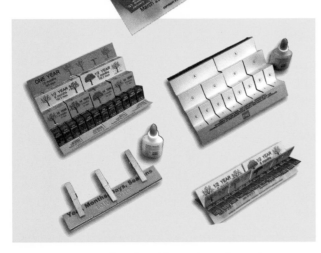

**EACH PACKET CONTAINS
12 IDENTICAL SHEETS**
EF1 **Mixed Set:** One of each, 16 sheets total
EF2 **1/2, 1/4, 1/8** (+decimals & percentages)
EF3 **1/3, 1/6, 1/12** (+parts of a dozen)
EF4 **Percentages** (+fractions and decimals)
EF5 **Decimals** (+percentages, fractions)
EF6 **Hour** halves, quarters, minutes, seconds
EF7 **Money** dollar, half-dollars, quarters, dimes
EF8 **Gallon**, quarts, pints, ounces, (+ml)
EF9 **Cup and Ounces** (+tablespoons, milliliters)
EF10 **Liter** (+quarts, pints, ounces)
EF11 **Mile** (+meters)
EF12 **Kilometer** (+feet)
EF13 **Meter** (+inches, feet, yard)
EF14 **Yard** (+centimeters)
EF15 **Music** Whole, half, quarter, eighth notes
EF16 **Year** (+seasons, days, solstices, equinoxes)
EF17 **Pounds, Ounces, Grams**
EF18 **Custom Mixed Packet:** Two titles, 6+6, your choice
EF2 thru EF17...$14.00
EF1 & EF18...$18.00

EASY TO MAKE Quickly and easily make a classroom set. Pop out the diecut strips, fold the sheet like an accordion, and glue the back to make a three- dimensional **Equivalency Flip.**

To order call 1-800-99DINAH or visit www.dinah.com

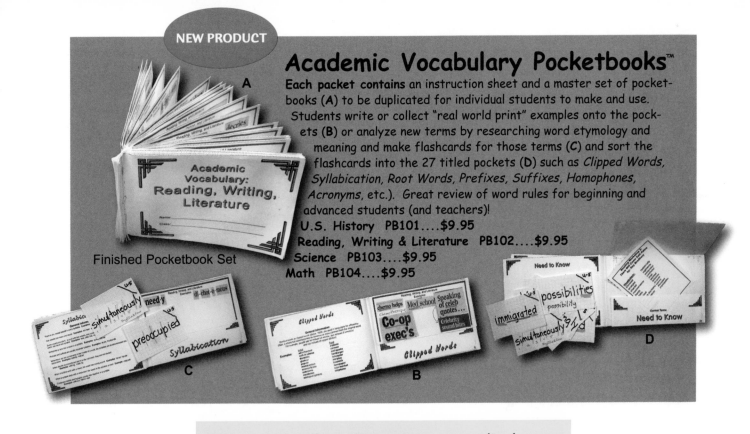

Line Art Library CD   Over 1000 illustrations!

Introduction

We commissioned an illustrator who loves working with kids, Becky Hall, to draw **over 1000** different illustrations appropriate for language development activities with PreK to 2nd grade students. The art on this CD fits perfectly on Foldables® and VKVs®, or it can be enlarged and used on posters and charts. Many of you purchased this book with the CD. Those of you who did not can purchase the CD separately if you think in hindsight that it will be helpful.

CD-101...................... $20.00

Organization

Line Art Library CD is organized in easy to use folders:
- Antonyms
- Blends
- Compound Words
- Consonants
- CVC
- CVCE
- CVVC
- Digraphs
- Diphthongs
- Heteronyms
- Homophones
- Homographs
- Phonograms
- Prefixes
- Suffixes
- Syllables

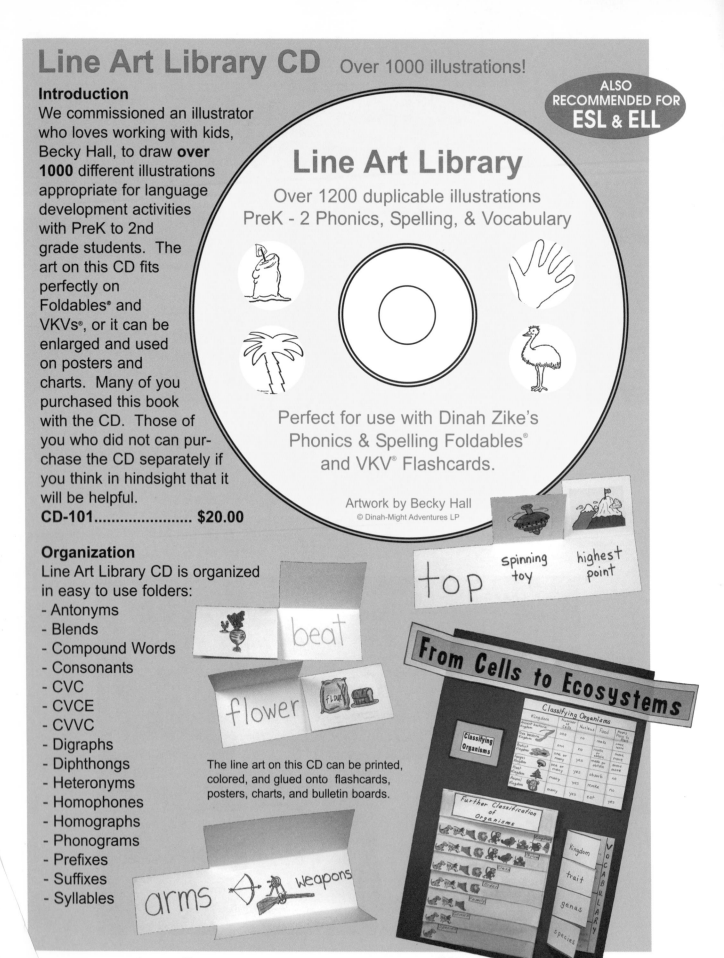

Line Art Library

Over 1200 duplicable illustrations
PreK - 2 Phonics, Spelling, & Vocabulary

Perfect for use with Dinah Zike's Phonics & Spelling Foldables® and VKV® Flashcards.

Artwork by Becky Hall
© Dinah-Might Adventures LP

The line art on this CD can be printed, colored, and glued onto flashcards, posters, charts, and bulletin boards.

To order call 1-800-99DINAH or visit www.dinah.com